W9-ARU-085

THE KILLING OF
ANNA NICOLE SMITH

Judge Larry Seidlin

THE KILLING OF
ANNA NICOLE SMITH

Published by Transit Publishing Inc.

Copyright © 2010 by Larry Seidlin

The reproduction or transmission of any part of this publication in any form or by any means, electronic, mechanical, recording, or otherwise, or storage in a retrieval system, without the prior consent of the publisher, is an infringement of copyright law. In the case of photocopying or other reprographic production of the material, a licence must be obtained from the Canadian Copyright Licensing Agency (Access Copyright) before proceeding.

ISBN: 978-1-926745-33-6

Cover design: François Turgeon
Text design and composition: Nassim Bahloul

Cover photo:
© James Bareham/CORBIS Outline

Back Cover Photo:
© Lou Toman/SUN-SENTINEL
/POOL/epa/CORBIS

Transit Publishing Inc.
1996 St-Joseph Boulevard East
Montreal, QC
H2H 1E3

Tel: 514-273-0123
www.transitpublishing.com

Printed and Bound in Canada

Editor's Note: All testimony and all interviews in this book are reproduced verbatim. Square brackets designate an editorial addition to maintain clarity. Emphasis has been added.

Contents

ACKNOWLEDGEMENTS

I want to acknowledge my wife Belinda, and my daughter Dax, who has been so patient and is the most important person in my life. I would also like to acknowledge Dax's grandparents, omie, papa and mamaw; and my parents Dave and Betty, who are now in the heavens.

I want to thank my publisher Pierre Turgeon and his son Francois, for believing that we would hit a home run. And my editor, Clare McKeon, who possesses a spirituality that is reflected in her existence and her work. Sometimes I wish we could surround ourselves with people who exhibit only the beauty and truth of the world.

To Diane Sawyer, for being so patient. She is even more beautiful, charming and intelligent in person than she is on television. When she met with my wife and daughter in her conference room, Dax started to spin in one of the leather chairs, and Diane responded by spinning in her own chair, making Dax and all of us laugh. She handwrote a note to Dax's teacher explaining her absence from school.

To Larry King, for bringing Dannielynn on his show as a suprise for me, and for allowing Dax to participate in the encounter. The segment was titled, "Three Larrys and a Baby in Los Angeles." I enjoyed getting together with him in New York and thank him for granting a private interview.

To Fox and Geraldo Rivera, and his brother Craig, for treating me like family during my guest appearances as a judicial analyst.

To Greta Van Susteren, for sitting through my trial and for having the insight and fortitude that made our exchanges on contemporary legal issues so satisfying.

To Judge Napolitano, for representing the judiciary on the highest standards and for understanding the truth about how a judicial proceeding takes place.

To everyone at NBC's *Today* show for making our visits so comfortable during my appearances as a judicial analyst.

To CNN's Wolf Blitzer and Suzanne Malveaux for my time in Washington as a judicial analyst.

To the E! Network, and Ken Baker for his sensitive and compassionate interviews.

To *Access Hollywood* and Tony Potts for that fun interview on the tennis courts in Pasadena.

To Jane Velez-Mitchell, whom I always look forward to working with, for her depth and analysis of timely issues.

To the staff of *Showbiz Tonight* for making our interviews and analyses so interesting.

To the staff of *Inside Edition* for allowing me to express my analysis of the celebrity cases.

To the *Saturday Night Live* cast members who emulated me. We found it quite enjoyable.

To my close friends and family who gave me support during many a storm.

To the families at my daughter's school, Pinecrest, a wonderful educational environment. The teachers, parents and students have been supportive and kind to all of us.

And finally a big thank you to the people on the streets and in the towns who continue to inspire me and show me love and encouragement. As the Beatles once pointed out, "All you need is love."

PREFACE

Valentine's Day, 2007. I was in my car with my wife Belinda driving to a Greek restaurant for lunch, when my judicial assistant Joanne Gallo called to tell me that the Clerk's Office wanted to set up an emergency hearing for 1:30 p.m. I asked her who the hearing was for, and she told me it was for Anna Nicole Smith.

"Who is Anna Nicole Smith?" I asked.

"Who is Anna Nicole Smith? Are you kidding me?" Belinda said.

And I came back with, "If she played second base for the Yankees, I'd know her."

Anna Nicole Smith, as I later learned, was a former Playboy Playmate and 1993 Playmate of the Year, a model, a reality TV star, and the widow of billionaire Texas oilman J. Howard Marshall. She died the week before at the Hard Rock Hotel and Casino in Hollywood, Florida, at the age of thirty-nine. Her body was lying in a South Florida morgue and was decomposing at an alarmingly rapid rate. And I had to decide where to bury it.

My chambers, located on the 8th floor of the courthouse, were the size of a bowling alley, as big as some of the courtrooms. All told, there were twenty-nine lawyers present, many of whom had never previously appeared before me. I spent the rest of the day with these attorneys, as they continually checked in and out, and constantly took or made calls on their cell phones. They had hearings in different parts of the country and in different divisions of my own courthouse. They came in and out as if they were at a turnstile in Macy's department store.

I looked them in the eyes and I could tell they were distracted, and anxious, like horses at the starting gate before a big race. They were everywhere and nowhere. Their minds were flying and they were hyper because this case had so many issues, and these issues were being tried in different jurisdictions. It seemed at times that Anna Nicole's body was like a pinball being bounced around in a pinball machine.

At this point I felt it was essential that: (1) all parties and their attorneys stay focused on the task at hand; (2) that I get their attention in a forceful manner; and (3) that they know who was in charge. There had to be one person with the guts and the fortitude to make the necessary decisions.

So I told them, "This body is not leaving Broward County. This body belongs to me now. I am not releasing it. That baby's in a cold, cold storage room."

What it boiled down to was this: I had jurisdiction over all the issues. I believe this set the tone for the trial, and put the lawyers on notice that one judge, one arbitrator was going to decide the fate of Anna Nicole Smith's body and where her final resting place should be.

These words played big on the front pages of newspapers and on TV screens all over the world. I realized that my words might have seemed gruff or insensitive to the beauty and warmth that had been Anna Nicole Smith, and therefore I apologized for that language on the record the following day. But it did accomplish my goal, which was to bring the parties together for this difficult journey, this six-day slug fest which I refereed, mediated and ultimately ruled upon.

Differences aside, the bottom line for me was that we show respect for Anna Nicole's body and, at the same time, balance that with the legal issues that had to be resolved. My primary concern was always the best interests of Anna Nicole's baby daughter, Dannielynn, and how this child's life would be improved by the proceedings.

When I rendered my judgment on February 22 that Anna Nicole Smith's body was to be buried in the Bahamas, it should have been case closed. Since then, however, many red flags have popped into my mind about how she died and why. After going over the trial transcripts and reviewing the testimony from later proceedings that involved many of the principal characters who testified in my case, I have questions and I have concerns.

The case of Anna Nicole Smith set the precedent and opened the flood gates for law enforcement to begin examining doctors who are writing false prescriptions, prescribing excessive amount of drugs, and conducting themselves in an unprofessional manner. We opened the gates of hell for doctors and so-called loved ones who are enablers, both of whom may really have an intent to destroy the celebrity, whereby they would be charged with manslaughter: *the killing of another individual through reckless conduct.* Some of these doctors do it purely for money. Others want a piece of fame. They desperately want to be in the showbiz environment, and want the high that goes with it. Some may argue that Howard K. Stern poured time and energy into Anna Nicole. Some might even say love. But when you mix it all together, he was named in the will as the executor of her estate and, as we see in Michael Jackson's case, great sums of money and power flow from that position.

Did we, as a society, kill Anna Nicole Smith—as well as Michael Jackson, Heath Ledger, wrestler Eddie "Umaga" Fatu and even Elvis Presley? The same elements were present in all those deaths. Everyone knows that in the entertainment industry, there are too many drugs, too many needs, too many hungry pharmacists, too many hangers-on. Television networks pay incredible money to some entertainers, even though the network brass know they need therapy but are hesitant to request it because they are afraid they will lose the talent and the advertising dollars that go hand in hand with them.

Overuse and illegal use of prescription drugs in professional sports has been making the front pages of the media for years. Pro wrestling in particular, which attracts 20 million TV viewers every week, may be the sport with the worst track record of overuse of prescription drugs, yet there seems to be a veil of secrecy regarding the premature death of any wrestler from prescription drugs, especially painkillers.

In an article by John Swartz that appeared in the April 8, 2010 issue of *USA Today*, Canadian-born former pro wrestler Rowdy Roddy Piper—a WWF superstar from the 1980s—said, "I experienced what we in the profession call the silent scream of pain, drugs and loneliness. You're in your hotel room. You're banged up, numb and alone. You don't want to go downstairs to the bar or restaurant. The walls are breathing. You don't want to talk. Panic sets in and you start weeping. It's something all of us go through." The article also cited research that the newspaper conducted, revealing that pro wrestlers are about twenty times more likely to die before they reach the age of forty-five than are pro football players.

During the 1980s, Piper was one of the most popular figures in the world of pro wrestling, but he stated something very odd in the article. A wrestling promoter told him, "If you die, kid, die in the ring. It's good for business." And yet, Piper described a practice of one of the doctors on the pro wrestling circuit that is eerily similar to Howard K. Stern's duffle bag of drugs. "The doctor had shopping bags with our names on them that were filled with steroids and prescription drugs," said Piper. If you want an even more vivid example of the abuse and torment that pro wrestlers like Piper went through, check out Mickey Rourke's Oscar-nominated performance in *The Wrestler*.

Criminal charges were later filed in Anna Nicole's case because the world was watching and was sickened by what arose from the testimony during the six-day trial in my courtroom. Eventually, the California Attorney General reacted appropriately by slamming the doctors and enablers who were responsible for her death. And when the trial of Howard K. Stern, Dr. Khristine Eroshevich and Dr. Sandeep Kapoor begins on August 4, 2010 in Los Angeles on charges of illegally providing Anna Nicole Smith with sedatives and opiates, we will then finally get the answers to the questions that I have raised in this book: who and what— killed her?

I believe Anna Nicole Smith, like Michael Jackson, was given a toxic mix that led to her death. I believe someone committed manslaughter, through reckless conduct. Her son Daniel, who traveled to the Bahamas from California to be with his mom on the occasion of the birth of Dannielynn, was also given a toxic mix. He arrived late in the evening and was dead by morning. Where did he get these drugs? Reckless conduct also led to his death. I also question if we buried Anna Nicole in the right place.

Howard K. Stern was present at both deaths. He arrived the same day as Anna Nicole did in the Bahamas, a place where the police department operates like the Keystone Cops. They then traveled together to Seminole Hard Rock Casino, which also has an ineffective law enforcement agency. And speaking of the Seminole Police Department, its Chief, Charlie Tiger, stated he had reviewed "hundreds of hours of tapes and found nothing unusual"; therefore, Anna Nicole Smith died of "an accidental overdose with no other criminal element present." Chief Tiger, basing some of his conclusions on tape, in my opinion is utterly ridiculous. Anna Nicole was on tape only when she entered the hotel because, as we discovered, she never left the hotel room. When she did leave the hotel room, it was on a stretcher, dead as a doornail.

Stern admitted in my courtroom that he obtained Anna Nicole's drugs and got these drugs in other people's names. As a matter of fact, the nine bottles of prescription medications that were found in her room at the Hard Rock were prescribed in his name. I believe that Howard K. Stern actively participated in obtaining these highly addictive prescription drugs for Anna

Nicole. I believe that Howard K. Stern exercised a great amount of control over Anna Nicole by maintaining and reviewing her drug desires and addiction.

This control goes even further. Stern wanted to be the legal father of her daughter Dannielynn, even knowing that there was substantial doubt if not high probability that he wasn't the biological father. Obviously, if Howard K. Stern was the father on paper, he would be in control of the Marshall inheritance, for potentially hundreds of millions of dollars. Furthermore, as I recognized in the trial, he was, and still is in the catbird seat, because, I believe, he is the wizard behind Anna Nicole's estate.

What concerns me is that Stern admitted during my trial, and in later testimony and statements, that he got her drugs while she was pregnant with "his" child in a hospital setting under a doctor's care, which he smuggled in via a duffle bag. Who would give drugs to a pregnant woman who is carrying his alleged child? Someone who has a fiduciary relationship with and a supposed love connection to the victim? This is not only bizarre, it's also not sustained by common sense. The question is: do these enablers have an intent to keep the "star" hooked on drugs, so that they can remain with them and, in effect, continue to help control their person and property?

In this book, we will explore whether Anna Nicole Smith died from an accidental overdose, as announced by Dr. Perper, the chief medical examiner for Broward County, or from foul play. Why did Howard K. Stern, as an alleged enabler, allow Anna Nicole to remain on drugs? Was it so he could remain with her and control her person and property? Read this book carefully and you, my reader—the juror—will decide.

After three years, Anna Nicole Smith and her son Daniel need to rest in peace, and I think I have found the path for their souls to receive this peace.

Judge Larry Seidlin
Fort Lauderdale, Florida
May 2010

ONE

"THIS BODY BELONGS TO ME"

At the beginning of the trial, two of the principal parties, Howard K. Stern and Larry Birkhead, were outside my physical jurisdiction. Birkhead was in California and Stern was in the Bahamas. Krista Barth, Howard K. Stern's attorney, stated that "unfortunately, recently the injunction was entered in the Bahamas and that precludes Mr. Stern from leaving the country. At this time, it's Mr. Stern's concern first and foremost for the safety of Dannielynn, for his little girl. He did not feel it was in her best interest for him to leave her at this time." As a result, I allowed both parties to appear in court via telephone. Thereby, the court resolved its first issue.

In order to prevent this case from bouncing from state to state in different courtrooms, we bit the bullet and decided that this court was going to have jurisdiction over the body of Anna Nicole Smith. The death investigation was ongoing throughout my trial. I knew that the Seminole Indians owned the Hard Rock Hotel and Casino where she died, and that they had their own police department, which would not turn this investigation over to an outside police agency, which would have been the Broward County Sheriff's Office.

The Seminole Police Department is rudimentary, without the sophisticated and expensive technology that is needed to investigate a potential homicide. Like thousands of police departments all over this nation, it is good at telling you how to get to the public library and adequate in issuing a citation for running a red light. But we're talking about a highly publicized death here. Adverse publicity concerning her death at their Hard Rock Casino in room 607 was not something the tribe wanted. And speaking of room 607, I recently contacted a few of my inside sources who are closely tied to the Hard Rock with a simple request: get me pictures of room 607, the room that Anna Nicole *never left* during her stay there. They called me back, and each of them reported that the room is *among the missing*. Another source told me that they couldn't find the original room. Somehow, some members of the Seminole tribe changed the room numbers, refurbished the room, and took it to a higher plateau by sending their medicine man into the room to ritually remove the evil spirits.

This action screams of cover-up. Basically, the Seminole tribe did everything in its power to erase the existence of the original room 607 because it is embarrassed by the sad story of Anna Nicole Smith and her final days. This approach is the exact opposite to what another major North American hotel did to preserve its place in history. At the Queen Elizabeth Hotel in Montreal—where John Lennon and Yoko Ono staged their "Bed-In for Peace" in May of 1969 and where they wrote and recorded their legendary song "Give Peace A Chance"—the hotel's management practically turned Suite 1742, where the

"Bed-In" actually took place, into a tourist attraction. It's even been renamed the "John Lennon Suite." That one simple action by the Queen Elizabeth Hotel helped to cement John Lennon's legacy to the world of popular music. What the Seminole tribe did with the original room 607 at the Hard Rock Casino was to wipe out part of the memory of Anna Nicole Smith.

I remember sitting in my French class at Hunter College, reading a play that dealt with a labyrinth. Basically, we were in such a labyrinth now, and we had the added tension or burden of having this case played out through the media in front of the whole world. A case that is media-driven takes on different dimensions from a case that has no public interest. So I stated in court that everyone involved in this case was caught in this French labyrinth. "When you look at the center of the maze," I continued, "it all points to one issue, what's in the best interest of the child. This little baby, this little girl that was born and you guys [the attorneys] touched upon it yesterday, the child, and that is what we are going to have to focus in on. And it's always going to come back to this issue, what is in the best interest of the child."

Krista Barth then reminded me that "Florida does not have jurisdiction over Dannielynn Hope Marshall Stern." But I played Columbo. I wanted to keep the net wide. I wanted to resolve as many issues as I could regarding what was in the best interest of Dannielynn. I knew how certain issues in the court system get bogged down. Delay is not the exception, but the rule. I wanted to expedite the resolution of who Dannielynn's true father was.

Ms. Barth continued, "Dannielynn was born in the Bahamas.

She's never been to the United States. She does not have a United States passport. Her mother [Anna Nicole] was domiciled in the Bahamas and was on vacation in Florida, here merely for several days to pick up a boat." Barth also made the point that "they had an order in California that said: do not touch the body so we can get some DNA. That issue is properly before the California court where Mr. Birkhead brought his original paternity action."

It's important in a court proceeding to keep the parties positive and relaxed. Walter G. "Skip" Campbell, considered one of the finest trial lawyers in the country, a former state Senator and candidate for Attorney General, agreed with my approach and in a statement to the Miami Herald after the completion of the trial said that I was "one of the more compassionate persons I know. He genuinely wants to do what is right, regardless of who the parties are."

You can always accomplish greater things if the team is in a relaxed setting. Focused, of course, but comfortable in their environment and surroundings. I was able to establish such a setting in Family Court, where dysfunction is the rule, where parties and witnesses come in a distressed state, where they let their hair down and allow emotion to prevail over logic. In criminal court, the defendants come in trying to look good, dressed good, speaking well, trying to impress the court that they will turn their life around. In civil court, the parties try to impress the judge and jury about what upstanding citizens they are.

Family court is the toughest court. I was the Administrative Judge of the Family Division and was one of the architects in creating the Family Court for Broward County. I gave up the administrative post, and in politics you don't give up power willingly. You hold on to it. But I felt that, at times, it was impossible to accomplish my goals. I soon learned that if the case involved big money, then the attorney would take me from Manhattan to Queens via Staten Island. This detour took longer, which was another way of saying we need more discovery. I knew that was a code word for more attorneys' fees.

The attorneys would set a motion, the parties would be there, I would turn to the parties and say we can resolve the case now. I had a bulletin board and I would begin to chart the distribution of their assets, who would get primary custody of the children. Unfortunately, one of the lawyers would always say you are prejudging the case. We haven't completed our discovery and we need to have a four day trial. I knew this was just baloney and couldn't stand the waste of money and the continued destruction of family members. We needed to end the proceedings, divorce the couple and begin the healing process. There were certain attorneys I didn't need at the buffet table. By and large the vast majority of the attorneys that appeared before me were beautiful individuals with good hearts. But, unfortunately, in some of the cases that involved big dough, the attorneys were heartless. They manipulated the children and misstated the facts to keep the journey going.

The first afternoon of this trial was a prelude to a kiss. It was an opportunity to meet the attorneys and the parties who were present for the hearing—except Howard K. Stern and Larry Birkhead—to familiarize myself with the issues, and get a feel for them. This French labyrinth was a real puzzle, like the Michael Jackson case, and I had no roadmap. The issues of paternity, residency, burial, guardianship, cause of death would be examined. I would open the floodgates and set the precedent.

In my courtroom, I was able to elicit testimony that would lead to the charges against the doctors and Howard K. Stern. The public was shocked by the cavalier attitude in the videotape of Anna Nicole, who was fully pregnant, with her face painted, in a drug stupor, while Stern was questioning her as if she were on a mushroom trip. Public outcry affects government supervision and authority and I believe it caused them to take a deep long look at the factors that brought Anna Nicole Smith to her death. When I viewed the videotape, I actually had to turn away from the screen because it sickened me. I tried to think about something calming, like ocean waves hitting the sand. It is hard to absorb this kind of visual destruction. How can a grown woman be pregnant and have so many drugs in her? We all know drugs affect the unborn and can cause untold physical and mental ailments to the fetus.

After the first day of the hearing, I knew I had to put some of my own players on the field. You recall in *The Godfather*, when Michael Corleone went to visit his father in the hospital, where the police department was supposed to be guarding him, and there was no one around. He knew it was odd. He immediately called his brother Sonny and within minutes their own people secured the hospital so no further harm would come to their father. I also recall as a boy growing up, there was a great softball pitcher, Eddie Feigner, the King and His Court. Eddie would play the best teams around the world. He pitched. He also had a catcher, first baseman and shortstop. He was able to dominate and control the outcome of the game with his three men even though teams consisted of nine players.

I wanted to appoint independent attorneys in the Anna Nicole case who would advocate what was in Anna Nicole's and her surviving child's best interest. These attorneys would do splendid work and be beyond reproach. I knew this case would be moving at a very rapid pace. I knew I needed skillful lawyers available to me, who would work into the midnight hours. I did say at the beginning that Anna Nicole's body was on ice and it wasn't going anywhere, but that was to divert the lawyers from trying to throw everything plus the kitchen sink at me at one time, to reduce the tension and let them feel that all their arguments and testimony would be heard, which was ultimately the case. The lawyers I brought into the case were not foaming at the mouth. They attempted to resolve the case in an equitable and reasonable fashion.

Some time ago, I had been summoned by my administrative judge of probate to a hearing where Richard Milstein was representing a client. The probate judges seemed to be objecting to the procedures that Milstein's client was advocating in court. I observed Richard Milstein advocate his client's position without hesitation. I saw him hold his ground and prevail against these mighty forces. While I watched in silence, I was amazed by his tenacity and knowledge of the law. At the end of the hearing I did something I never did before. I asked this attorney for his card. I stuck it in my wallet and said to myself that one day I was going to need a warrior like him.

Richard Milstein is a quality person. He had passion and compassion, and he excelled in what he did, probate and guardianship. I later found out that he has dedicated much of his adult life to volunteering and helping people. When I am in battle, this is the guy I want in the foxhole with me. This guy is not going to retreat or capitulate. There are no white flags in his back pocket. This guy had no fear. He didn't back down to a judge. Some judges at the beginning of their careers, and some throughout, have what is called Black Robe Fever, a power trip, which I fortunately never had. I saw myself as the common man doing God's work like a minister, preacher or rabbi trying to help people. I just love helping people and I love interacting with people.

So here we are, the King and His Court. I am anointing myself the King, the pitcher, and Richard Milstein will be the catcher. It's funny. When I was a substitute phys ed teacher in high school, I made myself the pitcher and batted 3rd or 4th in the batting order. If I was a student with this group, I would have probably been sitting on the bench. If you have the power and authority you might as well use it for a good cause.

I was about to make a pitch, a very important pitch; one that I desperately needed to protect the integrity of my case, and one that would have great implications for Dannielynn. The primary focus of the biggest case I ever had, and would ever have, because I knew I would be retiring shortly thereafter. I called Milstein at 7:00 a.m. that morning on his cell phone. I didn't have time for idle chat. I told him that I had a case and I needed help. I told him I was going to appoint a guardian ad litem for Dannielynn. My concern and worry was unnecessary. Milstein wanted to help. He wanted to help the court but most of all, this kind soul wanted to help the child. He said, "I start at 6:30 in the morning, but I will see you later in court, Your Honor." That was the last ex party communication I would have with him and the only direction I gave him was do what you think is best.

My next pitch was to the court. "I am going to do some housekeeping. I am appointing a lawyer who I met in a case one time . . . you want him when the hurricane comes. He doesn't move. He is going to be the guardian ad litem for the child in the Bahamas. You can object if you want on the record. I took him because he fought us one time on something and he did not bend. I called him earlier this morning and he was in his office. I called at 7:00 a.m. and I said all I want you to do is a good job, that's all. I asked him to do this and his name is Richard Milstein. My only connection to him is that we both graduated from the University of Miami Law School. Maybe a little bit before I did and I went there for the last year of law school. Otherwise, I don't know him from a hunk of coal."

So, the pitcher, the catcher. Now I needed a 1st baseman.

There is another expert probate lawyer—he wrote the Bible for probate. Rohan Kelley. I knew his son Shane, an apple that didn't fall far from the tree, an absolutely lovely person who has a master's degree in taxation and with whom I had an excellent rapport, someone I would talk to at the end of a hearing in open court.

I called Kelley Law Firm and his answering service had him call me back. Would Shane Kelley too easily acquiesce to his appointment as administer ad litem? During the trial, Stern's attorney would cite Kelley's $600 an hour fee to ask him a question. Rohan Kelley, the probate guru, sat most of the time throughout the trial behind his son and I had a strong feeling that when he wasn't in the courtroom, he was watching the televised version.

After the first day, I realized Broward County's chief medical examiner, Dr. Perper, knew his stuff and would be a great ally in getting the right results in this matter. I knew he would be an extension of the court's eyes and ears and would make sure everything having to do with Anna Nicole's body was done properly.

But I was still missing the shortstop, a third lawyer to scrutinize, a third set of legal eyes to make sure we were dotting all our *i*'s and crossing all our *t*'s. I was looking for the perfect result.

So I called another lawyer. A lawyer with a deep baritone voice, and he couldn't say no fast enough. He told me that he couldn't take the heat. I knew I could not shop this around any longer. This lawyer would remain silent, but I didn't want the word on the street that I was recruiting and not succeeding. You must always have the aura of success and the ability to accomplish. It's interesting to note that the vast majority of people don't want their lives scrutinized because they can't take close media attention. As I learned fame and fortune brings both good and bad. And nuts come at you, nuts that are jealous, envious, and they will even admit that they are jealous, and they will say anything. They will lie, as they did against Michael Jackson when he was accused of being a child molester. These people have nothing to lose. They are judgment proof. They have no standing in the community, so they don't care about their reputation, or they believe that by attacking you, they receive a piece of your fame. I have learned that more and more of these famous people are being stalked. I have learned in the green rooms of TV studios and radio stations that these famous people have frivolous lawsuits and actually have the FBI or private security protecting them, because they have stalkers, real lunatics who are threatening their welfare and safety.

So back in the courtroom, here we go again. The lawyers are attempting to throw everything at me the moment I appoint Milstein. Susan Brown, the attorney for Larry Birkhead, stated that she filed in both courts a motion for DNA testing and this court had jurisdiction over a limited portion of the paternity action in California.

"Under the . . . Unified Child Custody Jurisdiction Enforcement Act, the Florida court has the authority and should act at the request of California to enforce California orders," she said. "There is still a DNA testing order in existence and we are asking Your Honor to enforce it. This court also has jurisdiction under chapter 55.502, which provides for full faith and credit of foreign orders and judgments. And I think Your Honor should hear everything, and I think you can. Under the unified family court you can hear everything. And this court does have jurisdiction."

I found it somewhat amusing that their attorney is quoting me about the unified family court. I remember being at a BBQ at the state capitol in Tallahassee. Rosemary Barkett, the first female state Supreme Court judge, expressed the objections she was getting as chief judge of the Supreme Court of Florida. In my opinion her number one agenda item was to create a family court division for every circuit in the state, in which the families of Florida would have *their own* family division, and not have to share their time with the more prestigious and money cases in the civil division and effectively be put on the back burner.

I said to Rosemary that she was doing the right thing and anytime there is a substantial change, the bureaucrats will holler and scream. Even brilliant people have some hesitation and need a positive chorus behind them. My agenda was always what was in the best interest of the individual asking the question. Like a question you would normally ask your mother and father. You know their answer will have your best interest at heart.

Here I tried to go through the back door. I really wanted to know who was Dannielynn's father. I wanted these two fellows, Larry and Howard, to come to the plate and give their DNA. It's easy. There is no perspiration and it clears a major hurdle, which is who is in charge of Anna Nicole's body. Because at that point, the father of Dannielynn would be the spokesperson for her; therefore, it would render Milstein's position as moot.

Plus, in these tender months of the child's life she would know who her father was, because she would have contact with him immediately. This was the point at which other men around the country, for example Zsa Zsa Gabor's husband, were coming forward, saying that they were Dannielynn's father. And here I stated on the record that "you look at the statute and the statute says next of kin is the child. So now we have a guardian ad litem that is going to speak for the child. We have Mr. Milstein.

"Let me pose this now. The child, if we knew who the father is of this child, then the father would be the natural guardian of this child, could then inform the court what the child, as the natural guardian, would want to do with the body of Ms. Smith. Is that logical?"

I posed the question. But I already knew the answer. There was no way in hell that at this juncture of the trial, and at this juncture of Stern's strategy, they would agree to this. But I wanted to continue the body punches, wanted to play Columbo. I wanted to continue to wear them down.

Krista Barth, Stern's attorney, replied, "No."

Sue Brown, Birkhead's attorney, then added that they were happy with the appointment of Richard Milstein. "That's a brilliant suggestion," she concluded.

That evening, I was standing on the balcony of my condo in Fort Lauderdale, chomping on a cheap cigar and reflecting on what went on in my courtroom just a few short hours ago. A lot of things went through my mind about the opening of the trial, and I didn't like what I saw. In fact, I thought I smelled a rat—and believe me, as someone who grew up in the Bronx, I have come across my share of rats, both in the animal and non-animal form. And that's when it hit me, during that bit of reflection on my condo balcony, that the Anna Nicole Smith trial I was presiding over was not going to be your average, open-and-shut case.

TWO

WE ARE GOING TO TAKE THE HIGH ROAD

At 8:20 a.m., before the second day's hearing began, the court administrator knocked on the back door of my chambers, and asked me to move from my chambers to a large courtroom.

"I have been in these chambers for a long time holding court," I replied. "They are large and they will accommodate everyone." At my level of power, I was able to tell her no.

However, ten minutes later, my judicial assistant Joanne Gallo rang me and said that two legislators were sitting in my office. These legislators helped control the state wide funds of the judiciary, and they both told me that Tallahassee—implying some of the Supreme Court justices, administrators, as well as several powerful lawyers from around the state and the country—wanted these proceedings to be held in a courtroom. Obviously, I would be sitting up high and the parties and litigants involved would all be in a normal courtroom setting.

I began to retreat, but after they left my chambers, I wasn't convinced. Then the chief judge, Dale Ross, called and told me that I was going to courtroom 850. I asked him what time he wanted me to begin the proceedings that morning, because I never said no to a reasonable request from a chief judge. I served as an administrative judge for five chief judges. Each of them was different, but they all allowed a healthy discussion of an issue. But when they made their decision I joined in supporting it.

Funny, but this reminded me of a time when I was living in a hotel for the first fifteen years I was on the bench. The place was full of characters. Like Pat. He dressed like a wannabe gangster, complete with black shirt, white tie, and he always had a chauffeur driving him around in a limo, like a big shot. I was told he was called by an entertainment agency and they had a part for him. He thought he was going to be the lead actor, but they told him the part was to call the horse races. He refused to take such a small role, but the agency told him that it would pay $5000. Pat replied, "Two minutes to post time."

I stated on the record that "we were in my chambers for the first few days, I don't want to lose that intimacy with the attorneys and the parties. I think we are developing a certain bond. We are moving ahead and getting a lot accomplished."

In court, the judge doesn't have to decide the answer to every issue. Sometimes the passage of time and good lawyers will resolve the issue.

Virgie Arthur, Anna Nicole's mother, was represented by Mr. O'Quinn, whom I referred to as "Texas," and an excellent lawyer out of Miami named Stephen Tunstall. I gave nicknames to people and sometimes I mispronounced names badly because— can you keep a secret?—I can't read words phonetically. We learned in school to read phonetically, which is the proper way. But the only way I could read was by memorizing the word, memorizing the sound of the word. Names you have never seen before or pronounced before, someone like me is going to mash them and destroy them. With O'Quinn, I didn't know if it was "O'Quinn" or "Awkin," but he was tall and big like the state of Texas. And then I had Dr. Perper, the elegant gentleman from Eastern Europe whom I called "Dr. Pepper." Tunstall let me know that Milstein was able to get the parties together and now there was sufficient DNA sampling that was preserved by the medical examiner. Ms. Schwartzreich, who was and continues to be the legal advisor to the Broward Sheriff's Office, stated that "in light of the detailed examination of Ms. Smith's body performed by the medical examiner's office, the detailed documentation of that examination, as well as the sample collection performed by medical examiner's office, it is our position, since all that has already been performed, embalming would not compromise any potential, future criminal investigation in this matter."

I always had concerns about burying Anna Nicole, because I knew there would be a criminal investigation into her death. I didn't want any exhuming of her body. When she was laid in the ground I wanted it to be for perpetuity. "I want complete finality," I said. "I have been in the system long enough to know, I want every loose end tied up. I want peace and tranquility, not only for the dead, but for the living and the living want to visit her site."

I was a hands-on type of judge, always trying to mediate, massage and resolve the disputed issues, so I stated on the morning of the second day of the trial: "I appreciate all the attorneys meeting with me in the room back there [the jury room] and we tried to hash out the other issues that are going to be coming up and it is difficult. It's difficult issues. They are emotionally charged and I just appreciate your efforts and your patience and I had to give it one try at mediation. And I want to be true to myself. If I did not give it the good old American try, to try to resolve it in a mediated form, and I appreciate all your efforts and it gave us a little time to catch our breath."

In most reality TV courtroom shows, the action is live to tape, and the tape is broadcast later on TV. In a trial, you have attorneys taking depositions of the witnesses, reviewing all documents that will be admitted into the trial and developing a strategy that will prevail upon the court. However, I told everyone in the courtroom, "You do discovery, you call witnesses before the trial begins. But we are doing the trial as it is happening, just as it is happening, we are doing discovery right at the time of the trial, but we are doing it because of speed . . . we have a spiritual requirement to move forward. We cannot be bogged down and that's what we have been doing." I then continued, "because the burial is of an emergency nature, you are all going to be with me in this courtroom until we finish it up, there is nothing that is going to intervene with that, because it is pressing, it is absolutely pressing, and I want to get that resolved."

This prompted Krista Barth to stipulate that the medical examiner will keep possession of the DNA samples until an order was issued by the court in California.

Once again, I began to get philosophical, because I knew we had reached another good juncture in this case. The stories that I told the attorneys and the parties involved gave them the opportunity to relax for a minute, gave them a breather, and if I was lucky created a laugh or two, if they didn't laugh out of politeness. I then told them, "you know in this game, in this life of being on the court, you don't rule until you have to. That means, let's not bring the cart before the horse. Let's wait. Let's not worry. We got enough to worry about."

The attorneys were again worried about the DNA. Whether another judge would hear that argument, and whether that DNA ruling would occur in my courtroom. Being a seasoned judge, one who knew he had his leg on a banana peel and was about to retire from the bench within a short period of time, I shared another bit of curbside philosophy: "I serve at the pleasure of the lawyers and the public. That's the way I always perceived it. I look at the judicial economy. We worked hard to make a unified family court, which means probate, juvenile, family court."

I wanted to reinforce that I was the director. I was going to run this show and stay focused. Mr. Tunstall got the message and told me, "I think we all agree, you got the whole enchilada." The lawyers started to appreciate my approach. Ms. Barth added that "the family law is your paternity issue, the collection of the DNA, which Your Honor has already kindly heard and we have that issue resolved. We have the collection of DNA [and] we have agreed that the DNA will be maintained."

I knew that ultimately the California court would require—as it did with Howard K. Stern—DNA testing in order to find out if Stern was actually Dannielynn's biological father. Ms. Brown said in court that "the court finds respondent [Howard K. Stern] is granted an option to designate a proposed location, time and date, inside or outside the Bahamas for the genetic testing." I knew that Larry Birkhead would also be tested and the order further provided that "Mr. Birkhead was allowed to designate a Florida location or department" for the DNA testing if he so desired.

In court, lawyers try to warm up to the judges. They try to discover something that appeals to them. In Florida, so many of the judges attended the University of Florida, Florida State or the University of Miami as an undergraduate or for graduate school, some bell would ring for that. So a story would be told to bring that into play, because a lawyer wants to get a read on the judge prior to a hearing, what the judge likes, or dislikes, or how to get a handle on this court. So when California attorney Debra Opri, another one of Larry Birkhead's lawyers, got on the phone with me, I called her "California," to which she replied, "Your Honor, I am from New York like you, and I am going to be very specific." I liked her; she was forthright and clear in her pronunciations, and she was feisty.

It's essential in a courtroom to maintain order and a level of respect for one another. It's a cardinal rule that once the judge walks into the courtroom, the opposing attorneys do not speak to one another. An attorney should always speak through the court to address the other attorney, otherwise you wind up in a laundromat with a lot of screaming. As a judge, you want to prevent one attorney from name calling another attorney, because personal insults and nastiness slow the case down and just create a lot of tension, with no result. So one of the lines I used was, "We don't want to characterize the lawyers anymore. That is a closing statement to a jury, where we want to drum up some emotion. We want to get to the facts. We don't want to characterize each other. We got to live together. We want to take the high road here.

You are all fine. We are going to take the high road."

I was setting the table for Tuesday's hearing.

Here I began my wrestling match. I wanted Stern in my courtroom for Tuesday and his lawyer, Ms. Barth, is telling me that "they [Larry Birkhead's attorneys] filed a restraining order saying that Howard K. Stern can't take his baby out of the Bahamas. He can't leave. He can't leave her there. You want him to leave that baby alone? Are you kidding me? Look at what is around you. He can't leave her alone."

The court was then told that there was a break-in at the house Anna Nicole and Stern shared in the Bahamas.

But I still needed to get all of the parties involved in the case in my courtroom and that wasn't easy. It was like Harry Houdini breaking off the chains after being dumped into the ocean. I didn't want to use subpoena power or contempt power, because they may have disregarded it anyway, and there would be hearings and appeals. I had to phrase my language to show that I wanted them there, but I didn't want to imply they would lose if they didn't show, because that would be grounds for recusing me.

I stated: "You are at a disadvantage, wouldn't you say, not to have your client here?" Ms. Barth responded, "Absolutely." Mr. Tunstall added that, "Stern has chosen to exercise the jurisdiction of this court. I want him here. There is no reason why he can't be here." I then questioned both attorneys. "What is the injury if he comes? What is the conflict if he comes here?"

The tension mounted for me. I had to nudge Howard K. Stern to appear in court without being overbearing, and with him watching me on television. I wanted him to feel I was reasonable and gentle. Ms. Barth responded to my questions, that "the conflict if he comes here is that he has to leave Dannielynn alone because they filed an ex parte injunction . . . Your Honor has said, you wrote it big on the board, you said the first day the baby is paramount and everybody is saying I don't care about the baby."

I knew the answer to my next question, but I wanted to keep going. I asked Ms. Barth if Stern didn't want to bring Dannielynn to Florida at this point in time. Barth replied that he couldn't because a restraining order was filed and granted—that he had to keep the baby in the Bahamas. Tunstall wanted to continue to turn the screws on this issue and go for the jugular. He said that Gulfstream had a flight to and from Nassau that took only forty-five minutes, which would enable Stern to fly to Florida in the morning and take another flight right back to Nassau when his testimony was done. "So, there is no severe prejudice," said Tunstall. "I don't get it. He chose to be in this court, where is he?"

I felt that Barth was beaten up enough, so I turned to her and asked her what she wanted to do. When she deferred the matter over to me, I resolutely decided that *He is going to come here on Tuesday morning. The court rules that he be here physically present.*

Now this was a court order that had as much power as a lion without any teeth. I directed that he appear in my courtroom, but it was a complete and utter bluff. I was not going to issue any contempt proceedings towards him. It was simply a plea or request to appear.

Actually, I was begging for his appearance in court.

When Barth requested if Stern could be taken out of order,

so that he could be over and done with his testimony as quickly as possible, I replied that, "he will be here Tuesday morning [at] 9:30. We start, we wait for no one. I want him here. Because you know, this is a struggle for all of us. Let everyone perspire here." And to guarantee that Stern would appear in court on Tuesday, I stated the following in court, to sweeten the deal: "Let the record reflect that he [Stern] is here on the limited purpose of testifying on the issue for Tuesday." To which Barth added, "which is the burial issue?"

I accomplished what I wanted. I knew that Larry Birkhead would be flying in and Virgie Arthur was already in the courtroom. So Tuesday would be the time when all the major players of this drama would appear.

THREE

LIGHTNING LARRY

I knew that this would be the one and only time all the parties would be in the same courtroom. I knew that this would be the last time the attorneys, all twenty-nine of them, would be in the same courtroom. I wanted to seize the moment and accomplish my primary goal, which was to make life better for Dannielynn, Anna Nicole's last and only surviving child . . . a baby.

Howard K. Stern, an attorney, allowed his emotions, his love and obsession for Anna Nicole to trump and overrule his scholarly legal mind. Did he think he was coming to a wedding or bar mitzvah?

The appearance by Stern, and his eventual testimony, would sink him. I believed with the testimony that he was about to give, that those statements by him that were admissions against interest according to the street vernacular—would hang him, hang him real high. I believed that the California Attorney General and his assistants, basically the general law population in Los Angeles, were viewing this trial at the same time, or would later review the trial transcripts. I believed that this trial would set a precedent, whereby the general population of America would hear live, unaltered and brutally blunt evidence that people with money, power and fame can get drugs from enablers.

Little did Howard K. Stern know that announcing his name in my courtroom would eventually take him from a law-abiding citizen at least on the record book or the police blotter—to an individual charged with multiple felony counts.

The day began with the usual greetings and pleasantries among myself, Stern, and his attorney, Krista Barth. I even told him that it was nice to have him in my courtroom. Everyone felt the tension. You could cut it with a knife.

I told everyone gathered in my courtroom to settle down, take a seat and take a deep breath.

Virgie Arthur, a lifetime police officer, was there, holding her husband's hand. There is a genuine sweetness about Virgie that somehow was never projected into the media stream, but I witnessed it. I saw a certain love and concern that she displayed for her granddaughter Dannielynn, and for her deceased daughter and grandson.

Larry Birkhead was an upbeat, energized young man who exuded confidence and love of life. He was always respectful to the court and really didn't have a dog in the fight of where Anna Nicole should be buried. I told everyone that "we are going to give you all a chance to speak. Let's relax and feel our feet. "

Richard Milstein then proceeded to say that he was able to reach both counsels, and a confidentiality agreement was reached between both counsels and the funeral home embalmer in Palm Beach. He assured everyone by saying, "I was told by communication with the medical examiner's office on Saturday morning that at 8 o'clock, the embalming started, and spoke to them at 10 and we spoke again a little before 12, the medical examiner informed me that they would inform you that the embalming has been completed by them. As a result, the body is now safe and secure. It's back under security at the medical examiner's office . . . we are now awaiting what needs to be done further on this."

Milstein was a meticulous person. He is a judge's lawyer, totally honest, with no hidden agenda. "We do not want the funeral home embalmer to indicate anything that occurred that day," he added.

A sickening moment had just taken place in my courtroom and all the parties and attorneys were deflated. We just embalmed Anna Nicole Smith, the blonde bombshell who had been so young and so full of life. It was time for another story, to divert attention from that moment of sadness.

It went like this. "I am the product of a college in the Bronx, it is Hunter College that produced school teachers, and I was a teacher, [a] substitute teacher for elementary school and high school. And then upon graduation from law school, I taught here in a local college, a college for a master's program/law school. I was an adjunct professor there. And I guess it was no accident that I did this, I have a love of students and children . . .

"We have talked about there being a maze, that we are in a maze, in the center of the maze. Can we turn that board around, would you do me a favor, Mr. Stern, I got a magic marker. Would you write that little girl's name down under the word 'child,' because I am not sure how you spell her name. Could you put it right here . . . I guess my teaching is still coming out in me.

"We want to give respect and peace to Ms. Smith's body. That's one of the overriding considerations. But, the most important matter in this courtroom is the welfare, the well being and the stability of this child, Dannielynn. I want you to keep that in mind as we proceed, that's my overriding issue. Some of you want to box the court in, we can't go there. But when you look at this in a logical way, I remember when I was in Hunter College. I was taking, it was a philosophy logic course, there was an old professor, towards the end of class, and he said 'Seidlin, I don't know whether to give you an A or an A+. I have never given an A+ before.' I said, 'Set precedent, professor.'"

I was setting the framework to get these parties Stern and Birkhead—to belly up and give me DNA, so that I could find out who Dannielynn's father was. I then continued:

" . . . When you go through this, it's like when you took a course in college or law school, you had 140 pages in notes and then as you started to cram, you knocked it down to 10, and then you put everything on one page. It all came down to one page. When you look at this logically, in the center of the French labyrinth, in the center of the maze is Dannielynn, what is in her best welfare, what is in her best interest. Because we need to give the peace and respect that we are now giving Ms. Smith's body. We want to give this to this child. We ask, why are we spending so much time here, because we are here to save one child. That's why we are here."

I got a little hoaky, I got a little corny, but I was elected to be a judge in Broward County at the age of twenty-eight, in a county of close to one and a half million people. This was a major undertaking, this job as judge. It was an enormous responsibility and it was a 24-hour-a-day deal, so I believed God allowed me this wonderful position. A position that dictated whether grown men would go to jail, go on probation, or go free. That evicted the poor immediately, or gave them time to vacate the premises. A position where I could pass judgment on a traffic ticket for people of average means, and make the fine so high, that they could not pay their other bills, and eventually their licenses might get suspended and that would lead to jail time. A position where I was putting Humpty Dumpty back together again in family court, helping people who were in utter despair.

I hit a lot of racquetballs, a lot of tennis balls, and believe me, "Lightning Larry" got outside plenty of times. But I had the reputation of being kind, gentle and patient to all who came in front of me. I always reminded myself to be as patient as a saint, because I was performing the job of a priest, imam, rabbi or pastor. I had people's lives in my hands. I never displayed robe fever, as some judges might have. I never displayed arrogance. I remained true to myself. I remained a guy that enjoyed hanging out in a public park.

So, hoakey and corny. I then got spiritual. "Somehow," I said, "we were all selected to be in this room at the beginning. We are climbing a mountain here. We were selected to do a job, and since we are here, we are going to do the job. The lawyers have all agreed one way or another that you want me to handle the jurisdiction . . . but you wanted the court to take over the matters that you all filed earlier this week. I sat there when we were doing the uniform family court; I sat there with the Supreme Court judges in Florida and I was friendly with a bunch of them, on a personal note. They said, let's bring them all together. Let's bring juvenile court, family court, probate court, delinquency, dependency, it's under one roof, because we do not want the parties to be running from courtroom to courtroom. We don't want to put the child through so much turmoil. We don't want to put the families through so much turmoil that they have to educate another judge, [that] they have to warm up another judge as to the facts. Be that as it may, if there is no objection by the parties here today, I am going to assume jurisdiction of the paternity matters."

Although I stated in court that I was going to handle the paternity issues, all I could really do was convince Stern to give it up, meaning that he had to give his DNA to the California court, and let that DNA be matched up to the child Dannielynn. I wanted to bring Howard K. Stern to this conclusion, so I continued to do my dance.

Nancy Haas, Larry Birkhead's co-counsel, assured the court that many of the witnesses who would be testifying and much of the information that would be presented was intertwined with what lay in the best interest of the child. "So in that way . . . we do not want to do this twice, because many of the issues that you will be confronted with today, with regard to where Anna Nicole should rest is also intertwined in the paternity action and what we are seeking to establish, which is what is in the best interest of this child. Who is the natural father of this child? We believe the court can deal with all of these issues at once," she stated.

I continued to set the framework. I knew that these lawyers would be seeking DNA from Stern. Let's face it. Life is a chess game and you have to look way beyond the next move. I looked towards the end result and knew that this was always the goal. Let's get that DNA, and let's try to have a friendly relationship among all the parties that are connected to Dannielynn.

Again, I got philosophical. "We got the sons and daughters in Iraq, they are in Afghanistan, let's give them Godspeed and let's note we are working on the case. We are looking to saving one child and there is a ripple effect. Every time I save one child, I save another child that can go to college and contribute to this community and to humanity, so let's keep that in mind." I reminded the parties that the burden associated with this trial was heavy for their clients. And I decided to give them some practical—and healthy—advice.

"I need you so very healthy. Both of these men, you both had a relationship, somehow, someway with Ms. Smith. I need you fellows healthy, I want this child in a healthy environment. Not washed out and beat up everyday, [because] this legal process wears you down too. That is how cases settle, people get worn out. It's like Muhammed Ali, sometimes you have to wait the whole ten rounds. Sometimes it was one round. I don't want you wearing out. I want you to have the strength. Why? Because I want you to have the strength to care for Dannielynn. I am not making any decisions this morning. I am just happy to have you both here. Just relax, keep your feet on the ground and relax."

And then all hell broke loose. Krista Barth exclaimed, "you just did say to us that we were not going to personally attack each other. I just can't sit here because Ms. Opri did make a statement to my client that he actually killed Ms. Smith." I told her that there wouldn't be any personal attacks in my courtroom, to which she replied, "it needs to stop because I have to protect him [Stern]."

We had many chamber sessions outside the presence of the public and the media. This is done all the time by proactive judges who seek to get to the bottom line, and thereby save the resources and personal emotions of the parties. I then announced that "it has been indicated to the court one of the parties wants to physically meet in the ante room and discuss the case outside the presence of the media. I think it is a good step and we are going to do it now."

The lawyers at least some of them—were starting to get antsy, and I warned them that they were getting animated for no reason at all. "You were getting stressed for no reason," I sternly told them. "We were on different signals, twice now I am going to get you some juice, have a seat. We have been doing so well together . . . you had an issue [and] we talked it out."

Remember, Daniel died in September of 2006, and now a few months later, we had the death of Anna Nicole, so I reminded them that there was "a little bit of a healing process going on."

These chamber settlement conferences bear fruit, and they continue to resolve certain thorny issues. As the record reflected, outside the presence of the public and the media, we had been able to resolve the issue of embalming, who would perform that service, the timing of it, the location and similar issues addressing the preservation of Anna Nicole's remains as well as to maintain the dignity of the proceedings.

And again, Ms. Brown reminded me of the need to know who Dannielynn's natural father was, so that her rights could be asserted. She insisted that someone should go to the Bahamas in order to take a DNA swab test from the child. And of course, they wanted similar DNA tests to be conducted on Stern and Birkhead.

I told Ms. Brown that when I received the case the previous Wednesday, I anticipated everything about the case and what it involved.

"This begins like a chess game, which is a game you got to know where each move is going to be and hopefully you stay a few steps ahead," I said. "And the two alleged fathers came here in good faith, Larry Birkhead and Howard K. Stern. I don't want to really set a bear trap for them. One of the issues the court would have considered, Milstein hit on the nose is you [Milstein] are a stranger, you are a guardian ad litem, you are a good stranger, but you are a stranger. Like when I entered this building in 1976. But be that as it may, if we knew who the natural father was in this limited area, meaning where we are going to place Ms. Smith's body, it would help the court and be relevant. It would help the court if I knew who the natural father was to speak on behalf of Dannielynn, it would help me tremendously. But in good faith, I made an offer to both alleged fathers, if I could say it without insulting anyone, I knew they would be here this morning. And I am not setting a bear trap, saying now you are here, now I got you. They don't want to do it [the paternity test] and I don't want to say who but right now, the moment is not right. So I am going to proceed in this trial, without that bit of evidence coming in. And there is still plenty here to help me decide where to go."

And then there was the matter of Anna Nicole's disputed will, which, if it was probated and then contested, could take between two to four years to litigate in probate court. "So on this piece of paper, it is a purported will, whether or not one determines in its finality whether it is a real will or a valid will," I told the parties. "I don't know if I am going to reach that in this proceeding, it will be just another document. It is just another piece of evidence that you obviously are going to attack. At some point it will be admitted, but at some point you are going to attack the admissibility [and the credibility of the will]."

I allowed the document to be introduced in court. "Normally . . . he would attack the witness who wrote the will, that brought the person to write the will, etc. How far we get into that [the contesting of Anna Nicole's will] is another matter but the clock is moving. . ."

I turned to the parties and told them for the sake of giving peace and beauty to both Anna Nicole and Dannielynn, I would let them present their respective cases, but in a more abbreviated form, because the lawyers were at times getting blindsided by unfolding issues.

In a judge trial, you really just need a brief two- or three-minute opening statement. There is no jury that you need to pound continuously with your theme or your selling points. In a jury trial, an opening statement could last between fifteen minutes to a couple of hours. I told the parties that, "I pretty much heard this case. I know it like the back of my hand. I dream about it, I jog and think about it, I hit a tennis ball and think about it, and when I am looking at my little kid I think about it."

FOUR

WHERE ARE WE ALL GOING TO BE?

"Please state your name for the record."

"Howard K. Stern."

With that simple introduction began the explosive testimony of the most pivotal, controversial figure in the Anna Nicole Smith case.

At the beginning, the questioning was conducted in a straightforward manner between Stern and his attorney, Krista Barth. She asked him about his occupation [attorney], where he was licensed [California], if he was a member in good standing of the California bar [he was] and if he knew Anna Nicole Smith well ["I knew her very well, very well," was his answer]. Then Barth proceeded to question Stern about his relationship with Anna Nicole, and when he first met her.

Stern: Originally I believe it was back in 1996, she was a client of mine, we became friends, we spent a lot of time together. Ultimately, we became more than friends. This is years ago, we did not say anything at the time. She was pretty much my whole life, she was my best friend.

Barth: Could you describe the nature of your relationship?

Stern: She was my best friend, my lover, the mother of my daughter, everything to me, literally everything, my whole world.

Barth: If you could give the court more of an idea of the time that you spent with Ms. Smith?

Stern: Well, a lot of time I saw her daily and the last four or five months, I was with her everyday. Almost all of the time.

Barth: But prior to that since you knew her?

Stern: It would depend, you know, on what I was working on at the time, but I spent pretty much, saw her everyday and we spent a great deal of time together.

I decided to ask Stern where in California he first met her, which was in court, because he was her personal counsel in the litigation that involved the disputed estate of her late husband, the Texas billionaire oilman J. Howard Marshall, whom she married when she was twenty-seven and he was eighty-eight years old. Stern also served as co-counsel in the district court during that trial.

Barth then continued the questioning, this time regarding his relationship with Anna Nicole's deceased son, Daniel.

Barth: Did you know Anna Nicole's son Daniel?

Stern: I knew Daniel very well. Daniel was like a brother to me. We spent a great deal of time together, both at Anna's house and sometimes we go out to dinner and see movies. Daniel, he was a great boy. He was a wonderful, wonderful person.

I found it extremely odd that Howard Stern claimed Daniel was like a brother to him. Daniel was so young, and Howard was in his forties. Why wouldn't he state that he thought of Daniel as his son? It didn't add up. He knew him since 1996. That answer of his really stuck in my craw. Barth continued to pursue that line of questioning with Stern, about his relationship with Daniel.

Barth: Did Daniel have a father in his life?

Stern: Daniel, no, not really. He was estranged from his father since, I believe, he was an infant.

Barth: Can you explain to me the things you observed about Anna's relationship with her son Daniel?

Stern: Anna and Daniel were inseparable. Daniel was, without question, the most important person in Anna Nicole's life. From the time I first met her, everything she was doing was for Daniel, literally everything.

I thought to myself, if everything was for Daniel and her life was consumed with the love of Daniel, how can I separate these two people? I wanted to know more about the sexual relationship between Stern and Anna Nicole, so I approached the matter with him as diplomatically as possible.

Seidlin: Back up a minute. When did the relationship, when you as an attorney and then you were in a personal relationship, what year did that begin?

Stern: Well, we started spending a lot of time together in

1998. We became more than friends after that. It was probably around 2000.

Seidlin: In 2000 you started having a more personal intimate relationship with her?

Stern: Yes. It was not exclusive, because of my relationship as her attorney and we did not disclose it to many people, but she had other boyfriends in between. I wanted to make her happy.

Barth wanted to get back to the relationship between Anna Nicole and her son Daniel and how close they really were. She asked Stern if he could describe the relationship as a normal mother and child bond.

Stern: It was a little different, because Anna was so young when she had Daniel. In a lot of times they grew up together. They were friends as well as mother and son. When we would travel to different events, Daniel would always come with his mom. They were virtually inseparable.

I asked Stern about Daniel's death, especially the cause of it, to which he replied, "We had an independent pathologist."

Again, I thought this was a strange answer. I was merely asking him how Daniel died and he was very defensive, telling me that they hired a pathologist, which was too formal an answer. Stern hired an independent pathologist to make sure the Bahamian authorities didn't railroad him, didn't accuse him of Daniel's death. He wanted his own ace in the hole, because you will see that Dr. Perper played in an important role in determining the cause of Anna Nicole's death. Our prosecutor in Broward County really couldn't pursue manslaughter charges against Howard K. Stern or anyone else, when the Chief Medical Examiner was announcing to the world that Anna Nicole Smith died accidently from an overindulgence of drugs.

Barth started to question Stern about the circumstances surrounding Daniel's death, which took place just after the birth of Dannielynn.

Stern: Dannielynn was born on September 7. It was actually the night that Daniel came to the Bahamas to visit his baby sister was the night he passed away.

Barth: And how would you describe Anna's state of mind after Daniel died?

Stern: From the day that Daniel died, Anna honestly was never the same. I would say that physically she died last week, but in a lot of ways, emotionally, she died when Daniel died, and she initially [did] not accept that Daniel was gone and that's why for quite some time, that was the reason why she did not want to bury him earlier . . . And it was the most difficult thing that I have seen anybody go through.

I asked Stern about Daniel's age at the time of his death, which he stated was twenty, going on twenty-one. Stern also told the court that Daniel went to the Bahamas to spend some time with his mother. He admitted that Daniel was living in California with one of Anna Nicole's friends, and was close to completing a summer school class at Valley Junior College, but Anna was still supporting him. From there, Barth went back to the matter of Daniel's burial and Anna's fragile state of mind.

Barth: It took Anna quite some time to bury Daniel. Is that correct?

Stern: It did . . . It was quite a difficult process. You know, it was hard for her to talk about it and she went through a lot of thought in deciding what his plans would be and you know, throughout that time, the way she went about it, it was never where is Daniel going to be. All of the discussions were always in the context of *where are we all going to be?*

FIVE

THE TRIER OF FACT

Tuesday afternoon. We started with me again trying to have Howard K. Stern voluntarily submit to DNA testing, but it was like going through water torture.

"The probate statute we talk about [is] the next of kin. And Milstein is going to argue the next of kin brings Dannielynn first. She is first to decide what to do with her mother's body ... the guardian ad litem testimony is still a stranger to this family setting. So the court said, maybe we should take DNA of Mr. Stern and Larry Birkhead. So then we get the natural father and the natural father would speak for the child under the probate statute and the court would have that tremendous input," I said in court.

Again, I knew if I required Stern to submit to the DNA test, he would bolt from the courthouse on a recess. And there is nothing holding him to my courtroom. His lawyers can continue to argue where Anna Nicole should be buried without his presence. I continually state that they both should submit to the DNA test. I did not want to single Stern out. I didn't want to lose his confidence. I wanted him to feel that I would give him a fair and equitable hearing. And I stated, "I know if I said to them that they would have to give DNA, I was concerned about whether they submit themselves to this jurisdiction."

Ms. Brown, always being cute and entertaining, jumped up and said, "We volunteer Mr. Birkhead for DNA."

After that, Barth asked Stern to tell the court about Anna's feelings after Daniel's funeral.

> **Stern:** Well, Anna never got over Daniel's death. She would take almost like a poster size picture of Daniel, that is in a frame, that at least on ten occasions, she cuddled with it in bed, in our bed. She would literally cry herself to sleep and this was a constant thing . . . Anna had dreams.

Barth then approached the subject of the commitment ceremony that Stern and Anna held shortly after Daniel's death. That's when I said that they wanted to get spiritual, to which Tunstall replied: "I don't know how you can protect her spirit." I guess when lawyers begin to argue, they'll argue about anything, even about the spirit of an individual, as if they were Casper the Friendly Ghost.

Stern said that he and Anna did have this commitment ceremony, on September 23, 2006 on a boat in the Bahamas. A Baptist minister officiated, and about 15–20 people attended. Barth asked him why he decided to conduct such a ceremony. Stern replied that "Anna and I talked about it and she felt that she could not bear to be alone when Daniel was gone."

My bright friend O'Quinn was funny. He made me laugh inside when he stated that "Stern's reading her mind, telling us about her dreams." In fact, I had some funny exchanges with O'Quinn when he stood up for one of his many objections that day. One of my favorite replies to an O'Quinn objection was, "My friend, you've got to sit down for awhile. Save some shoe leather."

I followed O'Quinn's little aside with, "I am the trier of fact and it's whether or not I am going to buy into these positions and hopefully, I will be able to determine whether it makes sense or not." Stern stated Anna Nicole wouldn't be able to "put Daniel to rest unless we were together. She felt like she didn't have a family. She could not do it alone and Daniel was really who she thought was her only family."

I wasn't buying into this. She just had a baby, Dannielynn. Stern purports to be the father of the child and if he's not, then you have Larry Birkhead. It just didn't add up. But I knew the pieces that were missing from this puzzle, and they wouldn't fit in until later on, not in this trial.

For example, why wouldn't Stern give Anna Nicole a pep talk, tell her, "You have a beautiful new baby, who's carrying Daniel's name. When a child predeceases the parent, that parent shouldn't stop living." It's a heavy road to travel when a child dies. The statistics indicate when this occurs, the couple have a hard time maintaining their marriage, as I witnessed in family court. But how many people just do themselves in? Here again I see an enabler, instead of someone who kicks ass and takes names. In other words, pump her up and accept the consequences if she doesn't respond. In life, as in poker, you have to be prepared to lose what you brought to the table. But you must have confidence in yourself and not fear losing it.

It got strange again, when it came to the issue of husband-wife privilege. This privilege does not attach to activity that took place prior to a marriage. And Stern told the court that "the marital privilege, because of Daniel's death, … and I was wrongly advised that it applied to things prior to marriage, not just subsequent to marriage."

Now I was totally confused. I had no clue what Stern was talking about. I only began to understand this after the case ended and I spent the next couple of years investigating the deaths of Anna Nicole and Daniel. I admitted that I didn't know what the hell this guy Stern was talking about.

Seidlin: You missed me. I am missing this. Run this by me again … and I had a light lunch, so I am still strong.

Stern: Because her son had passed away and we did not want to give any perception that we were trying to hide any wrongdoing.

Seidlin: Wrongdoing? Because there were questions about the issue of his death?

All my antennas went up. You are talking about a kid like me who walked the streets of the Bronx. When you went jogging down those streets, when you go fast enough, they think you're stealing a TV set. I couldn't buy any of this. If there was a Baptist minister who presided at the ceremony, this marriage would be binding, because the courts look upon, and there is a public policy, that errors like this don't hinder the legality of the marriage. I thought that Stern was attempting to cover his bets.

If he needed the marriage to work for a husband-wife privilege, we are married. If the husband-wife privilege doesn't assist him in his agenda, then it was a spiritual marriage. Stern stated later on that he and Anna Nicole presented to the people that they were husband and wife. That is additional evidence to say that the marriage ceremony was a marriage. So the next logical question is: Did this marriage ceremony have anything to do with Daniel's death?

Stern: Well, there were questions by an initial coroner at the time. Well, a coroner came out and said the *death was under suspicious circumstances,* and then retracted that and said *whenever a 20 year old passes away, it's got to be because of something suspicious.*

Seidlin: I see, in other words, you did not want to get formally married with all the proper paperwork because...

My words there were unartful. I stumbled over the words. You are either pregnant or not pregnant. You are either married or not married. But I wanted Stern to continue testifying.

Stern: We did not want it to be perceived that we were trying to hide anything and this lawyer advised me that it would mean either she would not have to testify against me or I would not have to testify against her.

Seidlin: But that might not have been applicable, because it [marriage] was after the fact [after Daniel's death]?

Stern: It wasn't [the marital privilege].

Seidlin: So, I am right, the husband and wife privilege does not take place, because it was afterward, so she [Anna Nicole] still would have testified. So you went to a bad lawyer?

Stern: Exactly.

Seidlin: You are not having him working for you anymore?

Stern: Absolutely not.

This trial transcript is loaded with golden nuggets. I was criticized by some that the case took too long, but you would have to be an idiot not to see that we were pursuing many avenues. We are also looking at the death of Daniel, a twenty-year-old who arrives in the Bahamas at night, and lies in bed with his mother, and in the morning he is dead as a door nail.

I had an obligation to open all doors and allow any and all law enforcement agencies to review, investigate and charge whomever they thought was the proper party. But you had the Bahamas and the Seminole police departments responsible for the investigations of the deaths of these two individuals. Look at the law enforcement in Aruba. They are still trying to find the murderer of one young girl, Natalee Holloway. There are times when you need Babe Ruth or Mickey Mantle to bat fourth in the batting order, to be the clean up hitter. Here you needed a sophisticated, extremely competent investigative body to come back with the answers.

Also, major tourism areas don't want negative press. They depend completely on tourism and they don't want to be looking at any foul play. These police agencies work at the pleasure of the governing bodies, and the governing bodies would want a completed police report that is self-serving. If Anna Nicole's death was ruled a homicide, think of all the negative publicity that would generate. Look at the publicity that her *accidental* death just generated.

Stern then claimed in court that Anna referred to him as her husband to other people and he, in turn, referred to her as his wife. Then I began to think that these two were married: a minister performed a wedding ceremony and they hold themselves out to people as though they are married. If I married a couple, and if I failed to file the papers for some reason, this couple is still married.

> **Seidlin:** Were you then introduced as husband and wife at events and stuff like that?
>
> **Stern:** Well yes. Then it became so public that it wasn't legally binding in the Bahamas, that we had actually planned on getting married again.
>
> **Seidlin:** In the Bahamas?
>
> **Stern:** Legally.
>
> **Seidlin:** In the Bahamas.
>
> **Stern:** Correct.

I think that the parties saw I was somewhat flabbergasted, that I was busy with my shovel digging out all this BS, that this was just too much for me. So Barth tried to repair the damage by asking Stern, "When were you going to do that?" And Stern responded with, "the first marriage was at sea and I haven't researched what that means."

So here we go again . . . are they married? And why do they want to get married really, on the heels of the death of Daniel?

And Anna Nicole wasn't thinking clearly at this point. Barth asked Stern when he and Anna were supposed to get married. Stern replied, "We were supposed to do it this week." When I interjected and asked him if he was supposed to get married this week in the Bahamas, Stern just nodded his head in agreement.

I just got done with this marriage issue and now I tried to indicate what Anna Nicole's intent was, because they wanted to admit Anna Nicole's will into evidence, which she signed in 2001. The will didn't state where Anna Nicole wanted to be buried. But it appointed Howard K. Stern her executor and he would express Anna Nicole's wishes as to where she wanted to be buried. The will, therefore, was just an additional piece of evidence for the court to study in order to determine where she should be buried.

Barth tried to give Stern a stronger position: he is the executor of her will and he is speaking for what is in the best interest of Anna Nicole. And additionally, he had conversations with Anna Nicole about where she would want to be buried. So as the executor, Stern wears this additional hat and comes to my court with more power.

But this will is horrible. It's poorly drafted and is completely illogical, because one of the first clauses in the will is repugnant. Let's take a look at it. Article 1 of the will states that, "I am unmarried, I have one child Daniel Wayne Smith. I have no predeceased children, nor predeceased children leaving issue. Except as otherwise provided in this will I *have intentionally omitted to provide for my spouse and other heirs, including future spouses and children* and other descendants now living and *those hereafter born* or adopted, as well as existing and future step children and foster children." Look at this paragraph; look at this article again. Tell me it doesn't slap you in the face, because you will never see a woman anywhere in the world who has this clause in her will.

In Article 3 of this will, Howard K. Stern is the first executor. If he fails to qualify or ceases to act, then Ron Rale is second, and Eric Lund is third.

Finally, I told the court that Anna Nicole's 2001 will would be admitted "strictly as another piece of evidence to help us decide where we are going to lay Anna Nicole Smith to rest." I then turned to Rohan Kelley to ask him about the impact the natural father of Dannielynn would have upon the court and the decision process of where to bury Anna Nicole. I was really using Rohan Kelley, the noted probate expert, as another weapon to pressure Stern to take the DNA test.

Kelley told me, "that depends on Anna Nicole's intent. If it is Mr. Milstein's decision, one of the factors he has to decide is what the natural father would say, because this is where she [Dannielynn] would be living . . ."

I then had another little exchange with Texas—O'Quinn— when he was objecting about the rules of evidence.

O'Quinn: An emergency doesn't overrule the rules of evidence.

Seidlin: Well, you have an issue to appeal me on.

O'Quinn: I prefer to get it right the first time.

Seidlin: I am trying to get it right.

O'Quinn: I am trying to help you, Your Honor.

I am thinking to myself that this is one sharp dude. At another time and place, I could visualize myself downing a tall one with him. Texas reminded me of my judge brethren in the Florida panhandle. About twenty-five years ago, I was with some of them in a car, on our way to a country tavern, and somehow the conversation rolled around to my accent.

One of the judges said, "You aren't one of those Jews from New York?"

I said to him, "You don't think I am from Alabama or Tennessee? You don't think I am Greek or Italian? I guess my ancestors spent a longer time in the desert."

This judge had a thick southern accent and he told me, "You have to get the f--- out of the car! My mother and father would have rolled around in their graves if they knew a Jewboy was sitting in the car with me."

To which I replied, "Actually I would have your mom and dad laughing."

So this judge turned to the other judges in the car and said, "He is a character, I like him, let's let him have dinner with us."

As we drove back to the hotel convention center, they said to me, "Take off those shorts you are always wearing and don't look like a d---head, forget that Ralph Lauren look, put on a tie and a jacket and tomorrow morning just say yes. We are going to elect you the vice president of the county court conference for the state of Florida."

I was thirty-two, thirty-three years old. I was unopposed and served in that post as vice president for five years.

In life, it's important for us to embrace the differences that we all have. Look at me . . . a kid with a strong Bronx accent arriving in the deep south and being warmly received, encouraged, accepted, and essentially elected, appointed and loved by the citizens and power structure of Broward County, with a population of over a million people, which is larger than a bunch of states in the union. Really, our country exemplifies that our citizens embrace and assist one another's dreams.

It is important in a courtroom that all lawyers believe and feel that the judge is applying an even-handed application of equity for all. I didn't want, and never did want, a lawyer to feel that my Yankee accent made a difference, that a southern accent wasn't equal in my courtroom. I wanted them to know that I welcomed all attorneys into my courtroom, regardless of their backgrounds.

When I was on the bench early in my career, there were judges during the late 1970s who would not marry parties of different races. It is interesting to note that our Florida Supreme Court, as other courts around the country, has advocated that trial judges needed to take sensitivity courses to help them sympathize and empathize with ordinary people. Some judges have what we call, among ourselves, black robe fever. They act like monarchs. And not only to the litigants and attorneys that appear in front of them. In fact, I felt their wrath as an administrative judge for five different chief judges. As Tiny Tim would sing, "I had to tiptoe through the tulips." I had to kiss their behinds to get something done. So what you begin to do after a while is you leave them the hell alone, you let them run their court and you go to the reliable, dependable, good spirited judges. You wind up violating one of my rules, and that is don't take advantage of a friend, but when you have the public's life at stake, who can you turn to but caring individuals.

Barth's questioning of Stern now revolved around his knowledge of Anna Nicole's relationship, or lack thereof, with her mother Virgie Arthur.

Stern: When I first met Anna, she talked about Ms. Arthur. I knew that they were estranged, she told me that she was estranged from her family. I spoke with Virgie after Daniel passed ... I spoke with Virgie about trying to get pictures of Daniel that Anna wanted, that were in Virgie's possession.

Barth: What kind of pictures?

Stern: I know one was an oil painting. Another was pictures of Daniel's childhood, because Virgie kept those and did not let Anna have them.

Seidlin: In 1996 when you met her [Anna] did she have any contact from the moment you met her, to her death, with her mother?

Stern: There was an occasional phone contact.

Seidlin: Who made the phone calls?

Stern: The last time, it was Anna [who] left a message that Daniel was dead. And then Anna was very upset that her mother went to the media with that recording and said that Anna was clearly on drugs.

Seidlin: Was there any physical contact between 1996 and the time of her death between the mother and daughter?

Stern: Not that I am aware of.

Seidlin: Do you know when the relationship between the mother and daughter became strained, what year that happened?

Stern: I think it was during her childhood. I know that Anna left home at a very early age. That is what Anna told me. I know there were attempts to reconnect when Anna was married to her second husband, J. Howard Marshall, but those did not last long.

Barth: Anna was very upset for her mom for something that happened after Daniel was buried. Can you tell me what you observed as to why she was very angry with Ms. Arthur?

I knew the answer to this question was going to be a bombshell, and I wanted to lessen the tension and drama that would flow from Stern's answer, so I said that I would allow Stern's testimony in a limited scope, and although I realized that some of it was self serving, I was going to give him a little bit of leeway.

Stern: Well, there were a couple of things. One of them is that *it really bothered Anna when Virgie went to the media and said that either Anna or I had murdered Daniel.*

Seidlin: What is that? Run that by me again?

Stern: There is— *Ms. Arthur went to the media and said that I had murdered Daniel, either I or Anna murdered Daniel* and it just angered Anna. At that point she said, this woman will never see my daughter . . . and it was the absolute final straw.

I then began to battle with Stern. I was laying a foundation that I believed that Anna was in a drugged and depressed state and that she was not in a normal capacity.

> **Seidlin:** Now, when she was talking to you, wasn't she in a very depressed state? Also when she was talking to you about that?
>
> **Stern:** Anna was irate.
>
> **Seidlin:** Was she in a depressed state?
>
> Finally I got the answer I knew had to be given; the only logical answer there was.
>
> **Stern:** Sure, she was depressed, since her son died. But she was very irate.

I thought either Anna intentionally tried to kill herself, or there was some foul play. Things didn't smell right. I was really going off the charts with the next few questions. I can be too demanding, at times too aggressive. But being tough is sometimes necessary to get the job done right.

> **Seidlin:** Was she suicidal at that point?
>
> **Stern:** I would like to think that Anna was never suicidal.

Here is where I really went to town. This guy is either blindly in love with her, and sees no faults in her, or he is smelling different air than me.

> **Seidlin:** But she had just given birth to a child, she just lost

Danny. Wouldn't she be in a depressed state when she made that comment about her mother?

Stern: It was a while after, *she was distraught,* but she was more angry.

Seidlin: How do you describe distraught? She is talking about death and wanting to pick out cemetery places.

Stern: No, no. This was after, well, I can't say the exact date that Virgie Arthur went to the media, but it was pure anger at that point.

Then the prosecutor in me came out. I can't let go. I guess I am like a mad dog when I ask Stern, "What state of mind was she in when she made these comments and that is an issue, a big issue."

Barth sees I am foaming at the mouth and, as a good lawyer, wants to break the tension. So Barth propounds a question basically eliminating mine. I take a step back and allow it, because she is a good lawyer and a good person and we had a mission to accomplish in an expedited manner.

Barth: Can you tell the judge the one specific thing that happened after Daniel's funeral, a month after Daniel died?

Stern: Anna was upset that Virgie brought the media, brought Splash News to Daniel's gravesite to take a photo op virtually on Daniel's birthday.

Barth: When was the last time that you know that Ms. Arthur saw Daniel?

Stern: It was, I was told, it was during his childhood, he was probably five or six.

Stern wanted to prove to me that Anna had no interest in being with her mother, dead or alive, and so they showed me a tape that Anna made for *Entertainment Tonight*.

The ET reporter says, "Let's move on Nicole. Let me ask you about your mother, who has made some statements in the press. What can you tell me about the statements and accusations that she has made?"

And Anna replies: First of all, she is not my mother. She is my birth mother. Second of all, she doesn't know me, she doesn't know my son. I left home when I was fifteen years old and, I mean, she has not seen my son since he was probably five years old. And she doesn't know him, she doesn't know him or me. I have gone through—and making these ridiculous statements and me killing my son or Howard killing my son, who does she think she is? She is out there making money for herself.

Reporter: When was the last time you spoke with her?

Anna: The last time I spoke with her or the last time she beat me? The last time I got a beating from my mother, I think I was twenty-one years old. And before that, it was a big gap. I left home when I was fifteen and she came to me to live in one of my houses because her husband, I don't know what he did to her, she married—she has been married like twenty times.

Reporter: Did you contact her at all when Daniel passed?

Anna: I don't know any of my family. The only time my family tried to get a hold of me is when they wanted money or something, or they want a story about them or something. They somehow . . . the media wants to contact me to get me to give them a story. I was sedated; the doctor had me sedated. It was tough. It was bad. My son died. So I called my mother and all I could say is Daniel is dead. Daniel is dead.

Reporter: What did she say to you?

Anna: I said, Daniel is dead and I hung up the phone. I seen her on CNN telling everybody *that I killed my son or Howard killed my son.* And she kept trying to say that Howard used drugs.

Reporter: Why would she say these things?

Anna: She didn't know—she never wanted to know me, because she was so jealous of me. And she definitely did not know my son. What has she done to me? You want to hear my child life? You want to hear all the things she did to me, what she let my father do to me, or brother or my sister. All the beatings and the whippings and rape. That is my mother. That's my mom.

Reporter: What do you want to say to her?

Anna: I want to say to her, how dare you, bitch, how dare you. That is what I want to say. Come after me. Come on. Because you know what, I used to cry after you. I used to cry even after my baby girl. I cried for you and you ask Howard, I cried for my mom. When I saw her on CNN and saw how evil she was and evil she looked, all that is gone now and so bring it on, mom. Mommy dearest. Bring it on. That's all I want to say.

Reporter: I am sorry . . . will you ever talk to her again?

Anna: I will never speak to her again, never.

Reporter: She will never know Dannielynn?

Anna: Are you kidding me, she will never touch my child. She may have touched me, but she will never touch my child.

Reporter: Did Daniel know these stories?

Anna: Daniel knew. Daniel knew some of the stories. Not all of them, but he knew. Why do you think he had nothing to do with her? He was a big boy. He knew about my mom and me, how I was crying.

Reporter: You want to be a much better mother?

Anna: I am a better mother. I am a good mother. And I will be a better mother now.

Reporter: When your mother sees this, and she will, will she be surprised that you said that?

Anna: No, she will not be surprised. She will laugh, she will probably laugh.

Reporter: You never spoke about this before?

Anna: I never spoke about my parents. She opened up a can of worms and I am going to put a whoop ass on it.

Reporter: Do you think she will be surprised to learn this about you?

Anna: Yes. I tried to give respect, because that is what God says. But if she is going to say I *murdered my son,* she opened up the can.

Reporter: There is a lot of rage and anger?

Anna: Well, yes, about my parents, my mom, yes. She strapped me to my bed. I could tell you stories. I think that's enough.

When I viewed these tapes in open court with the rest of the world, I asked myself this question: Was Anna on drugs? She just lost her son, she was sick to the core at this point, and who else are you going to lash out at but your mother? No matter how long it has been since you have seen your mother or father, there is a bond there. God created a bond. When I was in dependency court, I heard about parents who did horrible things to their children, unspeakable things, acts that only a monster would perform, and these poor frightened children still wanted to be with their parents. Look at the facts here. The closest person to her is her son and look whom she calls right after his death . . . it is her mother. Anna still needed the connection to Virgie. Anna didn't want her mother going on the media outlets, and she also needed someone to lash out at, to vent her great loss. I had enough of these tapes, I didn't want to hear it anymore.

I spent so many years listening to the children who were abused and neglected, and in the twilight years of my judicial career, I wanted to leave that area and go into probate court, where the people are already dead and the files are quiet. But here I was again, embarked upon a tale of alleged abuse and neglect . . . and maybe murder, and possibly suicide. And somehow I blurted out in court that, "Just when you thought you were out of it, you are in it."

All the trials I had, probably thousands of judge and jury trials and hearings, the lawyers always wanted to do a perfect job. They always had one more question to ask, because they didn't want to leave anything in doubt. So here we are and Barth told me she had one more question. I did not allow that question, because it is never just one question. One question leads to an answer and that leads to another question. At some point, you have to close the door and, with your experience and intelligence, hopefully you will know the right stopping point.

Texas now had the opportunity to cross-examine Stern. You know he's been waiting for this since the inception of the trial. He is like a little kid in a candy store, or a hungry man at a hot dog stand. He wants to tear Stern a new rear end.

Texas: Is it correct you have refused to take any type of DNA test?

(Barth objects; I sustain the objection).

Texas: Have you permitted the child [Dannielynn] to have a swab taken?

Barth: Objection.

Texas: And then you represented that over time you [Stern] became her lover, true?

Stern: That's true.

Texas: That began in the year 2000?

Stern: Somewhere around there.

Texas: And do you mean by lover, that you had sexual relations with her?

Stern: Yes, sir.

Texas: Are you aware that it's unethical for a lawyer to have sexual relations with his client?

Barth: Objection.

Texas wanted to get into the purported will that Anna signed back in 2001 and he asked Stern, "Nowhere in this document does it say that you are appointed anything about being the guardian of Anna, or having instructions as to carry out her desires on being buried?"

Before I let Stern answer that, I wanted to rough it up a little bit with him, because in this document, Stern becomes the executor of Anna's estate. I tell him that "as an executor, it's . . . that could be a big sum of dough."

Stern replied "I did without a fee. She appointed me, because she trusted me."

Just like Michael Jackson. Even though the entertainer or star dies, there are still great sums of money to be generated from this personality and Stern recognizes that. He tells the court "what I would want to make sure is that somebody manages Anna's estate responsibly, because beside her lawsuit [regarding the J. Howard Marshall estate] is her name and likeness and someone to continue generating income from that for Dannielynn."

Stern's attorney wanted this purported will admitted into the trial. This purported will, signed by Anna in 2001, was a piece of garbage. I couldn't swallow the clause that leaves out her future children. It kept haunting me. But Stern wants to admit the will, in order to show that he is the executor, and as the executor, he would instruct the court where to bury Anna's body. Because the will might not be conclusive in proving Anna's intent as to where she wants to be buried. But I can't swallow this will: " . . . leaving out future children in the will. I never saw that in all my years."

Stern's attorney brings in probate counsel Bruce Ross, an attorney from Los Angeles, whom we later learned would admit Anna's will into probate court in California. The will is written by a different person. I just blurt out, "the clause," to which Ross replies, "No, it is extraordinary."

Seidlin: Have you ever seen a clause like that?
Ross: I have not.
Seidlin: Have you ever seen a woman write a clause like that?
Ross: No.
Seidlin: Would any woman?
Ross: I cannot imagine any woman writing a clause like that.

In the middle of all this, I get a phone call directly in the courtroom from Dr. Perper, the chief medical examiner for Broward County, who tells me on the speaker phone that the two embalmers who performed the embalming on Anna Nicole on Saturday said that they checked the body's condition, and they observed "unfortunate deterioration" on the body that's proceeding at a very rapid rate. Dr. Perper added that according to the embalmers, "If the body is to be viewed, the viewing should be done this week ... they cannot guarantee that there would not be changes that would interfere with the face of the deceased." I told the doctor, "This deceased is Anna Nicole Smith. She cared about beauty, doctor, as you are aware."

The thought of her body deteriorating at such a rapid pace was sickening. I never had to hear about this process, inside or outside a courthouse. Usually, by the time I get a case, the body is buried. I don't get into the details and the nitty gritty of a deteriorating body.

I had to expedite this proceeding. We had the embalming, now we needed a viewing and we were going to need to transfer the body to be buried. And I still had twenty-nine lawyers in my courtroom, all wanting their time in court for their arguments. I felt like a short order cook in a Manhattan restaurant...everything is cooking and percolating. I guess I know why I retired shortly thereafter.

I am looking at whether or not there is a will that is proper out of California. I am looking at who the father of Dannielyn is and the paternity suit. I am looking at potential murder charges for two victims, Anna Nicole and her son Daniel, or whether one or both might be suicides. I am working through a death—actually two deaths—along with the mourning and healing process of the family and friends. And, finally, the issue that is front and center, the one that gave me my original jurisdiction, which is where and how to bury Anna Nicole. All of this was taking place in a six-day hearing. And afterwards, my wife told me that some of the commentators, those talking heads, said I took too long.

Look how long, or short, a California Attorney General took to file charges against Howard K. Stern and the two doctors, and this was all done off-camera, not in a live courtroom with twenty-nine competent, qualified lawyers, all with their own agendas or strategies to prevail and witnesses to present. I am still amazed how this case turned out. They could teach a law course just on the issues and the fact pattern that were presented in this case alone. James Brown's body was on ice for months before burial took place because of the probate issues.

Back to Dr. Perper's phone call. He added, " . . . because shipping the body involves some procedure, which may take two or three days, that perhaps who has the custody of the body will agree to have the viewing here in Broward and then ship the body to the place of burial." The good doctor then tells me if there is a delay in rendering my decision until next week, it might create a problem, especially with the condition of the face. I cut him off in mid-sentence, because I couldn't bear to hear any more details about the deterioration of Anna Nicole's body. "The court is going to render an opinion by the end of this week," I said. "Let the chips fall as they may."

I couldn't have ended the hearing at that point. I still had to hear from Virgie and Larry Birkhead. How did the media expect me to finish up this case in a day or two? It would have taken 30 to 40 minutes just to introduce the twenty-nine attorneys. How about when an attorney needed to go to the bathroom? How about the fact that some of these attorneys were also involved in other cases? How about the fact that they were coming in from other states, such as Texas and California? How about the witnesses coming in from other states?

Really, anyone who argues that I should have had the proceedings completed in a day or two is a complete idiot. I didn't even have Stern in front of me until the third day. Remember, he was in the Bahamas being robbed, having his home broken into, as well as taking care of Dannielynn. It wasn't until Tuesday, because Monday was a court holiday, and I could bluff him into appearing for Tuesday. Was I supposed to make decisions based on no evidence? Maybe I should have used a ouija board?

When a judge takes a case and that case is aired on TV, it's like a Democrat/Republican debate. Half the commentators are going to voice pleasure with the way it is conducted, and half displeasure, because they are turning it into a media circus, perhaps because they feel controversy drives up the ratings. I didn't need any controversy to drive this taxi, because the passengers all came with their own broken suitcases. This wasn't a taxi cab, this was a third world bus, with everything hanging out the windows. But I liked the ride. It kept me on my feet and it made me investigate what really might have happened.

SIX

TO SAVE ONE CHILD

I knew that Stern's testimony was coming to a conclusion, but I wanted to keep him in my courtroom. I didn't want him hopping on a jet to the Bahamas. I wanted all three parties to be physically present when each of the others was testifying.

As the trier of fact, I wanted to look at their faces. I wanted to feel their electrical current and observe their body language. I told counsel, "Get the mother on the witness stand. I may not see Stern again. He is going to get back to the Bahamas."

Then I said something pretty wild, but somehow Stern bought it: "The mother is testifying next with Stern still physically present in the courtroom. We are doing it tonight. She is next. You suffered through his testimony. He is going to suffer through your testimony." I looked at Stern. We were playing chicken, two race cars heading toward one another, waiting to find out who was going to dodge first. I knew it wouldn't be me, because this is my courtroom and I am simply asking for his presence, which is a reasonable request. I really wanted to look at Stern's face when Virgie started screaming that he was a murderer. I turned to Stern, and told him, "Do you understand? So you are to take a breath and take some water."

In the middle of all of this, Milstein requested that maybe the parties involved would consider a stipulation, which means an agreement, to have Anna Nicole's body sent to a funeral home in Florida, which wouldn't prejudice anyone's decision making in case there would be a viewing of any kind.

I can't have this proceeding as if it was Israel and Palestine. I can't have one party so hostile towards me, because I still need their agreement and cooperation. I also have continuous housekeeping matters to complete, like the viewing of Anna's body. I asked, "Do we agree that family members can view?" They all agreed to the viewing, and of course, the logistics have to be worked out, especially the little details. Stern then added, "I want to make sure there are no cameras or pictures or media."

I am now in the funeral business. This was another big hurdle we just climbed. I am performing many kinds of tasks, but every successful business person knows you can't be afraid to lick the stamp to get the job done. One of my favorite lines is you can't have any ego if you want to get the job done. When I play doubles in racquetball, I take one of the best players and I say to him that I have no ego, take as many shots as you want, because I don't want to be sitting on the bench at the end of the game.

I got another agreement. Milstein announces that Anna Nicole's body will be removed from the medical examiner's office to the funeral home for viewing.

Meanwhile, through all this, Bruce Ross is still on the stand and we return to the topic of *the clause.*

Ross: The clause is unique, it is legally ineffective.

Seidlin: It's against public policy. So who would write a clause like this?

Ross (looking at Rohan Kelley): I am sure my colleague, called a scrivenor's error.

Seidlin: A clause like this, are you selling that to me now?

Ross: No, I am not selling it to you, or trying to sell it to anyone.

Seidlin: It's not just that clause. When you have a clause like that, the court says what kind of draftsman is there? Who read it? Did she [Anna] really read it? Did she read the whole will? If she read that clause, she would say take it back . . . there's no woman in America that would sign a clause like that?

Ross: I told him, Lund, that considerable attention, *shock*, and dismay has been afforded this will.

Ross was a very well spoken attorney, and extremely diplomatic in his response. I liked the way he explained such poor draftsmanship. I asked him what was Lund's answer. Ross told me simply, "It was a mistake."

And this is what I said about this will: "When a fish has a little smell you get rid of the whole fish. It's not just to take away the clause. You got to say did she read this will . . . what state of mind was she in? . . . And I will tell you . . . it has holes, it has plenty of holes and one day even the Bahamas or California, you will try to admit it . . . and let the chips fall as they may. It's a piece of paper that is purported to be a will. That causes me to lose more hair than I already lost, you know it and I know, because we can't fool each other, we are too good, we are going to move on."

Here, I'm going to jump forward in time to make an interesting point about the will. My investigation revealed that around June 19, 2007, former foes Larry Birkhead and Howard K. Stern sat next to one another in a California courtroom, as a hearing officer admitted Anna Nicole Smith's will to probate. Birkhead, father of the late model's daughter, was appointed guardian of Danielynn, while Stern serves as executor of her will. This began a process in which Anna Nicole's assets would continue to be accumulated (including the Marshall estate) and the court will determine the fees that Birkhead and Stern will receive and how the money will be distributed.

Meanwhile, the next larger than life figure in this play, a real live play, is Virgie Arthur, Anna Nicole's mother. "Texas" O'Quinn began his questioning of Virgie by touching on her career in law enforcement.

Texas: What do you do now?

Virgie: I am retired.

Texas: What did you do for a living before you retired?

Virgie: I was a police officer 28 years.

Texas: What duties did you perform?

Virgie: I worked in the jail for 3 years and other times, I worked in the streets, [as a] patrol officer.

Seidlin: You carried a gun?

Virgie: Yes.

Seidlin: Did you ride in a police car by yourself?

Virgie: Yes.

Seidlin: You made thousands of arrests during your career?
Virgie: Probably.

Being a police officer on the streets of any city is dangerous. The studies indicate that there really should be *two* police officers riding in a police car, but costs prohibit most police departments from following that caution. So Virgie had looked danger in the eye for over twenty-eight years. Her life was on the line each and every day.

I wanted Virgie to relax. She had come through a horrible double loss: first her grandson, then her daughter, who held a special place in her heart. And my instinct was right, because throughout our private hearings, outside the presence of the public, I saw her tears and her love for her family. I asked her about the police officer's pension and doing extra jobs, which Virgie revealed were two topics that were always discussed by her fellow police officers at practically every coffee break.

I started off the questioning with her well being in mind, probably as a result of my years in the family and criminal juvenile divisions. Whenever the police officer took the witness stand, as important as the matter was for the person charged, I just didn't like the police officer being grilled. So I would try to set the tone, ask the preliminary questions, and thereby set a pace and establish a sense of harmony, which would probably only last a minute. But it gave the officer a chance to settle down and put two feet on the ground.

After Tunstall briefly clarified with Virgie who was Anna Nicole's father—Donald Eugene Hogan—I asked Virgie a vital question about her relationship with Anna Nicole.

Seidlin: If you had one regret with your daughter, what would it be, one regret?

Virgie: That I was not able to get her away from drugs.

Seidlin: She left your home at a young age?

Virgie: Seventeen.

Seidlin: Was she on drugs at the time?

Virgie: No.

Seidlin: Why did she leave home?

Virgie: Because she was with the wrong crowd at school and she was getting in trouble.

Seildin: Where did she go?

Virgie: She went to live with my baby sister.

Seidlin: How long did she stay there?

Virgie: Six or seven months, but she quit school at seventeen. You can do that in Texas, and she went to work for Krispy Fried Chicken.

Seidlin: And he worked there too?

Virgie: Yes he did.

Seidlin: And did they get married?

Virgie: Yes they did.

Seidlin: How long after did the child come?

Virgie: She didn't get pregnant right away, so probably thirteen months.

Seidlin: How long did the marriage last?

Virgie: The baby was three months old when she left.

Seidlin: That's the boy that recently died.

Virgie: Yes, that's him.

Seidlin: Did you have a relationship with him?

Virgie: Absolutely. He lived with me for the first 6 or 7 years of his life, while she was pursuing her career.

Seidlin: As what?

Virgie: She worked in exotic clubs to begin with.

Seidlin: Then she was discovered?

Virgie: Yes.

Seidlin: What kind of relationship did you have with her during those first 6 years?

Virgie: Good. We went and got her hair done together or nails done together.

Seidlin: How far was she living from you?

Virgie: 15 miles.

Seidlin: Was she doing drugs in those days?

Virgie: No.

Seidlin: What happens next?

Virgie: She was still working there and she meets a guy. He wanted her to get into the photo shop, where she got into *Playboy* magazine.

Seidlin: And their relationship was?

Virgie: Boyfriend/girlfriend.

Seidlin: Then what happens?

Virgie: Well, she got in *Playboy* magazine and zoomed right on up.

Seidlin: That was her launching pad?

Virgie: Yes.

Seidlin: Did you continue to have a relationship with her?

Virgie: Yes we did.

Texas took over and touched on the subject of Anna Nicole's international fame as the spokesmodel for Guess Jeans, and then Tunstall continued the questioning.

Tunstall: Then what happens?

Virgie: Guess Jeans, she then met Howard Marshall, a millionaire [billionaire] in Texas.

Tunstall: Did you know him?

Virgie: Yes. He was a very good man.

Tunstall: Was he famous?

Virgie: He was a rich man.

Tunstall: So that made him famous?

Virgie: He was a very good man.

Tunstall: Were you worried about her well being in those days?

Virgie: Not with Howard Marshall, no.

Tunstall: What happened next?

Virgie: Well, she told me that he asked her several times to marry him, but she didn't want to because she wanted to pursue her career.

Tunstall: And then?

Virgie: She got famous. She did movies and modeling. She always wanted to model.

Tunstall: When did your relationship with her go sour?

Virgie: Probably '95 or '96.

Tunstall: What would you say [was] the cause of it?

Virgie: Drugs.

Tunstall: She started to take drugs?
Virgie: Yes.
Tunstall: In '95?
Virgie: Yes.

And now I went at it. I wanted to know what kind of drugs she was using, who was supplying them, and everything else about these drugs. I started by asking Virgie what type of drugs Anna Nicole took. Virgie answered, "She was on valium. I can't remember the names. She liked downers. She did not want to be up. She liked downers." I asked her, "And you started to worry about her big time?"

Now Barth told me, "I am going to object to leading. I don't know what else to say." Because I am the judge, and I was asking the questions, and Barth didn't like the phraseology and the leading nature of the question. So Tunstall kids around and wants to act as a judge and states, "Overruled." I didn't want to overstep my bounds, so I turned to the witness and told her, "I am going to turn it over to you." Plus, by asking some of the questions, I wanted to show Stern that I wanted to rush the proceeding in order to try and get him back to the Bahamas, whereby Stern responded, "Anytime tonight is fine."

Tunstall brought out that Anna Nicole had brothers and sisters who lived in the Houston area and they had children who were also living in Houston, in order to prove to the court that Anna Nicole would want to be buried with her family in Texas. His questioning of Virgie then continued with the subject of Anna Nicole's drug use, and how it affected their relationship.

Tunstall: Can you tell us, at least your observation of the relationship between when you observed your daughter doing drugs and when Mr. Stern appeared on the scene?

Virgie: OK. I had never met Howard Stern. This is the first time [I] probably ever seen him.

Tunstall: Have you ever talked to him on the phone?

Virgie: Once.

Tunstall: Your relationship with your daughter became strained in about '95? Did you and she keep in contact with each other?

Virgie: Off and on. Not very often. After she started drugs, every three or four times a month, she would call me in the middle of the night.

Tunstall: In what kind of condition?

Virgie: Drugged, she told me specifically, don't go to work tomorrow. I promise I won't go to work tomorrow. She'd say, because I think you are going to get killed. I go to work at 6 and this was 4 o'clock in the morning.

Tunstall: You would have raised him [Daniel] from when he was born?

Virgie: I think.

Tunstall: Then where did he go?

Virgie: He went to live with his mom. By this time, Howard Marshall was taking good care of her, he bought her a house and she could afford a nanny.

I then attempted to perform magic and asked Stern if I could borrow him for a couple of hours tomorrow morning, because I liked his presence in my courtroom, which helped me get a picture of the situation. Stern said, "What I would request is, I will stay as late as you want tonight, but I would really prefer. . ."

I interrupted him, because I knew where this was going. Over the years we have been instructed by the court administrator's office not to work beyond 5 o'clock. I stated, "These people are worn out and they do not want me to work people beyond 5 o'clock. They have their own family and children. I know I got to let them go home. Do me a favor, come tomorrow for a couple of hours. I promise you, I will let you leave at eleven."

Barth requested that Stern fly back to the Bahamas that evening. Stern promised me, "I will come back. This is important to me to carry out Anna's intent, I will be back."

Stern will show tomorrow, I am a hundred percent positive of it. He's going to show tomorrow, and the testimony that he gives tomorrow will change his life forever. I believe that the charges in California, which the California Attorney General subsequently filed against him, were brought because of the testimony that Stern gave in my courtroom the next day: admissions against interest. This testimony was just too damning. Stern's own testimony fulfilled the essential elements of the California Attorney General's charging document.

The California Attorney General did not overcharge him, that is, did not bring more severe charges. They had multiple counts, and some of those counts could be dismissed in a plea bargain. Therefore, if he pleads guilty in California, he'll be doing a little time. That would be an equitable resolution of those charges. The California prosecutors do not have jurisdiction over the more severe charge of homicide, of which there are different levels. The jurisdiction for Anna Nicole's death is Broward County, my home county, and the jurisdiction for Daniel's death is the Bahamas. Basically, these jurisdictions have the exclusive decision making power and they have the power to decide who and when to charge.

And if you, the reader, will indulge me for one more minute here, I have some significant information to bring to your attention. Don Clark served as a special agent of the FBI in Miami, New York, and Los Angeles. His assignments included violent crimes and other investigative programs. Mr. Clark supervised high profile FBI investigations, including the 1979 Iranian hostage crisis and the terrorist attack of the cruise ship *Achille Lauro* in 1985, which claimed the life of Leon Klinghoffer. His resume and assignments are as long as my arm. He would be admitted as an expert in law enforcement in any courtroom in the world. So here is some information that I dug up later. In a letter dated August 2, 2007 from Don Clark to Brian Cavanagh, the assistant state attorney in the homicide division of Broward County, Clark stated, " . . . however I and others in the law firm do believe that the investigations were not conducted in sufficient depth to determine actual motives. And more detailed actions of the individuals surrounding Ms. Smith from prior to her travels between the Bahamas and the Hard Rock Hotel on the Seminole Reservation. I believe that a more detailed look into individuals associated with Ms. Smith and the actions of each of the individuals prior to her clinical time of death will produce different results."

Clark continued: "Frankly sir, we don't question the coroner's [Dr. Perper] conclusion that Ms. Smith died of an overdose of various drugs, but we do question that her death was accidental. We find it extremely unbelievable that a person in Ms. Smith's mental and physical condition, which has been established by witnesses and according to Howard Stern, was never left alone, could have the quantity of drugs found in her body as a result of ingestion or by using a syringe herself."

But that took place after this trial.

I told the court, "We have a journey to give lasting peace and tranquility to Ms. Smith's body. A permanent resting place. Throughout these proceedings, the court is referring to Dannielynn and there is not much time, over the course of these proceedings, where all of these parties are going to be present again. I know this judicial system, I know the jurisprudence and I know there may not be another moment for a while where all parties are physically present. All the main parts of this equation are physically here. And therefore, I am not only having a proceeding but we are also grieving together. If you want to phrase it that way, it's a grieving process. All of us are recovering from it and feel the pain and weight of it. And as we proceed, I want us to remember that we are here to save one child."

We were within a day of shutting this case down, of coming to a conclusion. Not only were we winding down Anna Nicole's matters, but we were really closing down the largest chapter in Judge Larry's life. I had echoed or whispered to my wife that I was ready to get off the big white horse. I was ready to do something new. I was thinking of teaching, doing radio or TV, something that would get my juices going. Maybe even writing a book. But through this case, somehow, the Lord allowed me to get in a lot of my thoughts, my curbside philosophies, and state those to the parties and the world at once.

I continued in open court, "You have a terrific legal cast here, they are wonderful, they have been so cooperative, they have been reading me very well, but we must go beyond the battlefront, we must go and see how we can help Dannielynn. We have to merge our desires and wants with those of our partners."

Isn't a legal battle often like a mini war? Working with families, dysfunctional families, when the smoke clears and the ugliness of the dialogues that have been expressed by each party remains, someone, the judge, has to clean it all up. Someone has to put Humpty Dumpty back together again. That is why as a family court judge, I never wanted to reach new heights of hatred in my courtroom. I wanted some things unsaid. I wanted some things left out, because once these things are said, they can't be taken back and they scar the soul of the parties. I must be wearing pink sunglasses with this upbeat, happy approach. But I maintained it for twenty-eight years. I maintained this positive attitude every day.

"We have a grandmother here, who has a lousy time of that." I looked Virgie directly in the eyes, with her husband holding her hand, and stated "and that word does not properly describe the turmoil that you have had and I am going to come to you soon, because I am starting to figure a little bit of this out."

Little did I know then that it would take me years to unravel this puzzle, which had all the intrigue and mystery of a Shakespearean play. Anna Nicole was a queen and every monarch is surrounded by death, sabotage, and people who want to grab power at all costs.

" . . . So we have a father, we have another man who may be the father, or if he is not the father, at the minimum he is acting as the father and we have grandma. And if you three, if it was a case in a normal course of time, I, as a family judge, would require you, I *would take you to the woodshed a few times and demand, I would demand that you all be cooperative*, and somehow it would happen. I want you all to reflect when you leave me, because I *know the wheels of justice are not always round.* Those wheels, sometimes they are scary, it's a bumpy ride, like the old west where it's a bumpy ride, and I am not always going to be on that ride with you. So I want you all to reflect on those thoughts. I want you all to go beyond your personal needs and desires and remember this child Dannielynn. We don't want her to grow up in an atmosphere that we are experiencing now . . . so I want you to remember those words when you get up in the middle of the night and you are thinking. I want you to remember those words where we want to bring a bond here. So you all three trusted me, because you did not have to come here. But you came because you believed, you believed in the American judicial system and you probably took a look at this court and you said, this Judge *may be eccentric enough to get this thing done.* And somehow we have been getting it done, and we are going to keep getting it done."

Later, all three parties walked out to the front of the courthouse holding hands! It's a picture that is imprinted in my mind and that I remembered many times since.

I knew Stern was getting antsy again. He wanted to get the hell out of my courtroom, and now he has Texas coming at him wanting to cross examine him. I turned to Stern, because I have a feeling he just wants to bolt, and told him, "You have been respectful. You have been a tower. I am going to let you fly out at some point and time. I want you to notify the court two hours before you have to leave, you are not a hostage here."

SEVEN

PALACE POLITICS NEVER CEASE

I continued the questioning of Virgie Arthur, regarding her career as a sheriff's deputy in Texas. She told me that she started out as a deputy in 1977, at a time when there were 3000 employees in the Sheriff's Department—it has since grown to 8000.

Virgie: We were woman jailers, back then there were only four women on the street.

Seidlin: And you were one of those four woman deputies?

Virgie: Yes, I was.

Seidlin: And in those days, we did not have all the safe guards in the work place?

Virgie: No.

Seidlin: In those days, in the '70s, there were times when you were not treated equally with the other deputies, is that right?

Virgie: Yes sir you are.

Seidlin: You are in the deep south?

Virgie: Yes.

Seidlin: When you went to the deputy conferences and conventions, you were all over the country talking to woman deputies?

Virgie: Yes I was.

Seidlin: So it was in every village, hamlet, be it west, northeast, or south where woman deputies were not treated the same?

Virgie: Yes sir.

Seidlin: Would you say that that was a time they asked the woman deputies to make coffee?

Virgie: Yes.

Seidlin: You were also trained not to tell war stories that would look bad on the sheriff's department.

Here we have a direct parallel between Virgie and her daughter Anna Nicole, who are really two trail blazers. Virgie entered a dangerous world, a man's world: the police department. And Anna Nicole went into the entertainment world, where the business side is impossible at times, even for me. I have an accounting background and legal training and they still throw curveballs at us. It is hard to know what to believe and who to believe. The entertainment world is a body of water, infested with sharks. Add to that the element of time, because entertainers need to keep or maintain a certain youthful or young appearance. And this is even more unfair to the beautiful female star. Do you remember the interview with Gwyneth Paltrow? As beautiful as anyone in Hollywood, an absolutely elegant, class act, she takes a short hiatus from her profession to spend time with her child and expresses the fear that she wasn't certain if Hollywood would accept her again. These entertainers, these stars, are always waiting for a phone call. They are under tremendous pressure, thinking to themselves "am I there tomorrow, will I have work?"

Virgie told the court that she and her female colleagues in the law enforcement field had to be tough, and were not allowed to show their emotions in front of their fellow deputies—they even had to cry in the privacy of their police cars. Tears were a sign of weakness, so Virgie had to be tough, as she said to the court, "for the ones who come after me." I asked her if Anna Nicole inherited that same type of personal toughness from her.

Virgie: None of us are alike, not you, not me.

Seidlin: But your daughter was not tough like you?

Virgie: No.

Seidlin: How would you describe Anna Nicole's personality?

Virgie: When she was young, she was sweet, she was funny, she was very funny. She loved frogs. Frogs were her favored things. She was a tomboy, but she was a sweetheart. She was giving, she was loving . . . she was a good child.

Seidlin: Tell me, as the years went on, how was her personality?

Virgie: Well, she was always a great child and she always made us laugh . . . As she got older, kids get more serious and she became a teenager.

Seidlin: Why did [Anna] reflect on death so much?

Virgie: I never heard that. She never talked about death. She was a young person . . .

Seidlin: Later on in her life?

Virgie: I don't believe that. You can't make me believe that. She was too full of life. She loved to be in the public, so she loved life as she got older . . .

Seidlin: If you could have done one thing different with your daughter, what would you have done?

Virgie: When I knew she was really deep into drugs, I would have went and kidnapped her. I would have done everything possible. I went with her to the Betty Ford Clinic. I came down one time . . . she is in the hospital and she never went in the hospital under [her real] name, never . . . I took a week off of work to stay with her . . .

Tunstall took over Virgie's testimony, this time on the subject of Anna Nicole's deceased son Daniel, and what kind of person he was.

Virgie: He was an angel. I know I got him when he was three months old and he was an angel. I raised him until he was seven; he was just starting first grade. . . .

Tunstall: What was going on in your daughter's life at the time?

Virgie: She was trying to make her way into the world. She was dancing in the exotic clubs, which I did not approve of, but you cannot make your children. You teach right from wrong, you raise them and tell them, this is the path you should take, baby. And I kept her in church, she went to church after she moved out. . . . So she knew right from wrong and all my children, not just her, I have three other children and all of them loved her and they were raised together. It was not just me that she cut out, but she refused to see all of us, she was close to all of them.

Tunstall: Was it difficult for you when Daniel moved back with his mother?

Virgie: This is the time when she met Howard Marshall and he had bought her a house and he was making sure she had everything they needed. He wanted to get married, but she wanted to get a career in modeling. From the time she was five years old, she said she is going to be a model. I said, baby you can be anything you want to be ... I did not want to be a cop, I wanted to be a ballerina, believe it or not and that dream did not come true, but I did not want to become a cop.

Seidlin: It's never too late.

I could visualize Virgie, at night, telling Anna to follow her dreams, to do what she wanted to do. Virgie was in law enforcement all these years and she was just going through the motions. Just grab hold of your dreams and pursue them at all costs, I could imagine her saying, and don't compromise your desires. I entered a field that was no friend to females and I survived it. I felt Virgie was uncomfortable about this part of her testimony. She knew she was a middle-aged woman, that her youthful looks and slender figure were no longer there. But she too possessed that girl-like quality that was in her daughter's soul. So when she said it, I didn't laugh. I knew she was dead serious.

Tunstall continued to elicit from Virgie more details about her role in the mother-son relationship between Anna Nicole and Daniel.

Tunstall: From the time your grandson Daniel went back to live with his mom Anna Nicole, how often would you see him?

Virgie: Well, I saw him a lot while he was in Houston, but she moved to California.

Tunstall: When they went to California, how often would you see them?

Virgie: With her traveling around, not an awful lot, but once every three or four months, she would go on a shoot. And she would have him with her and she would get a hotel room for us ... would visit in the hotel room, my oldest son came down when she was in Vegas, [and] me and him and Danny went out and had a good time because she was working.

Here we go again. I have Dr. Perper on the phone again and I don't lose track of the fact that I still have to figure out where to bury Anna Nicole. It still sits in my craw that certain legal commentators wanted me to finish up this case in an hour. Did they want me not to have any witnesses, just have the attorneys submit written memoranda of law? How sensitive and caring I would have been, not taking the parties testimony, and leaving out Milstein and Kelley in the process. Those commentators should take a long walk on a short pier. With their advice, I would have made the wrong decision and the appellate court would have reversed me, and then I would have had to start all over again. These Monday morning quarterbacks should just remain on the couch and try to predict which football team is going to win.

Dr. Perper told me that Anna Nicole's body was in very good

condition. He warned me, however, that if we allowed more time to pass without burial, the discoloration changes on her body would progress and make it more difficult to show the body.

So I announced, "I am going to render a court's decision by Friday morning."

Here I had Dr. Perper, his voice resonating throughout the courtroom, like it was the play *Cabaret*, announcing the most gruesome details of Anna Nicole's deterioration. I imagine it sent shivers through the veins of these hardened, experienced, top notch trial lawyers. I know it did through mine. What I should have done after I got off the phone, was call a recess, so that Dr. Perper could drive to the courthouse, take the witness stand and have the attorneys question him. But time was of the essence, and it was becoming surreal at this point.

The cross-examination between Tunstall and Virgie continued.

Tunstall: And before she went to the Bahamas, do you know where she lived?

Virgie: California. She had an apartment. I mean she was with Howard Marshall, she had an apartment in New York; she lived in Marilyn Monroe's house ...

Tunstall: Now, I realize your daughter was traveling as you said, but until July of 2006, did your daughter have any connection to the Bahamas?

Virgie: No.

Seidlin: Did you ever physically go to the Bahamas?

Virgie: When my grandson died, yes.

I had some questions of my own about the relationship between Anna Nicole and Daniel.

Virgie: She loved him and he loved her.

Seidlin: Tell me about that love, without making you use tissues too much, try to be detached for a moment, if you can, I know it is hard. I am making you wear your police hat.

Virgie: She loved Daniel, you know they did fun things together. In fact, when they were together, she would act his age, they would do fun things. She was a comedian, she loved to make you laugh. She, you know, was always coming up with something cute and funny, just stories.

Seidlin: Did she absolutely adore this boy?

Virgie: She loved him with all her heart.

Seidlin: She absolutely loved him?

Virgie: Yes she did.

What a strange paradox. I spent fifty years enjoying the company of the opposite sex. And then at the ripe old age of fifty, I have a beautiful daughter and my days now are spent completely involved and consumed in the activities and fun of my daughter. I don't remember a life without her. And Virgie's words about Anna Nicole's love for Daniel brought me to my knees. I would love to go back in time, to be the judge that intervened before Anna Nicole's demise, to say what are we doing here, what are we doing with all these drugs. We are also allowing Daniel to be associated with these drugs, which will lead him down the wrong path. Why do you have all these meatballs around who enable you and dance to every tune you sing, getting you enough drugs to choke a horse?

The entertainment world is unforgiving. It takes a 24-hour body guard with a slew of professionals just to keep the scum out. Palace politics never cease. The players move constantly, always trying to surround and hijack the anointed one.

EIGHT

JUST A FEW CARDS LEFT TO PLAY

I had three primary parties: Virgie Arthur, Larry Birkhead and Howard K. Stern. I tried to analyze how each party interacted with the other two, in order to gauge how Stern and Birkhead would act towards Virgie, who is the grandmother to Dannielynn. Most states give a grandparent no rights concerning the grandchild, meaning a grandparent like Virgie would have no right of visitation. I believe the courts have taken this view because there is enough to resolve just with the parents and visitation. How far can they go with grandparents, aunts, uncles and cousins? Fortunately, for Virgie, California gives standing to grandparents. And once the defamation lawsuit, where Virgie is the plaintiff, against Birkhead, the defendant, is resolved, Virgie will file a petition for the right to visit her granddaughter Dannielynn.

So I allowed the following line of questioning between Barth and Virgie.

Barth: You went to the Bahamas after the death of Daniel; is that correct?

Virgie: Yes, and that's when I met him [Birkhead] it was not after Vicky's death [Virgie referred to Anna Nicole as Vicky]

. . . I went to the Bahamas before Daniel's birthday. So I went to his grave and I seen his [Birkhead's] card on there and he called me and I asked was he on the island and he said yes and I said Larry, can I meet you, I want to thank you for putting flowers on my grandson's grave.

Barth: How did you get to the Bahamas?

Virgie: A family member helped me. We all pooled our money together, that is why I video taped it so they could see.

Barth: Did you ever receive any money for the videotape of your service at the gravesite of Daniel?

Virgie: No, I have not.

Barth: You do not have an agreement with Splash?

Virgie: I do not have any money from anyone from that video.

Barth: Have you received any monies since the date of Daniel's death, from any news agency, from any magazine, TV station, you have no idea what I am talking about?

Virgie: No, I have no money. I was not given money. I have no money.

Barth: Have you ever, in any fashion, profited at all from the death of your daughter?

Virgie: I am trying to process that question.

I can't stand this line of questioning. The death of a daughter, profiting, the whole thing is sickening and turns me off. But I am the trier of fact and no matter how repulsive some of these facts appear, I have to be a big boy and sit through it, but I want to cut to the chase.

Seidlin: The question is, are you going to get income from her death?

Virgie: No, I am not getting any income; Howard is the one.

I am trying to make soup here. I am trying to make a heaping bowl of gazpacho. I am trying to get these parties to work together and I don't want all hell to break out among them, and I interject, "We don't want to do this." Then Tunstall has the audacity to claim that counsel wants to turn this trial into a circus.

Circus, I say to myself. I'm busting my tail. I am aging rapidly, and can I really afford to lose more of my hair? I have instructed other judges that come on the bench, because remember, I became a senior judge at a young age. And I never displayed any anger in this courtroom. But this led me to pop off. The circus was actually *outside* the courtroom, not *in my* courtroom. And all who sat in that courtroom would attest to that. I say this knowing that some of you will go out and interview someone who will want to voice a dissident position, because that is the nature of our present storyline.

"There is no circus, my friend, there is no circus."

Tunstall looks at me like I am a ferris wheel that just lit up and tells me, "I am not referring to you . . . I [am] referring to our friends back here."

I'm thinking again that I don't want all hell to break out among the lawyers and the parties, not to mention some of the witnesses and some of the members of the media, who are prepared to stoke the fire. They are looking for a good July 4th fireworks show and I am looking for a quiet day on the lake. So here I go, into one of my classroom professor speeches: "The lawyers are excellent, you included. You can turn to the fact that a lot of people are interested in the outcome, that's a given. But this is a very calm proceeding, it's a proceeding like I would handle in any other case. You have absolutely demonstrated professional conduct here. There is no circus. The circus would be it's just the attention, if you want to say circus. You say circus equals attention, but not the conduct of trial, not the conduct of the hearing. Everyone is being heard. We are just abbreviating the time span on how much time we want to spend on each witness. But the term circus is offensive to all of us. Don't use that term, it turns me off. It's not the way it is."

It was important to me for history to show, and for Dannielynn eventually to know, that as casual as I am, my heart wanted to render, in this case, as in all cases, perfect justice, even though at times that's an impossible goal. And I went on to say something that I have never said before. Because I didn't want to be like Tarzan in the jungle. I didn't want to pound my own chest and extol my own virtues, which is contrary to my Columbo-like fashion. An extremely casual approach can get a hell of a lot done. I said, "Maybe we are a little casual, but that is just to disarm us, so we can get a lot done in this disarming presentation. It allowed Stern to come in here. Stern never would have come here."

Now that Stern has been charged criminally by the State of California, in my opinion he hung himself when he testified before me in 2007. Stern fell on his own sword. Sometimes you should keep your big mouth shut.

I added, " . . . and Birkhead would come. And your client [Virgie] has been able to open up this court so we can get some grieving and later on, you are going to have me with a box of tissues, but we have had some grieving which is important for the memory of Anna Nicole Smith. And I want to get beyond that. I want to build the child. I want to build. . ."

Little did I know that, later, when I would pronounce the judgment of the court, I would become part of the grieving process and the building of a child. Did I become too attached to the parties and Dannielynn? Define "too attached." Can you ever be too attached to the outcome of what is in the best interest of a child?

Barth wanted to continue with the questioning: Did Virgie sell her soul to media outlets for money?

Barth: Are you going to receive any money from Splash News and Picture Agency? Did they come with you to the Bahamas?

Seidlin: You are making a compound question . . . [To Virgie] You know it is not a guillotine. We are not in the old 16th century France. You can answer that question and explain it, you are going to have your lawyer, who is going to rehabilitate you, and he is going to give you an opportunity to explain it.

Virgie: Because I don't know what the right answer is here.

Seidlin: There is no right or wrong answer. I am just trying to get through this big maze that they presented me. You remember when you had this big French labyrinth. That is all we are trying to do; answer the question to the best of your ability.

Virgie was cooperative and said "Ask me again." I rephrased the question: "Did you get any dough . . . from that company, Splash?" to which Virgie answered that she did not.

Barth: Did you ever agree from anyone at Splash News and Picture Agency that you are going to receive a $30,000 fee?

Virgie: Ma'am, I don't have $30,000. I never got $30,000.

At one point in the media coverage of this hearing unsubstantiated statements were intersecting with evidence and facts, and I didn't want to get into the nonsense of this kind of gossip. That stuff might sell newspapers and magazines and increase viewership in the broadcast outlets, but it has no standing in a courtroom. I spit out, "We are dealing with innuendos and rumors and that's not the world. We are in a courtroom. I appreciate you trying to submit it. You took your shot, she says no."

Barth: How about Babbette Agency, have you entered any discussion with her regarding selling film, video, your story or anything else have you entered?

Virgie: I don't know who you are talking about. The only one that made any money off of my daughter is that man [Stern] right there, he sold movie video to her. I heard that ET is buying her death funeral, that is why he wants her body, for a $1,000,000 bucks.

It was getting ugly. "I am not going to travel down this road, it is too windy, it's too long, it's almost a philosophical question. It's something I want to tell you, something, I want you [Barth] to have a seat for a minute because this is an issue that you keep bringing up. I am going to have you have a seat. You know, I believe the issue of her death and money is a personal decision to be made by every party in this courtroom. That's how you are going to conduct yourself. You are going to conduct yourselves accordingly. And the rules, that are the rules of decency and humanity, and you guys are going to decide where you go with that, and some are going to say they are going to spin it. It's an area that you are trying to profiteer, others will say I cannot pay my mortgage, I need some money. It's up to you, where you go. You know how you were brought up. You know the rules of decency, you know what is right and wrong. We are a civilized country, America. We have a rule of law and rule of decency. Not everything is adjudicated in a courtroom. It's adjudicated in the streets of New York, Texas, California, every state in this union . . . that is for that person to decide, that is for them to decide when they meet their maker, whether they cross the boundaries of decency and I am not going to allow this into the courtroom. That makes it a circus; that is what makes a circus. I am taking facts and that is all I am taking. I am not getting into money, and money—let's face it, money is the root of all evil—and we have to consider that in the overall scheme of things, but I am not getting into it and we are not going there anymore."

Barth, being a strong and competent attorney with a terrific personality, didn't want to let go and asked Virgie, "Were you paid for that [ET interview]?" to which Virgie replied "No. Don't look like it." This questioning brought me back somewhere I didn't want to be, so I asked Virgie, "What do you mean by it? Doesn't look like it."

Virgie answered, "Howard or someone in that capacity said that if I talk to ET that they [Stern] would not let them [ET] have the exclusives rights of Vicky's life, her baby being born, now her death. He [Stern] is the one that is getting the money, I am not."

This is a pimple with more puss coming out. "See this is unfortunate here, the whole thing because we really should be working all together. I would be banging heads together at this point, in the old days, I would take you in the back room [chambers] where we would chop down trees."

Stern attempted to address the court and I turned to him and said, "You have no podium here, Mr. Stern, I appreciate your being here though."

I had just a few cards left to play. "This is a time where, you know, you got to bang some heads together, because here is the mother, here is the gentleman Mr. Stern, at least who is acting in the capacity of the father, and here is the gentleman Larry, who may also be the father and you also. If we had some brain power here, the three of you with your attorneys would figure out an overall scheme of things and figure out, okay, if there is going to be money made in the future, let's make a foundation, help children and [the] primary focus of it would be for Dannielynn. There is nothing wrong with that, if we did that in a respectful, peaceful manner, but you all are not going to submit to my jurisdiction [for all the issues].

"So therefore, I am a realist. I want to do what I can really do here. But that is what the three of you should be doing instead of fighting. You should join hands, join hands because it is only in this country that you can join hands. We don't have these kinds of religious wars that take place around the world. We have a chance here to join hands and get a celebration of the life that Anna Nicole had. We can celebrate her death. Some religions celebrate death, we would celebrate her memory and make her life worth while, but then, we would focus in, as Milstein wants to do, on Dannielynn's life. You ought to really think about it, but if I had the power over you three, there would be some smoke coming out, we would get it done. We would have the three of you sit down and agree, have the lawyers around there and we would do it and you guys better do it, you better do it."

Barth then asked Virgie, "You have no reason to believe that your daughter does not want to be laid to rest next to her son, do you?" Virgie answered "No, all mothers and family need to be laid by each other, but . . . " Barth interjected, "That's the question. Thank you."

Virgie's lawyer, Tunstall, disagreed. I interjected and said, "Well I heard it, believe me. I have not missed a word here. She wants to exhume the body of Danny and bring it back to Texas. You don't have to get into the vivid pictures of that."

Milstein (to Virgie): You said you bought six plots when you were younger. Can you tell us who they were for?

Virgie: My husband, myself and our four children.
Milstein: Which husband?
Virgie: Donald Hart

Milstein: Is that who you are married to now?

Virgie: He is the one that helped raise our children. We raised our children together.

Milstein: So when you bought the plots, the intent was not for the same people that exists today, is that correct, in you[r] family?

Virgie: Yes, but we still have the plots.

Milstein: Did you anticipate that maybe your children would have spouses and they would want to be buried with them? . . . Do you think you would have control of where your children should be buried in the future should they marry?

Milstein's wise questioning allowed me to appreciate that many intervening factors had occurred since Virgie bought the plots. . . marriages, death, divorce, more grandchildren and Anna Nicole moving away from Texas. And there were only four plots in Texas.

Milstein: Do you know where he [J. Howard Marshall] is buried?

Virgie: He was cremated.

Milstein: He is not buried in Texas, is he?

Virgie: His ashes are in Texas.

Milstein: With whom?

Virgie: Half with his son and half with Vicky.

Milstein tried to make it a logical conclusion.

Milstein: So the ashes now would be with Vicky in Nassau?

Virgie: No, in California.

Milstein: Did you ever discuss with her where she wanted to place the ashes of her husband?

Virgie: She wanted to keep them with her.

They are talking about ashes and burials and I am saying to myself, I can't listen to this anymore. A probate judge, you would think, should be listening to this. But this is really never discussed. A probate judge, in the rare instance when a will is contested, decides who gets the assets, not where the body is going to be buried or burned. At this point I am trying to think of hitting a racquetball. Trying to think of making a kill shot. I don't want to be completely absorbed in this talk of death, it is just too depressing. I am a guy that wants to live life. I am happy when I am breathing. Here we go again.

Milstein: You went to see Daniel on his birthday at the gravesite?

Virgie: Yes.

Milstein: Can you tell us if the tape has ever been played in the media?

Virgie: I think pieces of it was.

Milstein: How did the media get that tape?

Virgie: My sister-in-law.

Milstein: Who gave her permission to give that tape to the media?

Virgie: It was her video.

Milstein: And you permitted her to videotape you at the gravesite of your grandson?

Virgie: Yes.

Milstein: You never instructed her that this was a private service for you and your grandson. That this should not be given to the media or be publicized?

Virgie: No.

Milstein: Do you have a granddaughter, Dannielynn, who has a brother who has died, did you consider what rights your granddaughter would have about having seen that tape on television [in the future]?

Virgie: Sir, I was so upset when my grandson died and I tried to tell everybody that *he didn't voluntarily die and I tried to tell my daughter that she was going to be next to die.*

Milstein: When did you speak to your daughter, you said you had not spoken to her in 10 years?

Virgie: No, she called me when the baby—when my grandson died. She called me and she was very upset and she was crying and she said Danny is gone, but I was on the other end of the phone. I have a phone at home that if it rings, if you don't pick it up before the 3rd ring, then it records. And I was there and I was listening to her, but she would not hush talking, she was so upset, she would not hush talking for me to say anything and when she was still talking, when the phone was hung up. So I did not get to talk to her, but she did call me.

Milstein: Did you ever describe that message on national news?

Virgie: I think when I talked to CNN . . . that's when I said, *please Vicky, Danny is gone and you are going to be next, please pay attention to what is around you. Please be careful.* I said that on national TV because I knew she was going to be next, my grandson did not overdose. Howard was there when he died and Howard was there when my daughter died. It's not his child and I am afraid for her life as well, please help us.

Now the red flags are rising like the humpback whales in Alaska. Two people die, a healthy young man and a beautiful young woman. And among the common denominators is Howard K. Stern who was present at both deaths. Remember that Virgie was a police officer for all those years, and she had a police officer's instincts. If she wasn't a woman, she probably would have been a police chief by then. So she wasn't looking into a crystal ball. Unfortunately, her fears about Anna Nicole's death came true within just a few months.

Milstein: The news media indicated that your daughter had an interest in Marilyn Monroe.
Virgie: It was her idol.
Milstein: How long was it her idol?
Virgie: Since she was six.
Milstein: Did she ever talk about wanting to be buried in the same area as Marilyn Monroe?
Virgie: Wherever the stars were buried that is where she wanted to be. I want to live this life and this is my road, I want to live this life and yes, she did mention that once that she would like to be buried next to Marilyn Monroe.

Milstein: That is contradictory to your statement that she wanted to be buried in Texas, because she is a Texas girl.

Virgie: She was younger then.

Seidlin: And then there is another moment in her life that she wanted it to be in California, right?

Virgie: When she was in the movie life, in her modeling life, yes, where all the movie stars [were].

NINE

IT'S NOT WHO TALKS LOUDER

The afternoon of the next to last day, I turned to Stern and said, "Mr. Stern are you comfortable coming back here one more day, tomorrow?" Stern answered "Your Honor, I would love to finish it up today." Stern keeps getting deeper and deeper, as you will see as his testimony unfolds.

The lawyers started bickering, addressing one another in my presence. These are fine lawyers and they know that is a cardinal sin. But they were getting tired and beat up. I was working them at a frantic pace and they continually had to shoot from unexpected positions. I announced, "I am the courtroom director. Everything to me. It's not who talks louder, it's who signs the report card at the end of the day. Stay loose as a goose." Stern was starting to get antsy again and I turned to him and said, "Stern, do not make a final decision on if you are coming back or not. Be flexible."

Had he not come back, he would probably not be facing the criminal charges that were later filed against him in California. His testimony continued to self destruct; basically it destroyed him. These statements he made in the courtroom will be utilized later by the prosecutor as admissions against interest. We are getting into discussions with the attorneys and with Tom Pirdle—who is working with "Texas," and whom I now nicknamed "Houston"—on the witnesses that might be called to the stand. I said, "I want to rock and roll . . . I think Larry [Birkhead] may have somewhat of a say here, that is why we are going to have him testify. He has been forthcoming. *He may be the father of Dannielynn.* And under some of these theories, he might have a right to speak."

Things are getting accomplished outside the view of the media and the public. I had Milstein, like Santa's helper, accomplishing extraordinary things and Milstein announced, "All the parties, namely, Mr. Birkhead, Mr. Stern, Ms. Arthur, met with all counsel in your chambers to discuss the viewing of Ms. Smith. Arrangements were made last night and this morning for this purpose and the viewing was held today. It is not a surprise to the media anymore, because there were three helicopters and enough press to let us know that everybody seemed to figure it out. I am pleased to say that family members have had an opportunity today to be able to view their loved one in a dignified manner, in the medical examiner's office. They were very professional. They set up a very comfortable room and things progressed properly."

Milstein argued to me that we needed a confidentiality agreement, so that the parties would keep their mouths shut about the viewing for eternity. I knew that I wouldn't be policing that into the future, because I was hanging up the robe permanently and there was no way I would leave such a task, a controversial one, for a future judge. So I said, "I cannot police this case into the next decade. Confidentiality will remain until this court pronounces its final judgment on Friday. Then you all do what you think your conscience tells you what to do within the bounds of society. But I am not policing it beyond that. You got another day and a half to remain mute on that issue."

Milstein then told me, "I am concerned that even though we are under a confidentiality agreement, that maybe someone is having some financial benefit from the death of Ms. Smith. I don't know if the court or you would permit me to inquire . . . but we had three helicopters and a lot of media and we believe that someone at least notified the media to be out where we were. They arrived before I arrived with Mr. Birkhead and we were the first ones there, so it was not like anyone followed us. Now, is it guesswork, maybe it is guesswork. Is it people tipping them off and getting paid? I have no idea. But I believe it may lead to the intent of the parties as to them having a pecuniary interest."

Tunstall responded, "Your Honor, when Dr. Perper called in, I mean he said, you know, in open court, if you want to view her—there is only one medical examiner. Why do we need to go there? It's done and over with."

I wanted to keep my lawyers in a framework that continued to show respect to the court system and I told the litigants and attorneys, "It's not a no-holds-barred operation here, but I am going to give you more latitude. I have to adjust my thinking as it unfolds. This is work in the making and it is evolving, and the court has not fashioned any final remedy for Friday, because it is evolving."

I didn't want this to become the wild west, with everybody drawing their six shooters. I reminded them that this was not a jury trial, where it becomes a dog and pony show. I am a weathered, hard nosed former cab driver that has unfortunately seen it all. They knew, even though I would need to remind them throughout the proceeding, that I was the trier of fact, not a jury, and I was the only one they had to convince of their position. Therefore, we could cut through all of the baloney, hot air and drama and stick to the facts and the legal argument.

As I looked at Virgie, my heart went out to her. I saw her holding her husband's hand. I don't think they ever let go of each other's hands. In my chambers, at the beginning of the hearing, five days earlier—by now it felt like five years—I told her husband that he could sit with his wife, that he could sit right next to her, and that he didn't have to sit in the back of the chambers. I felt their strong magnetic pull. I understand that they are still happily married, because these are again just moments in time. But this case, being a very high profile case, one of the most viewed cases, except for maybe the O.J. Simpson case, became imprinted on the minds of many people. It had all the ingredients—sex, *Playboy* magazine, many lovers, who's the daddy, an old man marrying a young woman and a judge driving the cab who took no prisoners.

Virgie looked beat up. She looked like someone who just lost her daughter and grandson, worn out. I said to her, "You know what I am going to do, mom? I know you are tired, but before you're totally zonked out, I will bring you up while you are still strong and have some juice. Let's put it this way . . . you will be done."

Milstein: In the interest of justice, I am going to ask Ms. Arthur, since the death of your grandson, have you received any financial remuneration directly to you from any news media?

Virgie: Plane fare.

There is a likelihood that Virgie may have received some sums of money, or in kind, gifts from media outlets. But this had no impact whatsoever on my decision making. I found it to have no real relevance to the issue of where Anna Nicole should be buried.

Barth (to Virgie): You have no idea how Splash came in possession of the tape of the memorial that you and your sister-in-law had and Mr. Lee [Splash] had together, correct?

Virgie: I guess my sister-in-law—no, I don't.

Barth: Was Mr. Lee physically present at the memorial service?

Virgie: Yes he was.

Barth: Did he know Daniel?

Virgie: No.

Barth: But you said Daniel was a good boy and you said he wasn't on drugs; is that correct?

Virgie: Yes, he wasn't.

Milstein: At any time, did you permit them to video tape you since the death of Anna Nicole Smith in the form of an interview, words, your trip from the Hard Rock Cafe or in any other manner?

Virgie: That one time.

Virgie received a bad rap for her media association, before and after Anna Nicole's death. I reviewed the media statements after the trial, and Virgie was just slammed in every direction. But recognize the fact that Virgie felt that her daughter's life was in danger, meaning the angel of darkness was at Anna Nicole's front door. According to Virgie's testimony, the only way that she was able to reach Anna was through the media. Howard K. Stern was shutting her down, and preventing her from having any form of contact with Anna Nicole. Unfortunately, Virgie's worst nightmare became a living truth. Her daughter did die, and under unexplainable circumstances, similar to the circumstances surrounding the death of her grandson Daniel. There has yet to be a full and fair investigation of either death. Experienced law enforcement individuals, the real experts in this area, have stated to me that both locations have done a poor and incompetent job of fully investigating these deaths. Neither one of these police agencies, the Bahamas or the Seminole Police departments, is equipped to handle this type of death.

Now Stern takes the witness stand again. I figure that Texas (O'Quinn), one of the wealthiest lawyers in Texas, who has carried a big stick in every courtroom in the nation, will carve him a new rear end.

Texas: Sir, you are licensed as a lawyer in the state of California?

Stern: Yes.

Texas: However, are you licensed as a lawyer in the country of the Bahamas?

Stern: No.

Texas: Have you ever owned any home in that country?

Stern: No, I have stayed with Anna at her house there.

Texas: Do you still live in Anna's house?

Stern: Yes, with our baby.

Texas: What is your source of income?

Stern: Right now, I am borrowing money from my parents to be here to fight for Anna.

Seidlin: When was the last time you earned your own income?

Stern: I had a law practice.

Texas: What year?

Stern: Until 2002.

Seidlin: What happened in 2003?

Stern: That is when the Anna Nicole Show started and I split up with my law partner.

Seidlin: In 2003, did you have any income reported on your tax return?

Stern: Yes. Well, there was from the Anna Nicole Show, there was income.

Seidlin: How much?

Stern: It was pretty small. It was like $12, 500. I was actually on that show, it was a reality show.

Seidlin: What other income did you have that year?

Stern: I was with Anna ... my income was with her.

Seidlin: You have no separate independent income?

Stern: No.

Seidlin: What happened in 2004?

Stern: Same thing, it was through Anna.

Seidlin: Was that show still on the air?

Stern: I think that was in 2004.

Seidlin: So you made another $12,000?

Stern: If that.

Seidlin: Where were you living in 2004, California?

Stern: Yes. I have an apartment in California that Anna paid the rent on, and I stayed at her house most nights.

Seidlin: How about in 2005, what was your income?

Stern: Same thing. All the way to today.

Here was a lawyer who had a very good reputation, yet he had produced very little income for the past several years. Stern placed himself in the position of having to rely on a woman who at times had shown instability and reliance upon drugs and overprescribed medications. And Stern knew about this, because he stated in my courtroom that he was with her all the time; she was his only client and the love of his life. For me, the $64,000 question was why would someone with his educational background become a valet for a star and have to rely completely on her generosity?

I asked Stern how much rent he paid while he was in L.A. He answered $950 a month, and that was paid by Anna.

Seidlin: When you went to a restaurant who paid the check?

Stern: Anna paid for most things.

Seidlin: When you bought a pair of shoes, who paid for that?

Stern: I did not buy too many pairs of shoes, but she did.

Seidlin: Did she give you a credit card?

Stern: No.

Seidlin: Would she give you cash?

Stern: Yes.

With Stern still on the witness stand, I said, "Is it the heart that is chasing this, or is it money chasing it, or both?" At that point, Milstein picked up the questioning of Stern, this time dealing with her will.

Milstein: If the will of Anna Nicole Smith is admitted to probate and you are appointed under the will as executor, will you be entitled to executor fees?

Stern: I would and I am going to say it right now. I am saying in front of the world that I am waiving any fee.

Seidlin: You keep giving me these gratuitous statements. I can't force him. He makes a statement. How can I force him to say we are going to put it here or there? . . . You were kind enough to come here, but I am not buying the Brooklyn Bridge.

Stern: Your Honor, that's the truth.

Seidlin: The truth will be what the court determines it to be.

Milstein: If you were entitled to a fee, will you accept a fee as the executor of the estate?

Stern: No, I will not.

Milstein: Under the last will and testament of Anna Nicole Smith, you were named as the guardian on behalf of her son Daniel; is that correct?

Stern: That's correct.

Milstein: Would you then be entitled to a fee as the guardian of her property?

Stern: I don't know if I would. . .I would waive that.

Milstein: Under the last will and testament of Anna Nicole, you are also named as trustee on behalf of Daniel; is that correct?

Stern: I believe so.

Milstein: Would you then be entitled to a trustee's fee under that will?

Stern: Same answer, I don't know, but if I would be entitled to it, I would waive it and I am saying it here, right now in front of the world.

Milstein: Mr. Stern are you still at the time of the death of Anna Nicole Smith, were you representing her with regard to any of the litigation involving the estate of her late husband, J. Howard Marshall?

Stern: Yes.

Seidlin: What is the potential return on that?

Stern: Well, right now we have a judgment in the ninth circuit that is worth approximately $100,000,000 [one hundred million dollars], but it is on appeal.

TEN

IF THIS ISN'T A JIGSAW PUZZLE

Texas continued to tear another strip off Stern, asking him how Anna Nicole was going to support him financially, now that she was no longer around.

Stern: She is not going to. I am going to go back to work, I am not an incompetent person.

Texas: Where are you going to go back to work?

Stern: Sir, I went to a good college. I went to a good law school. I have skills. Now, in terms of what I am going to do, honestly, right now, I am trying to deal with the death of Anna Nicole and I have not thought about it.

Texas: What did you do to help Anna Nicole as a different person [after the death of Daniel]?

Stern: I tried to be there for her in every way. . .Sir, you can try to mock me, but in my entire time with Anna, I have always emphasized that everything had to be in her name and only her name.

Texas: Did you know that there were a number of medications that she was on? Did you help her in that regard?

I think this question and the following line of questioning

sunk Stern in the eyes of law enforcement, as he just continued to bury himself even deeper.

Stern: What do you want—did I help her?

Texas: If she was on medication?

Seidlin: I want to get into that.

Stern: Sir, she had doctors.

Now the doctors are going to be hit over their heads with a brick bat. I firmly believe that the California Attorney General's office, Jerry Brown and his assistants, looked over this transcript with a fine tooth comb and now the doctors are going to be criminally charged. Just read the answers given by Howard K. Stern. But I wanted to get a timeline: where, when, what, why. As any good investigator would.

Seidlin: Was she on drugs during the period of time, in the almost 11 years?

Stern: Your Honor, I mean, I would prefer not to talk about Anna and her medical history and try to muddy her, which I know Ms. Arthur's counsel is trying to do. She always had a doctor.

Seidlin: What drugs was she on in the last 10 years?

An argument then ensued between the attorneys and the court on whether we should get into Anna Nicole's drug use and I began to quote Socrates: "I have got one honest man, if there is an honest man among us." Because I was seeking the truth and no legal technicality or argument was going to prevent me from knowing Anna Nicole's mental condition when she entered into her will in 2001 and when she made the decision to bury Daniel in the Bahamas, and whether she was able to form the intent to state to those around her that she wanted to be buried in the Bahamas. I was beginning to get the impression that her mind was cloudy. Her faculties were confused and she was not operating in a normal state of mind. I concluded, "I believe that her capacity is at issue. It's absolutely at issue."

Then there was the matter of the video of her interview with CNN, and what her state of mind was at the time she conducted that interview. I said, "You were going to say what was her capacity when the video was filmed. Was she sober or under the influence of alcohol or drugs? Were her normal faculties impaired?"

Debra Opri stood up and told me, "And Your Honor, I think you have the power and courage to make the order that . . . we take a step to the side and say, look we have a video to impeach . . . we have to get into the state of mind, because in the last months of Anna Nicole's life, she was isolated and by the way, was she depressed or suicidal and we need to know this, because her intent speaks for itself."

I told Opri that I planned to take it a step further, that I was going to look at whether Anna Nicole was under the influence of drugs. Kelley, my court appointed administrator ad litem chimed in, "If she was under the influence of drugs . . . she could not form intent." To which I replied, "In probate, we would be looking at intent and we would be looking at whether or not she was under the influence of drugs, it's painted all over, we know it."

Texas O'Quinn was so cute, he wanted to ask some questions

119

of Stern again. His big brown eyes were looking at me, the eyes of Texas were upon me as he stands up, this tall tree, and says to me, "Why can't I ask? I am the only lawyer that is not allowed to ask my own questions."

Texas is the lawyer's lawyer—handsome, sophisticated, well dressed, with a tongue that is sharp as a knife. But I knew he possessed the most important thing in the courtroom: honesty. So I gave him one of my dumb analogies. "You know, when I used to teach tennis, you used to wear white shorts and a white top. It always looked, you look good."

Texas said, "Thank you."

Texas knew I was in a tough situation, a precarious situation. All these issues were revolving around me, with little or no jurisdiction to resolve most of them. He knew we were in a big poker game and I was bluffing on some of these significant issues. But he allowed me this latitude because in his heart he knew, and I knew, we were only seeking justice. I was sick to learn of his death a couple of years after the trial. A big tree had fallen, a big pillar of the justice system had fallen, a man from a different era.

The prosecutor in me resurfaced as I asked Stern if Anna Nicole took drugs for the past three years.

Stern: Anna Nicole was on prescription medication at different times. When you say drugs, I don't want to say she was using anything illegal.

Seidlin: Was she abusing these drugs? Was she taking too many of them?

Stern: I am not a doctor. I am not a doctor. What I would say is this, is that. . . .

Seidlin: These drugs were prescription?

Stern: Yes.

[There was a proposal for me to read the names of these drugs.]

Seidlin: I am not going to read them, because I cannot pronounce them.

Texas: Narcotics.

Seidlin: What prescription drugs did she partake in?

Stern: You are talking about after Daniel died?

Seidlin: I am talking in the last three years.

Stern: Anybody who cares about Anna Nicole, would not go through this inquiry.

Seidlin: Well, you guys, he makes these free running statements. *You got to advise him not to, because he is going to fall into a bear trap.* I can call his bluff.

I remember all the stars, all the celebrities that have died from drug use—too many doctors, too many prescriptions—over the past few years. There should be a master registry for them and the drugs they take. I think enablers should be punished even though no enablers have been charged with criminal activity in the past. But the whole world was watching this trial. This was being televised all over the world, and the media loves to run with a negative story.

Stern is worried about her legacy in death? That we shouldn't know about her drug use since she died? How ironic. How about keeping her off drugs while she was alive? He was with her every day; how about saying No, and if she kicks your ass out, then good bye and good luck, because if everyone takes that strong position, then we have intervention and drug counseling and we won't have all this celebrity blood on our hands.

But remember, Stern displayed a confidence in testifying because, as a lawyer, and a California lawyer at that, he never heard of any person being charged for giving drugs to a star. But California Attorney General Jerry Brown has now set a precedent. He had the guts to set a new standard. California has led the way in many areas of the law and Brown has just blazed another new trail.

I continued to question Stern regarding Anna Nicole's drug use, particularly the medications she put into her body between 2000 and 2007.

Stern: Your Honor, I could not be sure of every medication that she placed in her body.

Seidlin: Tell me a few.

Stern: I know at one time she was on a medication called Topamax. . .Your Honor, is this really necessary?

Seidlin: Well, you know, you came knocking on my door . . .

Stern: . . . It's not right to do this to somebody after they have died.

Seidlin: (to Barth) I think you need to instruct your witness to respond to the court's question, because I don't want to get into an argument with him. . .(to Stern) Were there times that she went into drug rehab centers?

Stern: She went into [the] Betty Ford [Center], I am not sure of the exact year, it was before I was around.

Seidlin: Did she go into rehab centers after 1996?

Stern: Not into a rehab center, no.

Seidlin: Did she have more than one doctor prescribing these drugs?

Stern: Not that I am aware of.

Seidlin: These drugs all came from one doctor?

Stern: Well, at different times, she had different doctors.

Seidlin: I am asking, did she have prescriptions drugs at the same time from different doctors, where they get multiple drugs from doctors. Did Dr. A not know Dr. B was prescribing drugs?

Stern: She had more than one doctor. I believe the doctors knew about each other.

Seildin: Could you have stopped her from taking these prescription drugs, could you have stopped it?

Stern: Your Honor, after her son passed away?

Seidlin: Prior.

Stern: I talked to her about it. I talked [about?] it and she did not cut down a lot on the medication that she took. *Can anybody stop someone else entirely*—we are jumping the gun here because ...

Seidlin: I am not jumping the gun. I got a gun to my head and I got to decide by Friday at noon.

Stern: Anna, when she made her decisions, she was pretty clear on her decisions and I don't think medication influenced her decision. It was not like Anna was medicated all the time or she could not talk. She formed an intent and she had made it clear to many people.

Seidlin: That video that we saw the other day, is that her normal state of addressing someone?

Stern: What you saw on the video, yes, that is how Anna Nicole talks. That is how she talked since I have known her, I mean, there are times when she is more impaired than that.

I thought to myself holy cow, Anna Nicole seemed off the wall the other day on the video. If I had a loved one like this, I would immediately seek intervention. I couldn't operate in my world with someone so impaired. I then interjected, *"More impaired. . .was she impaired? You said more impaired, more impaired, was she under the influence then?"*

Stern replied, "No, I don't think so." To which I rebuked, "Well you said she was more impaired than that."

I found Stern less than candid. This was like a game of cat and mouse and I was getting tired of it.

Stern: I am saying that her. . .

Seidlin: She was impaired a little bit?

Stern: No, no. What I said was she formed her thoughts, she knew what she wanted.

A little knowledge is dangerous. Stern's central and primary thoughts were to convince me that Anna Nicole had an intent, and the intent was to be buried in the Bahamas. He didn't know that I was opening up every other area about Anna Nicole, and how can you form an intent when your mind is so drugged up? I went back to drilling Stern, but in a softer manner.

Seidlin: I can have a court reporter read this back.

Stern: By more impaired, I did not mean she was more impaired. When you asked me that statement, you asked me was that her normal frame of mind and what I was trying to get across. With medication she was impaired but in terms of where she wanted to be laid to rest.

If this wasn't a jigsaw puzzle, and Stern was trying to fill in the pieces, telling me okay, she may be on medication, she might be drugged up, but it didn't reach the level of influencing her intent to where she wanted to be buried, after telling me he is not a doctor. Cagey, but illogical. I am just not buying it. Do they think I have been sitting on the bench too long? That I have had too much sunshine here in Florida? That I hit too many tennis balls? That I sat through too many trials? I told Stern not to give me any conclusions, because it was up to the court to make the ultimate conclusion. I then asked him if Daniel tried to stop Anna Nicole from taking drugs.

Stern: Yes.

Seidlin: Did he talk to her about it?

Stern: Yes.

Seidlin: Did he have any success for any day?

Stern: It's not like she was impaired.

Seidlin: Answer that question. Did Danny have any success when he spoke to her about drugs?

Stern: She would go back and forth, depending on what was going on in her life. When she was more stressed out, she would take more medication.

Seidlin: Did she ever get psychiatric care or psychological care?

Stern: Yes.

Seidlin: How recent was that?

Stern: She had a psychologist.

Seidlin: What year?

Stern: Actually, she had a psychiatrist after Daniel's passing.

Seidlin: How about prior?

Stern: I believe she had a psychologist.

Seidlin: Give your impression of her mental status.

Stern: I think that Anna had a very clear head at times. I think at other times, her head was not as clear.

Seidlin: Why was it not as clear?

Stern: Well a lot of times, it would be from stress. A lot of times it would be just because she could not deal with the pressure that she was put under.

Seidlin: And when her head was not clear was it . . . was drugs contributing to that fog?

Stern: Sometimes, sometimes not. Sometimes not, but. . .

Seidlin: Was it difficult for you to pull her out of that maze?

Again, I was thinking of my French classes. I would think of the beautiful French landscape. I wanted to put something positive in my mind and, of course, I always think of food, and I thought of all the delicacies that I would eat in France. When I walked the streets of France, I would eat some French bread and brie cheese and wear it on my clothes.

Stern: After Daniel passed?

Seidlin: Prior to Danny's death.

Stern: The court litigation [during the Marshall case] put a lot of pressure on her.

Texas then specifically asked Stern about the type of drugs that Anna Nicole used, starting with methadone.

Stern: She took methadone, but not during, in my presence, not over the last five months.

Texas: She took it prior to the last five months?

Stern: She did.

Texas: Who was the doctor that you say prescribed the drugs?

Stern: It was a doctor named Dr. Kapoor.

Texas: Was he in the Bahamas?

Stern: No, it's all over the media, Kapoor.

Texas: Did she take hydromorphone or morphine? Did she also take a narc for hydromorphone or a Dilaudid?

Stern: Dilaudid, there were times when she took Dilaudid. I am not familiar with the other one, but it is possible.

Texas: On the matter of drugs, other drugs.

Stern: She did not take all of these at the same time.

Texas: What day did she die on?

Stern: February 8.

Texas: Did you all leave the Bahamas to come to Florida before that death, on Monday of that same week?

Stern: Yes.

Texas: And she was in Florida for three days and died,

correct?

Stern: Yes sir.

Texas: And you were with her at that time, were you not?

Stern: No, sir. I was not with her when she died.

Texas: Were you staying in the same hotel room or not?

Stern: Yes.

Texas: Were you doing things together or not?

Stern: She did not leave the hotel room.

Texas: So from the time you got here on Monday, she did not leave the hotel room on Monday, Tuesday, Wednesday, up until she died in the hotel room on Thursday, is that your testimony?

Stern: That's correct.

Texas: And Anna was having problems fighting drugs herself?

Stern: I would not define it that way, but she did take medication.

It was now Opri's turn to cross-examine Stern about his involvement with Anna Nicole's drug use.

Opri: What were all the names Anna Nicole Smith used?

Stern: She only had a few. Anna Nicole Smith, Vicky Marshall, Vicky Hogan, Vicky Smith. Then doctors, some doctors prescribed things to her in different names, even though they knew it was for her. One of those names was Michelle Chase, another name was Susan Wong. These were at different times, though. At hotels, she went by Mrs. Flintstone. I mean, she went by a lot of different things in different context. She went by Norma Jean.

Opri: Did you often pick up prescriptions for her at various pharmacies under these names?

Texas (interjecting): It's the trump card.

Seidlin: One at a time. Texas, you got your line in. Have a seat.

Stern: In Los Angeles, Anna did not drive.

Opri: So the answer is, yes, sir?

Stern: I picked up prescriptions for her yes, other people did.

I believe these admissions by Stern lead the California Attorney General to criminally target Stern. Because doesn't a reasonable person have one doctor and maybe one or two specialists, and one pharmacy? Why so many doctors and more than one pharmacy? The answer became obvious as the trial unfolded. I am hearing Mrs. Flintstone; where are Donald Duck and Mickey Mouse? It becomes bizarre when it's all an effort to provide Anna Nicole with the drugs that ultimately lead to her demise.

Opri: ... You can laugh at me all you want. Are you or are you not the biological father of Dannielynn under the laws of this state?

Opri was a mighty force in a courtroom. A diminutive individual, but she packed a mighty dagger. She spoke well, clear as a bell, with a big smile and a sense of confidence that was Hollywood. And in Los Angeles, you either got it or you don't. And Opri had it. I wanted to set the tone and reduce the burners a little bit. I told her, "I don't want you to inflame it. You are strong medicine, but I don't want the dark meat of the chicken. I want it soft. I don't want to inflame." My Opri, ever the feisty one, but one you want sitting next to you when you are in battle, responded, "With respect to Your Honor, it's impeachment."

I never feel challenged or threatened. To succeed in a proceeding, or in life, you have to put your ego aside. And do what is in the best interest of the mission.

> **Seidlin:** You came up with arms to bear and I understand that, but you are going to take a deep breath. We are not going that way. You know, we are not going that way, I will let you ask more questions, but not on that issue. Don't start dropping any bombshells here. We went through it. I think you are finished.
>
> **Texas:** Are you going to give a final argument?

This fine bunch of lawyers was accustomed to giving final arguments in front of a jury. I answered in one word: "No."

Texas starts to move around like a fine Texas thoroughbred ready to run in the Kentucky Derby. I have taken a hankering to him, and I turn and say to him, "Texas, you sit there. That chair looks comfortable for you."

I am getting ready for the next day and I want all three parties present throughout the final hearing. Opri said, "We are requesting Mr. Stern to be present tomorrow." Stern then turned to me and asked, "So you are ordering me to be here?" I reply, "No, I am going to talk you into coming." Stern responds to my request by saying, "This is important enough for me to be here."

ELEVEN

BABY, YOU TELL ME WHAT YOU WANT

Larry Birkhead is now called to the witness stand.

I quickly slipped in to all the attorneys that I would like a proposed final judgment from all three parties for tomorrow afternoon. I adopted this policy or procedure because it would allow me, before I wrote my final judgment or pronounced the judgment in an open hearing, to look at what the parties wanted. I look at what they want and compare it to what I think makes an equitable result, and sometimes we are not that far apart. I utilized this procedure often in highly contested family and probate cases. How would the parties want the judgment to read? How do they want the matter to be disposed of? And it really puts them on the heels for what kind of result they are seeking. It separates the hot air and baloney from the real result. It is easy to complain and disagree. But baby, you tell me what you want. . .you be the judge.

So I tell all the attorneys present, "You will submit it [final judgment] . . . and I am going to fashion a resolution and try to place finality on these issues into eternity."

Milstein then proceeded to question Birkhead, and began with the subject of his income since Anna Nicole's death.

Milstein: Since the death of Daniel, Anna Nicole Smith's son, have you received any direct financial remuneration from any source from any press or any media?

Birkhead: In my profession, I'm a photographer and a reporter, the answer would be, yes, in the sense that I have photos that I have taken over the years. In this situation, of Anna Nicole and also her son and Mr. Stern or anybody that was around us for the last few years, that has been on archive with my employers and different magazines, newspapers and archived photos. So in that sense, I have ...

Milstein: Have you sold any likeness or pictures of Daniel or Anna Nicole Smith since the death of Daniel?

Birkhead: There have been sales of those photos.

Milstein: You directly.

Birkhead: Not directly. I wanted to know if this guy was a deadbeat.

I wanted to know if this guy can stand on his own two feet. Can he make a living without leeching off Anna Nicole? Is he like all those people who hang around the heavy weight fighters? Those large entourages that are worthless, because all you need is one good person around you. And I wanted to go to town now. I wanted to open up Birkhead. I wanted to peer into his soul, to see what makes him tick. So far he is winning me over because his answers aren't on a slippery slope. He appears to answer every question in a forthright and truthful manner. It is refreshing when you hear the truth under oath in a courtroom. Sometimes I would sit in a courtroom and watch people put their hand on the Bible or raise their hand to swear to tell the truth, the whole truth, and nothing but the truth. I would say to myself, what an exercise in futility. This churchgoer, this person who holds himself out to be a religious person, who is also active in the community, but can espouse such lies in a courtroom—whether as a witness or an attorney—would just turn me off. I decided to ask Birkhead what his income was for 2006, according to his tax return. At first, he couldn't remember. So I prodded. At first I mentioned $30,000 to him, which I thought was a respectable amount. I was thinking of school teachers, managers of department stores. When he said more than $30,000, I was soothed. So I mentioned $50,000. When he said more than $50,000, I was starting to get a good impression of Birkhead's creative ability.

Seidlin: $80,000.

Birkhead: It was greater than that.

Seidlin: Where you live, do you pay rent?

Birkhead: I do.

Seidlin: What is your rent?

Birkhead: It is like $1500 a month.

Seidlin: Do you live alone in that place?

Birkhead: Yes, sir.

Seidlin: When did you meet Ms. Smith, what year?

Birkhead: 2003.

Seidlin: And what event was it that you met her?

Birkhead: I met her at that Barnstable Brown, in conjunction with functions at the Kentucky Derby. She was there in 2003 and I had no contact until 2004 and after that event, Mr. Stern and I had contact about a future event and I was invited by Anna Nicole via Mr. Stern to attend that event and take photographs. And after that, I was asked to go to another event personally by Ms. Smith and our relationship went from professional to a personal relationship.

Seidlin: They hired you as their private photographer?

Birkhead: Yes.

Seidlin: And to sell them.

Birkhead: To sell them, which I continue to do so.

Seidlin: Was that successful?

Birkhead: Yes, sir.

Seildin: When did it become professional to personal?

Birkhead: I would say in July and August of '04.

Seidlin: July of '04.

Birkhead: Yes sir.

Seidlin: It became a personal relationship?

Birkhead: Yes.

Seidlin: What was Stern's relationship with her at that point in July of 2004?

Birkhead: Well, he was her attorney, he was her publicist, her manager. He was her friend. He ran errands. He did personal things for her and he. . .he was kind of multitasking her.

Seidlin: Was he her most significant person that she relied upon?

Birkhead: In what respect?

Seidlin: Who else did she depend upon?

Birkhead: She did depend on Mr. Stern for his advice and input in her personal and professional matters.

Seidlin: Did you know whether or not they had an intimate relationship?

Birkhead: No, they did not, because I moved in with Ms. Smith in August of 2005.

Seidlin: Well, were you exclusive during that year?

Birkhead: Yes, sir.

Seidlin: What was Stern's reaction with regard to your relationship with her?

Birkhead: He interfered with our relationship.

This guy's candor and his lack of resentment towards Stern amazed me. Birkhead didn't come in with all the anger and hostility that I have seen so often in family matters. He's been battling Stern and Anna Nicole for DNA. He wasn't present at Dannielynn's birth, a special occasion, and now he hasn't seen Dannielyn for months since her birth. Birkhead could have come in like a bulldozer, but he didn't. I used the word. You spend years as a prosecutor developing trial skills so your questions would not be leading. This is a great word for that. I said, "Describe."

Birkhead: There were times when Anna Nicole wanted to do public events and there were a couple of instances where he cancelled tickets that we had for basketball games. There were times, because he was fearing that we would be seen in public, which is what I was told by Anna Nicole.

Seidlin: Tell me about when you moved in with Anna.

Birkhead: At her request, Mr. Stern, he had his own apartment at the time and he would come over after noon and sleep on a couch down below our bedroom or he would have his run of the house, and sometimes he would stay there. Sometimes Anna Nicole would be ... I would ask him to leave or we would have to try to ensure our privacy in some way in our own room, but I stayed living there until April 2005 ... the relationship did not end, well not really because what happened was Anna suggested that because of the tension inside the house, it was not just Mr. Stern and there were other people in the home and we did not have a lot of time. She suggested the possibility of us obtaining a place through another part of the city for us to go to, kind of a safe haven or place to retreat to that I would have my things at because basically we were running out of space where we lived, so it was a better fit.

Seidlin: Did you find another place?

Birkhead: Yes, sir. I moved my belongings.

Seidlin: But you still remained in the home?

Birkhead: No, sir, we went back and forth.

Seidlin: To both homes?

Birkhead: On occasions.

Seidlin: With Anna Nicole?

Birkhead: Yes. Most nights, yes, sir.

I said to myself where is Howard K. Stern sleeping? He is sleeping in the same residence as his so-called lover, who is sleeping with Larry Birkhead. How much crap is Stern willing to eat to be in the presence of Anna Nicole? Is it a question of spiritual addiction to her? Is he chasing her dough? Does he want to control her life by remaining with her at all times, even at the actual moment of conception with another man?

Once in a while I would date a woman and, for some reason, just get attached to her. But I knew I wasn't going to marry her and it was an arm wrestle. She would say she was dating someone else, just break my heart and force me to make that classic choice: if you don't propose, I am taking the magic carpet ride. So I would suffer the consequences. Finally, at age fifty, I guess the pain would have been too great to allow the departure of Belinda. But, never, ever would I want to be physically in the same facility with a woman that I had feelings for if she was banging someone else. That is why golf, tennis, and racquetball exist, so you don't have to confront something like this. This guy Stern is lying downstairs on a couch with these two rocking and rolling upstairs. It just doesn't add up, it just doesn't.

Birkhead: I got my own place and our main place, the place was in my actual name but it was suggested by her and agreed upon by both of us because Anna Nicole had suffered a miscarriage with my child and it was creating tension and she miscarried in February of 2005.

Seidlin: Then what happened? Another term you learn as a trial lawyer that is not leading, another magical line is, "What happened next, if anything?"

Birkhead: She thought I blamed her for the miscarriage. We had some tension and also because of interference internally in the home, we decided we wanted to break away from some of the things in the home and felt it was best, because I wanted

137

to be an individual and maintain my own place and have my own place. Because I had come from Kentucky, to be in a relationship with her to be based on mutual feelings. . .

Seidlin: In April of 2005 you found that new place to live?

Birkhead: Yes, sir.

Seidlin: How long did you remain in that place?

Birkhead: I am still there.

Seidlin: Was she picking up the rent money?

Birkhead: No, sir.

Seidlin: When does the Bahamas come into play?

Birkhead: After the miscarriage and all that we had, of course, a time in between, there is a long time frame in between and we maintained our relationship. There was a time in November and December of 2005, where Ms. Smith went to South Carolina. She [was] distraught over a video that aired and she said she wanted to get away.

Seidlin: What video?

Birkhead: On *Primetime Live,* where her husband or late husband said he did not promise her half of his estate.

Seidlin: This oil fellow?

Birkhead: Yes, sir. He said it was all gifts.

Seidlin: There was a video of that?

Birkhead: And she was very distraught and . . .

Seidlin: It affected her.

Birkhead: Yes, sir. She medicated. . .she was medicated and she was kind of not herself, and so she took off to there and we stayed in contact. I told her I was upset about her going . . .

Seidlin: She takes off. Where does she go?

Birkhead: She went to see a wealthy gentleman in South Carolina that I had introduced her to on a vacation.

Seidlin: You knew this fellow?

Birkhead: Yes, sir.

Seidlin: You think she might have had a personal relationship with him?

Birkhead: Yes, sir.

Seidlin: In November of 2005?

Birkhead: Through Christmas, through New Year's of 2006.

Seidlin: How long did she stay in South Carolina?

Birkhead: For over a month. She came back New Year's Eve. When she came back on New Year's Eve, we reconciled.

Seidlin: What were you doing while she was gone?

Birkhead: I spent Thanksgiving eating cheeseburgers, because we were supposed to spend it together.

Birkhead gives you real answers, because I remember when my little girl Dax was two. My wife was pissed at me for getting up early on Christmas morning to go play racquetball and she left a message on my cell phone, which was, "Don't bother to come home." I know her personality and I know she has to cool off, so after the game I wound up sitting at a diner eating a turkey sandwich with mashed potatoes and watching the big screen TV by myself. So when Birkhead would speak, you receive a vivid picture of his reactions. You see he is a man. He wants to have his own joint, his own nest with her.

Seidlin: How was your emotional state?

139

Birkhead: I was upset because, you know, it was my understanding that we were in an exclusive relationship and she told me to come from a job that I was working on, on the east coast, to spend Thanksgiving and her birthday.

Seidlin: She comes back to you after New Year's?

Birkhead: Yes. We reconciled our differences from the fact that she took off to South Carolina. I told her that I did not agree to some of the things. She was sending me some text messages and instant messages from South Carolina.

Seidlin: And are you back to having the same relationship prior to her leaving?

Birkhead: Yes, sir.

Seidlin: How long does that go?

Birkhead: Until she took off to the Bahamas.

Seidlin: February of '06. What happens then, if anything?

Birkhead: February in 2006, prior to Anna Nicole was preparing to go to the Supreme Court to fight for her late husband's estate case … Anna Nicole informed me that we were expecting another child, since we had previously had the miscarriage.

Seidlin: When did she inform you of that?

Birkhead: Right around Valentine's Day.

Seidlin: How long was she pregnant?

Birkhead: She did not know for sure, but we were trying to figure out the time frame.

Seidlin: Whether it was you or South Carolina?

Birkhead: Well, I asked her and she smacked me and said, I am not a whore, you dummy. So I took it as that and I made an inquiry to the man in South Carolina.

Seidlin: Is the man in South Carolina single or a married man?

Birkhead: Single.

Seidlin: Did you say he is a friend of yours?

Birkhead: I would not say he is a close friend.

I was glad he said not a close friend, because do you want a close friend, a confidant, to be sleeping with someone you love? And then I asked him, "Surely, you don't like him anymore? Did you have any conversation with him since?"

Birkhead: Yes, sir, because of the chain of events that's happened since then. What happened after February of '06 is, we stayed . . . I stayed in the relationship with Anna Nicole. She became agitated because once she told me she was pregnant. I tried to—I wanted to—continue working and doing things that would make me financially independent still and also would allow me to help take care of the baby.

Seidlin: How old are you?

Birkhead: 34, Your Honor.

Seidlin: Any marriages?

Birkhead: No sir.

Seidlin: Any children?

Birkhead: One.

Seidlin: How old?

Birkhead: Five months or six months.

It dawned on me that my boy Larry Birkhead was being a little cute with his judge, but he is a sweet guy. I asked, "That's the little girl we are talking about?" Birkhead replies "Dannielynn."

Seidlin: I am glad you are keeping your sense of humor.

Birkhead: So after, I guess February on down to up until the time she left for the Bahamas, we planned for the child. We picked out baby names. We shopped for things on the internet. She asked me to pick out a wedding ring for her. The day she got on the Supreme Court, she got on the Tiffany website and asked me to pick out a ring for her and I told her that we might need to go to a different website.

Seidlin: You are looking for Target or K-mart?

Birkhead: She wanted 10 carats.

Seidlin: You would have to sell a lot of pictures.

Birkhead: So we, you know, it was. . .I was a little nervous, excited.

Seidlin: Because you thought you were having your first child?

Birkhead: And also because of the previous marriage. So at the same time, like I said, I tried to do things that would allow me to be financially independent and she became agitated by that at me and took it that I did not want to spend time with her, that I was not excited.

Seidlin: Now, Stern, where is he in February of 2006? She tells you she is pregnant. Where is Stern?

Birkhead: Well, I saw him a few times on the couch that he would sleep on, on the level below us. I saw him, because he claimed he was working on the Supreme Court case that was represented here.

I said to myself if he is on that couch, he is not sleeping too well, because his world will be changing in enormous ways. There will be a new baby coming. And Birkhead, as kind as he appears, is still strong and he wants to be the man of the house, or at least share in the decisions with Anna Nicole. He is not going to put up with Stern lying on a couch. Now I want to know about the third party in this play.

Seidlin: How about her mother?
Birkhead: I didn't meet Ms. Arthur. At that time, I did not know her.

I like this guy's southern hospitality and his being respectful towards everybody. Even people who might be undermining his life's agenda, which would be to marry Anna Nicole, have their baby and live happily ever after. Is he not pursuing the American dream? The world dream?

Seidlin: But she embraced you one time in my courtroom?
Birkhead: I met her since the passing of her grandson and her daughter.
Seidlin: Did you form any impression about her from your conversations with [Anna] Nicole?
Birkhead: Yes, sir.
Seidlin: Was it that impression on the video?
Birkhead: No. Let me try to backtrack. I tried not to form an impression. I listened to what Anna said about her mother,

but I am the type of person that likes to observe personally ... before I make a decision of the type of character a person is.

Seidlin: And Anna Nicole's impression was similar to what the video showed?

Birkhead: No, sir.

This surprises me, that the video doesn't reflect the feelings of Anna Nicole about her mother.

Birkhead: ... Anna Nicole always told me that she and her mother did not get along and they had their differences. But one of the first people, when she got pregnant, she cried out for her mother, because she sent me a text message and said, I want my mommy.

Seidlin: She told you that?

Birkhead: Yes.

Seildin: Did her mommy call her on the phone?

Birkhead: No, sir. Because at that point, she was getting ready for her appearance in the Supreme Court ... on other occasions she mentioned her mother and I mentioned the possibility of a reconciliation. And sometimes she would say absolutely not and sometimes she would be more able to listen.

Seidlin: This video that we saw the other day, what was your impression, of someone who knows her so well, what was your impression of the state she was in?

Birkhead: It became ... it appeared to me by looking at the video that that was now becoming her normal state.

Seidlin: We will go slow, your accent is as thick as mine.

Birkhead: It became clear by looking at the video that it brought back bad memories of her normal state, but I don't mean normal. What I consider normal but normal to her . . . her voice seemed slurred to me and not, you know at times she seemed shaken, but I will say she is saying things about her son and what she perceived as statements from her mother about her son.

Seidlin: Well, her son.

Birkhead: Passing.

Seidlin: Alright, let's come back a little bit. February of '06 she is pregnant. What happens next, if anything?

Birkhead: We planned, we prepared, we talked a couple of times marriage, we talked about the future, what it was going to be like. She sent me out to get things for the baby. I bought her presents for Mother's Day, some maternity clothes. I bought her . . . she asked me to get her a wedding ring. She said she did not want to be a single mother, that she had done that before and she did not want to do it again and she said, come on, let's talk about marriage and all that stuff.

Seidlin: Marriage?

Birkhead: Yes, sir.

Seidlin: Were you still breathing when that issue came up?

Birkhead: Yes because the subject was approached multiple times, but now it had a different meaning because of the baby.

Seidlin: Were you considering that?

Birkhead: I was considering that, but I did not want to do it for the wrong reasons. You know because we just got over this two month incident where she took off to South Carolina. And I wanted a more solid, grounded relationship where I did not want to do it just because she was pregnant and I wanted it to be the right time and I knew Mr. Stern's feelings about me and the relationship. I don't read the magazines but I did not want a Britney Spears 55-hour wedding and I wanted it to be genuine.

Seidlin: When did she leave you?

Birkhead: Not until we got into an argument a couple times before she left.

Seidlin: Well, now she is pregnant what happens next?

Birkhead: In April of 2006, she called me to come to the hospital.

Seidlin: Were you still with her many of those nights?

Birkhead: Yes. . .because she was having pains and she had told me that she got rushed to the hospital and I was worried that something was wrong with her and the baby. And she said don't worry, I am OK, the baby is OK and Anna said, you want to know what the baby is. I said you went to the doctor without me because we were planning to go together. She said, don't get mad, I had to. I said, what is wrong, she said I am OK but I saw the baby, do you want to know? I said, no, I will wait until I get there and I came to the hospital and she was in the hospital for two weeks, because she was trying to get off medications or she was having an adverse reaction to the medications from the hospital, or previous medications she had taken before she went into the hospital. And at that time, I stayed with her for two weeks and slept in the hospital bed next to her while Mr. Stern slept on a cot.

At this point I am thinking of that classic Marx Brothers movie *A Night at the Opera*, when they open up the tiny ship's stateroom and all three Marx brothers, not to mention a ton of other people, fall out of the room. Think of it in a logical manner. What is Stern doing sleeping on a cot in the hospital again? Is he the proverbial cat that always finds a place to sleep near the master? I mean what is he doing there? Especially destroying the moment of a union between two young people—Anna Nicole and Larry—where they are attempting to have a loving relationship with a baby coming into the picture?

Seidlin: Then what happened, if anything?

Birkhead: At one point, she was—they had her on a drip trying to wean her off—am I allowed to say the drug name? And what happened was, Mr. Stern and she had packed a duffle bag.

Seidlin: She is pregnant and taking medications?

Birkhead: She was taking medications before and during the pregnancy.

Seidlin: Were you concerned about that?

Birkhead: I was very concerned about that.

Now I ask Birkhead the next question. But obviously I knew the answer and everyone knows the answer. And any matzoh ball would know the answer, which is "No." You don't even want someone to be near a cigar smell.

Seidlin: Why?

Birkhead: Because we had already had one miscarriage and every time she put something in her mouth, I thought that that's it.

Seidlin: It would affect. . .

Birkhead: Yes, sir.

Seidlin: The welfare of the child?

Birkhead: And her as well. And so we had a couple of clashes in the hospital room because she and Mr. Stern brought a duffle bag and when they were not administering through the drips. They were taken out of the bag and taken on top of drugs and thwarted the efforts of the hospital to get her off the medication.

Objections are raised, which I overrule and tell Birkhead to proceed.

Birkhead: OK. So after that, she was at one point on a suicide watch in the hospital and I caught her getting up and she was ripping the IV out at night. I tried to help her back and forth in the bathroom and Mr. Stern was assisting her at the same time while we were in the hospital. She had good times and bad times, depending on how she was reacting to the treatment plan. She maintained a book, a baby book and put my thumbprint as the dad and she put her thumbprint as the mom. And I felt sorry for Mr. Stern, because I knew his interest in her and I did not want to offend him.

Twelve

U–Turns

If anything, you would expect Larry Birkhead had an ax to grind against Stern and would want to paint a dark cloud of Stern's personality and motives.

Seidlin: So you believed in his bona fide friendship, that he was a friend and love partner? . . .Describe it.
Birkhead: Well, yes. Can I tell you where I was going?
Seidlin: Okay.
Birkhead: So at that time, I asked her, Howard is here [and] I feel bad for him. And she said to him, you put your thumb print in the baby book here, and she put Uncle Howard next to it.

I have it in black and white that Howard K. Stern is not the father of Dannielynn, and he knows it. It's clear to him. Anna Nicole knows it. It is clear to her that Birkhead is the father, as it is written in the baby book. So why all these shenanigans about who the father is? Why is there a trip to the Bahamas to subterfuge the answer?

Birkhead: And we stayed in the hospital and she had complications from the plan they were putting her on. Her body was not agreeing with it. One time she tripped over the IV cart and she was pulling out the IV. I said—she said I was yelling at her, but I said her name loud because I did not want her to fall. And she got up as I was sleeping and when I got up, she took that as me yelling at her and she was sensitive as hell, and she asked me to leave or she would push the security button. And then two days later, she called me and said, where are you. I said, you asked me to leave, and she did not remember.

Seidlin: Did she speak to her mother during that time in the hospital?

Birkhead: Not that I am aware of. But after that stay in the hospital, she returned home, to her home in Studio City. And I came back and I think that was around right before Mother's Day, the first week in May, and there was still some, I guess agitation about medications. So I would oftentimes correct her and say, *please don't take this* and she would take the medication against. . .she would not follow the labels on the medication. She would sometimes double whatever dosage she felt she needed. And I asked her why she did it and she said she had a high tolerance. And I told her that it could affect the baby, *please don't.* And sometimes as a substitute to the drugs, even though they were prescription drugs, I suggested why don't we try something that would be over the counter that would be less harmful to her and the baby as a substitute.

Sometimes she would break out in a sweat from pain and she would thank me for helping her and I would massage her pregnancy pain as a substitute for any kind of medicine. And then there were other times when she would send me to the store to get her something that she was craving and I would come back like 30 minutes later . . . and one particular point she slipped into what I call a seizure-like state, and I had to help her to the bathroom and pick her up and take and put her. . .

Seidlin: What date was that? Was that June of 2006?

Birkhead: May of 2006.

Seidlin: Were you living there in the home with her or your own place?

Birkhead: Technically I had my own place, but I was staying there 24 hours a day.

Seidlin: Where was Stern?

Birkhead: A lot of times he was gone. He was working for the Marshall case. In May, I got in an argument with Mr. Stern and Anna Nicole. She was at a hair salon and she yelled at me because she wanted a pair of sunglasses and it was kind of irrelevant.

Seidlin: At the hairdresser place?

Birkhead: Yes, sir. And she was visibly pregnant at the time and we were kneeling down from where she was to get her hair done because she wanted to take a photograph to market on her website, of her pregnancy and her. And while she was there, we had gotten into an argument. I was trying to go invoice for photographs so once again, I could say. . .could stay financially independent and she got upset because I took that path rather than getting her a pair of sunglasses. She said she would get her own ride home. I called Mr. Stern, [and] I got into an argument. I did not want to leave her, he said he would come and get her and that is the last time I saw her.

Seidlin: What month and year?

Birkhead: May of 2006. . .After the argument and he [Stern] picked her up, it became a back and forth fight about some possessions that I left in the house. There was a diamond cross necklace.

Seidlin: He would pick up loose ends for her?

Birkhead: Yes, sir and he said if I did not get over there and act right that she would be with the real father. I said, excuse me, if you are saying I am not the father of the baby, then I don't want to go over there anyway because I have been over there cooking, helping watching over her, caretaking basically, and I am having an attachment to this child that she is telling me this is mine and there is no point in this. Why don't I get over there and act right? Why would he state that, if she is going to be with the real father? Then I found out that Mr. Stern took her or suggested. . .I will not say suggested because it is hearsay . . . Mr. Stern, she told me Mr. Stern later took her to the Bahamas. First to South Carolina, to the man she was with in November or December, that it was his child and then later on I found out she was in the Bahamas and [I] made contact with her even though we had an argument.

Is this a bait and switch? Are Stern and Anna Nicole now

telling Birkhead that he is not the father to get him off the scent? Birkhead is not going to buy this. He is a shrewd southern boy and no slickness will camouflage his instincts. Birkhead knows he is the father. He even smells the fact that he is the father, and nothing and nobody is going to get in his way.

The other side of the equation is this: did Anna Nicole and Stern tell South Carolina also that he was the father of the child? Once we get that answer, the plot will thicken. Because I think she told him that so he would feel guilty and provide his Bahamian house. So this little web that is being woven knocks down two bowling pins. It deals Birkhead a knock-out punch so he will no longer pursue his desire for the child; and two, it gives them a free refuge in the Bahamas. The Bahamas is a difficult place for Virgie and Birkhead to get to. Flights and hotels are expensive, not to mention that the laws are convoluted and the corruption is so great. Plus, as we discover later on, their law enforcement mechanism is close to horrible.

Seidlin: You maintain contact?

Birkhead: Telephone IM [instant messaging] internet.

Seidlin: No personal touching. I mean being in the same room?

Birkhead: No, sir. Because she went to the Bahamas and she had the baby there and all these other events unfolded and so. . .

I had other terrain to cover. I wanted to understand

Anna Nicole's relationship with Daniel, through the eyes of Birkhead. Somehow I felt that Birkhead gave me information that was unfiltered. I am not saying he was as pure as the white driven snow of Switzerland and Austria. Here, I am pulling a real U-turn, and my cabbie instincts took over.

Seidlin: Tell me about Danny for a minute, tell me about Danny. Where was Danny sleeping when you all were together?

Birkhead: In the lower level, two levels below our bedroom or Anna's bedroom.

Seidlin: What was Anna's feeling toward Danny?

Birkhead: She loved her son.

Seidlin: Did they have a healthy relationship?

Birkhead: Yes sir.

I wanted to look into Daniel's soul, using Birkhead's eyes. Daniel died in the Bahamas from an overdose, an over supply of a toxic mix. Easy to believe that he had the same fondness for drugs. That it was in his genes, as it was in his mother's. Or was it just in his environment where he was growing up?

I know that with alcoholism and drug abuse, people who suffer from these two addictions often have the devil chasing their children. My mentor, the sheriff, was a recovering alcoholic. He directed me to be involved in this alcohol or drug community. Every city has a powerful inner circle of people that are involved in groups that cater to and assist recovering drug addicts and alcoholics. This recovering group will amaze you—judges, police chiefs, newspaper editors, and congressman that attend, and are involved with the A.A. meetings and support groups. I attended some of these meetings, but not A.A. meetings. I also served on the boards of some of these drug and alcohol commissions, and one of the oaths that you take in A.A. is not to disclose those who are in attendance.

As we investigated this boy Daniel, we concluded that he had no drug problems and the methadone that was found in his body was foreign to his constitution.

Seidlin: Did Danny have an impression about her prescription drug use?

Birkhead: That from what I witnessed, was when Anna was ever on any prescription, it was at a level where she was not herself. I would still need to shut the door and not let him . . . not ever lock him out, but not welcoming him into the bedroom because either an assistant told me, or Mr. Stern suggested that Daniel should not see her like this or he would get upset if he saw her like this. So this would be the only conversation that I would have about any prescription drugs.

Seidlin: When Danny died did you go to the Bahamas?

Birkhead: No, sir. I tried to contact Anna Nicole afterwards and I talked to her a few days after and I sent my condolences.

Seidlin: Did you ever get to the Bahamas before her death?

Birkhead: Yes, sir.

Seidlin: Why?

Birkhead: I was court ordered [that] the paternity was to be completed on or before January 23.

Seidlin: In the Bahamas?

Birkhead: Yes, sir. And when we went there . . . the Bahamas was a place of convenience . . .

I was looking for another pearl, so I proceeded to open one more oyster shell.

Seidlin: Did she talk about death with you?

Birkhead: Yes, sir she talked about that. She always said she was going to die at the same age that Marilyn Monroe died.

Seidlin: Did she ever talk about where she wanted to be buried?

Birkhead: Yes.

Seidlin: Where?

Birkhead: Where Marilyn Monroe died. Ever since I met her . . . I never had a conversation about where she personally wanted to be buried after May of 2006, but I had conversations with her about the fact that I disagreed with Daniel being buried in the Bahamas since his death. And she told me that, she said well, of course, reiterated the reason she was there was to avoid the paternity case and if I would put down my fight against her and did not want her to pay my legal fees, that she may let me see the baby. I said, why don't you bring Daniel home; that was not his home.

So my instincts were right. Anna and company took flight to the Bahamas to avoid the legal quagmire. Was the Bahamas really going to be her permanent home? I doubt that. She thrived on the media. She was addicted to the media. And the Bahamas is a lovely place. You get sand on your feet and enjoy the crystal warm water, but there is no way you are going to run a media empire out of that island. So is the trip to the Bahamas just a negotiating tool to get Birkhead off her back? I think so. In fact, I am sure of it. But then Daniel dies. He is buried in the Bahamas. And I am stuck with that decision. I am left trying to put the pieces together. He is buried in the Bahamas and I have no jurisdiction. And not to repeat myself: I can't exhume his body.

So maybe it was an error. Maybe Anna Nicole made an error in burying Daniel in the Bahamas. But our hands are tied and I don't want to separate mother from son. Unfortunately, however, I have separated mother and brother from daughter Dannielynn. I think when she gets older, she'll understand and forgive any decision that was not perfect. Meanwhile, Birkhead is open and he is singing like a bird. . .I want more impressions from him. I take another U-turn.

Seidlin: Stay with me a minute. The father of Dannielynn had to be either you, Stern or South Carolina?

In fact, every meatball around was now stepping forward. We were bombarded with letters and phone calls saying, "I am the father." I had jailbirds sitting in the can telling me they were the father. It was at this time that Carol Eddy, the supervisor of the court deputies, and Joanne Gallo, my judicial assistant, witnessed messages left on my courthouse phone threatening my life. I may have taken them seriously, but I didn't want to be separated from my family. I didn't want 24-hour security and, basically, I didn't give a damn. If you walk the streets of the Bronx at nighttime, if you drive a taxi cab during the graveyard shift, the midnight shift, what threats could make you blink? I knew I still had one last shot. I had my gun in my ankle holster.

Birkhead: No, sir.

Seidlin: I say it would have to be one of those three, it cannot go beyond?

Birkhead: Say me, one or two, if you want to include him [South Carolina].

Seidlin: Therefore, in your eyes, it had to be one of those three?

Birkhead: Yes, sir.

Seidlin: South Carolina?

Birkhead: Who had a vasectomy. So we are narrowing down here.

Seidlin: We are narrowing down. But you know, they have been known to fail once in a while.

Birkhead: Well, he is willing to be here to expedite the situation.

Seidlin: So you are starting to sound like a lawyer. So it is you and Mr. Stern?

Birkhead: Yes, sir.

I pull one more extreme U-turn. And the question I ask is a potent one. It's the big enchilada.

Seidlin: If you were the natural father of Dannielynn, according to some of the arguments here, you would stand in a stronger position than my guardian ad litem [Milstein] being a stranger to this child? Do you have a recommendation where I should put Anna Nicole Smith's body?

Birkhead: Yes.

Seidlin: . . . What do you think your little girl would want?

Birkhead: I would say I do have an opinion, but it is not just a cut and dry opinion. I would say that since she always had a desire to be in California and that was her home outside of just the paternity battle, that's where I would prefer her to be.

Seidlin: In California?

Birkhead: That is where I prefer her, since her son has passed away. I know he did not want to go to the Bahamas and he called California his home. I hate that he is there, so I am having a tough time with the decision.

This guy, Birkhead, is having a tough time with the decision! He knows all the parties personally. And here I am trying to cook an omelet. Put in all the right ingredients. He's touched them, felt them, smelled them. And when he is given the gavel to make the decision, he is perfectly candid and still rubbing his head.

Seidlin: You are, how about me?

Birkhead: You are starting to sound like a witness.

Seidlin: (To the court) He has a charming way about him. (To Birkhead) I saw it in your gait a few days ago, that is why I always wanted you to stay here.

Birkhead: I don't have enough suits and ties.

Seidlin: I am glad we can have a little softness. You're here and Stern is here as the potential father also. As serious as this is, you got to realize that we have to keep our personalities about us, right?

Birkhead: So to finish that, you know, if I am in a perfect world, they would still be here. . .

Seidlin: In a perfect world, I would have them all here. I would have jurisdiction over everything. If there was a perfect world . . . I would resolve everything. I would mow it down, but we do not have a perfect world.

Birkhead: But you know, since Daniel is there [the Bahamas], I mean, I guess the problem that I am having with it is, is that I am a California resident and if and when I get the daughter, that I know I believe is mine, she will not live in the Bahamas. So is that a place she is going to travel to see her brother and mother's grave? . . . Bring Daniel back here [the United States] and I hate to do that.

Seidlin: But that is a serious matter, exhuming a body, because it is a serious matter. It is something that we will talk about.

Birkhead: You know, I don't want to separate the mother from the child however . . .but I don't want them in the Bahamas, so I am having trouble with that.

Seidlin: . . . I am going to give you guys a chance to cross-examine, but he put a lot of meat on the bone here, in terms of presenting me a picture. You see, I am trying to fill in this canvas that we talked about.

The day is about to be recessed and I want to make sure Stern is there for tomorrow. I asked him if he was going to be back in my courtroom for tomorrow. Stern replied, "You ordered me back. I will be here."

Seidlin: Fine. You are not going to testify anymore.
Stern: If further testimony is necessary, I will.

However, another witness is going to testify the following day: Ford Shelley. He is the person who is in a dispute over the ownership of the house in the Bahamas. As well, he has in his possession the video of Anna Nicole in a clown costume while she was nine months pregnant with Dannielynn.

Thirteen

A Clairvoyant And A Crystal Ball

It's the last day of the trial. I started the morning off by letting the parties know, "We've liberalized the rules of evidence in this case. And we have done that because the candlelight is burning for us. Time is of the essence."

The drama continued with Debra Opri stating she wanted to do a little housekeeping. "An event happened yesterday and it was all over the news and I am concerned about it," she said. "There was video and recording that Ms. Barth removed my client's drinking cup from the stand and I just would like to know what that was about?"

I stopped any diversions. I stopped any shenanigans. This ship was on course to accomplish our mission. And there were also objections concerning the media zooming in on the lawyers' notes that were privileged and on their desk. The ride continued to be wild. I stated, "I'll tell you what, I'm not getting into this. I'm not getting into this, I've been impressed by the conduct of the attorneys in this case. I want to keep this dignified with decorum and respect."

Larry Birkhead retook the stand and I started to question him regarding his concern about Anna Nicole's use of medications.

> **Birkhead:** I stated the concern from the inception of the relationship.
> **Seidlin:** During that period of time, were you telling her not to utilize all these medications?
> **Birkhead:** I was telling her and also telling Mr. Stern that it was a problem.

One time, I had a chief judge, an old southern boy, who had been wounded in one of our wars and was left with one bad leg. He would call me up to his chambers and say to me, "Larry, tell me about the county court, exactly what do you do down there?" I didn't vote for him for chief judge when he first ran for the post, but we started to enjoy a mutual fondness for one another. And when the opportunity arose for him, he bypassed another judge who had supported him for the chief post and appointed me administrative judge of the county court. But we all knew that the judge he didn't appoint would maybe one day go out of the courthouse through a window, with his robes flying. Here I was, five years into my judicial career, and I became the administrative judge for nineteen judges at the ripe old age of thirty-three. One night he told me "Larry, I don't want you worrying about these cases once you decide them. You go home and you spend your time with your family and you start fresh in the morning." And I said, "Lou, is that what you do?" He said, "No. I think about them even after I decide my cases, but I am telling you to do it because you are young and you have a long career ahead of you."

Earlier in the morning, before the court session, I had taken a long jog along the beach and I was trying to put everything together. The media were taking my picture on my run back, so anybody would know there is no way you can divorce yourself from cases that rip your guts apart.

I turned to the lawyers and told them, "Now the dots are starting to fill in. Now we are starting to understand the personalities a little bit. You lawyers are trained to try to find a smoking gun. Who's the villain? Who's the hero? We came here, or at least maybe one of your purposes may have been, who is the bad guy or bad person here? There's black, there's white and there's a lot of gray in this case. Let's look at these three parties for a minute because we have a short day. Let's look at these parties. All these parties are, obviously, God's children.

"We have the mother who 10 years ago had a relationship with the daughter. We don't know how solid that relationship was, but she had some relationship. She begins to tell the daughter not to do drugs. I, being a former member of the Broward County Commission on Alcoholism and dealing in the rehab world in and out, know that people that don't want to get rehabilitated are going to take flight from that person telling them to get off the drugs. Anna stays away from the mother. We're not certain why, but now maybe some of the facts are coming out because mama is not going to like her taking medication . . . over-medicated drugs. We've got Larry who now tells her, because she is pregnant, and he's concerned about the health and welfare of the baby to be born and we know all the studies show that the baby can receive the addiction of the mother in the womb. And Larry tells her not to do drugs . . . so Larry runs her out of California because she doesn't want to be told not to do medicated drugs. Now, stay with me, then we have Stern. Is he a bad guy? Or is he a fellow who has some form of a love for her? We don't know. It's a fact that will come out way beyond this writing but whatever relationship he had with her, he would be called, maybe an enabler."

Stern's lawyer then raises an objection, because I am peeling away a piece of the onion here and they don't want me slicing and dicing it. And I tell the lawyer, "Your objection is so noted." Which is a nice way to say in the courtroom take a hike because I am proceeding; I am marching on.

I continued: "He lived in the home and he may have known if he said to her, stop taking these drugs, and I am going to have you bring forth arguments and fact concerning this. But he may have said, if he put his foot down, and he loved her maybe in some form or another, she might have taken flight from Stern. So my attorneys in most cases, we try to portray in front of a jury good guy, bad guy, hero, villain. I am stating that these folks may not be bad. They may not be living the perfect life, but that's for other people to decide, the perfection of the way they perform their lives' duties. Anna Nicole loves Marilyn Monroe. Camelot, knights at a round table, all for one, one for all. Loyalty, strong loyalty . . . we have a support system. We have people that we know are brilliant. And when you find someone brilliant, like our medical examiner, you don't let go of him. And we know brilliance. We can recognize brilliance and you hold on dearly for that."

Anna Nicole was in a different world. One that had sharks

circling. It's hard to recognize the good from the bad. And in Hollywood, in this high maintenance, high visibility world, these enablers—these ass kissers—it's hard to recognize the fact that they might assist you back to the gutter and maybe even death.

I continued. "She leaves you [I looked at her mother] at a young age. Anna Nicole thinks of Marilyn Monroe, Camelot, knights of the round table, one for all, all for one. But we know life doesn't work that way, we know people are not always considering our welfare, we know also that there's only a few people that one can depend upon in a lifetime. There's only a handful I know ... Unfortunately, in her condition, at times as it's been indicated through the testimony, it's been weak at times and sometimes weakness begets weakness. Strength begets strength ... Now she gets thrust into the limelight. Our Anna Nicole Smith, this beautiful woman gets thrown into the spotlight, but unfortunately she is not as prepared for this storm ... She's not as prepared for the hurricane as we are because we continue to do our same routines, don't we?

" . . . She didn't, because unfortunately she didn't have enough foundation. I'm not blaming anyone but that's the way it unfolded. She didn't have enough people around her supporting her position. Anna didn't really realize that life is a roller coaster as we all know. It's got its ups, it's got its downs, but you've got to hold on tight. And as we talked about the other day, you've got to hope for tomorrow's a better day. You look forward to tomorrow. If it is so rough today, you say, all right, let's try to make today good, but tomorrow will even be better. It's unfortunate. It's unfortunate that she didn't have enough strength to fight the currents."

Let's jump forward for just a minute. Since I left the bench, I've been swimming in the entertainment world. I am one of the most famous judges in the world and when people see me or hear me, they recognize me. You are the Judge, God bless you. You showed so much compassion. This momentary embrace I welcome, but this entertainment world, the business end of it, is a tough piece of meat to chew on. It takes a clairvoyant and a crystal ball to separate the BS from the truth. But thankfully, my livelihood and my wife and daughter ground me. Some malcontents and dissidents come in your direction, because they suffer from the lack of a proper number of brain cells. They are swimming in jealousy and envy and want to bring you down. They want to pull the carpet from under you, but thank God that the good around us and the happiness around us prevails and allows us to march on. I think, for some reason, Anna Nicole selected me to be the judge that decided her final resting place. But when she put her hand on my shoulder, it changed my world too. This fame brings with it many crosses to bear, but I hope to continue to wear this fame with fun and dignity. Some people will say anything they want about you. You must believe in yourself.

Meanwhile, back in the courtroom, I started off the morning telling the parties and the attorneys, "This would take a couple of years to hear a typical probate case. I have not concluded anything yet . . . my mind is completely open. So we talk about the next generation . . . we want Dannielynn to have a better life, a healthier life, and not a dysfunctional life that Anna Nicole Smith may have suffered. We want her to have the foundation and we don't want these other motives taking place. I want the heart. That's what I seek. I want the good and the welfare of this child to prevail."

Milstein then continued, questioning Larry Birkhead.

Milstein: Mr. Birkhead, in the time that you spent with Anna Nicole, what efforts did you make personally to assist her in minimizing or rehabilitating herself from any use of substances?

Birkhead: For one, I hid some of the medicines that I didn't feel was necessary for her, some things that she was getting prescribed by doctors ... Dr. A, Dr. B and Dr. C all together. And I felt like cumulative effects would have a bad reaction. I'm not a doctor but I know...I mean, your brain is a computer and all these different medicines are telling to do and all these doctors aren't on the same page so that would have a bad effect. Like I said, at times I took her medicine and I was told by Mr. Stern to give it back to her because she needed it to live. And in addition to that, I just told her over and over, I said don't. . .something is going to happen. Something is going to happen.

Seidlin: Did this dominate the conversations you had with her?

Birkhead: No sir, it didn't dominate, but it resonated and I said over and over and over. You don't know how many times I had to help her and carry her back and forth to make sure she is okay. Sometimes I didn't even know if she was going to live and they kept bringing more and more drugs in the house and the pharmacist. And at one point, the time I knew it was really bad is when one of the individuals in that house came home and they said, they had my picture up in the pharmacy as [a] VIP customer and they thought it was a funny thing to say.

Seidlin: Who said that?

Birkhead: An assistant and her picture was on the wall at the pharmacy and I said, this has got to stop.

I thought to myself, this poor schlemiel from Kentucky, living a southern life, saying "yes sir" on just about all the questions. . .how did he fall into this scene, this mudslide? They have a drug mill going on in Anna Nicole's house and she is pregnant.

Birkhead: And I told Anna, I told everybody in the home and it didn't stop. I did everything that I could . . . and when I was pushed away. . .

Seidlin: Who pushed you away?

Birkhead: I got into an argument with Anna Nicole that something that could have been brushed over. It was something, on a scale from 1 to 10, the argument was like a 6 and it could have been brushed back over like many in the past that everybody or every couple goes through. And Mr. Stern got in the middle of it with us and he said, like I said yesterday, he told me to come get my stuff, he threw the plasma television out on the front porch and clothes and he won't give me back some of my belongings in the house and the next thing, like I said yesterday, he told me he was going to take off. . .

What I saw here was that Stern was meddling, almost like the proverbial mother-in-law in a comedian's joke. Or my own mother, Betty. When I first brought Belinda to live with me, one morning as I was about to bite into a bagel, I glanced up and I saw Betty giving Belinda a double middle finger. I said to Betty, "What the hell are you doing?" I thought I was watching a Woody Allen movie. So what is Stern doing? Is he waiting in the lurch to sabotage the relationship between these two young lovers? Or was Stern a jilted lover? Did he love Anna so much, at all costs, that he wanted to possess her, even against her own well being, to never say no and just keep feeding her the candy. Who better to ask about Stern's motives than his number one competitor?

Seidlin: Did he love her?

Birkhead: I think he did and does, but I think as a result of that, I think he didn't do the things he could have done to help her.

Seidlin: But she took flight when you were saying to her not to do drugs anymore, right?

Birkhead: Right, but Anna Nicole didn't have a driver's license. She didn't drive herself to the pharmacy and pick things up. She didn't call the doctors. Mr. Stern called the doctors and asked for the prescriptions.

Seidlin: But she could have replaced Mr. Stern with another individual, am I right?

Birkhead: If he would have told her no on the drugs, she probably would. And I said no and that's why I'm here today.

I don't have my daughter, I don't have anything...I missed the delivery of my child. I had to pay $4.99 for magazines to see what my child looks like. I had to call and send gifts, FedEx Christmas gifts for my child and I've missed everything that you can't get back ...

Milstein: Did you ever pick up any prescription medication?

Birkhead: No, sir.

Milstein: Did you ever ask her if she would go to a rehabilitation center?

Birkhead: Yes, sir. Milstein: What was her response?

Birkhead: She said, I'm not a drug addict and quit calling me one. She said these are prescriptions. I said, you're not taking them properly. She always said...it was her contention because if there was a doctor's name on the bottle, that there was nothing wrong with whatever she could take...when it was announced that Anna Nicole was pregnant, there was a behind-the-scenes war with me and Mr. Stern where he had called me and told me to deny that I was the father of the child on press time with a specific magazine and he called me like 200 times. I was working at an event and he was telling me the importance of me getting my name out of it, because my name was being attached to the pregnancy. And he said if this goes down and my name is out there, that this is going to be bad and just to deny, deny, deny. I said...I did say no comment. He said, no, I want you to go back and say if she's pregnant, you have nothing to do with it. And he called me so many times at a job that I was at that I finally just agreed to get him off my back. And ever since then, the magazines that printed it previously that I was the father, they're saying, okay,

The photo I took of the burial plot. Inside sources in the Bahamas stated to me that Anna Nicole and Daniel are buried on top of one another.

The cemetery was a lonely place, it was off a busy road and it was small. Two caretakers were present and a security guard, who I was told was tough as nails, never said hello and was only missing a broom. My guide said she is going to be screaming at you, but within a minute she recognized my bald head and started hugging me. I paid my respects to Anna and Daniel and left this heavily guarded last stop.

This photo represents the Bahamian local food—a beef patty from Esso. I ate one in the Bahamian taxi cab—it has a lot of flavor, but thank God, it wasn't my last meal.

Here I am, standing at the entrance to Esso.

Horizons is an estate that Anna Nicole lived in during her short stay in the Bahamas. As I visited this compound, I felt like it was an old ghost town. There is no way a pop icon like Anna Nicole would want to live there for any long duration of time.

As I made a surprise visit to the Bishop's House of Worship an assistant brought me back to a very unusual room that was the office of the Bishop's wife, where I spoke to her. This Bishop is like the Pope of the Vatican, a powerhouse in the Bahamas. The Bishop performed the spiritual ceremony of Anna Nicole and Howard K. Stern.

My research brought me to this body of water. It was at this marina that Anna Nicole and Howard K. Stern boarded the boat with a small group of guests, which included the Bishop on a voyage whose purpose included a "wedding ceremony."

Defendant Sandeep Kapoor, a doctor of late entertainment celebrity Anna Nicole Smith, arrives at the Los Angeles County Criminal Courts building for his arraignment in Los Angeles.

Defendant Khristine Eroshevich stands in the courtroom during her arraignment at the Los Angeles County Criminal Courts building in Los Angeles, California on May 13, 2009. She and two others pleaded not guilty to charges that they illegally supplied Playboy model Anna Nicole Smith with prescription drugs for years before her death from an accidental overdose.

Larry Birkhead is surrounded by media as he leaves Broward County Circuit Court.

Howard K. Stern (L), Anna Nicole Smith's mother Virgie Arthur and Larry Birkhead walk out of Broward County Circuit Court arm-in-arm after a judge's decision to release the body of Anna Nicole to be buried in the Bahamas.

The Seminole Hard Rock Hotel and Casino in Hollywood, Florida, where Seminole tribal fire rescue and Hollywood fire rescue workers tried to revive Anna Nicole Smith.

Celebrity Anna Nicole Smith, accompanied by her lawyer Howard Stern, arrives for her hearing at the Supreme Court in Washington.

Anna Nicole Smith with her late husband John Howard Marshall II.

Anna Nicole Smith, has just been announced a Guess jeans fashion model.

now you're saying no comment. Now you're saying you have nothing to do with it. And then he was releasing information that Anna Nicole wanted me out of her life and that I wanted 15 minutes of fame. And he posted something on her website that said something to same effect. . . . Before Daniel's death, I released photos because I told Howard and I told Anna Nicole that it wasn't fair for him to be saying that stuff about me and she said, you are not the star. I'm the star . . .

There is an issue about the compensation that Birkhead has received for the photos of Anna Nicole, and he said, "Anything that I make for any of the photos is going to fight for my daughter and if I have to sell more photographs, if I have to sell this shirt or this tie, I'm going to sell it. . ... I have people calling me saying books, movies, million dollars, two million dollars.. . .that they would give me tons of money to go down there [the Bahamas] and knock on the door and all these things that I declined to do."I take a moment to reflect, then openly state to the parties that they should fashion "a result that makes sense to this child but don't dig your heels in against these thoughts. You are talking to someone who has been a long time here. I don't have the power to impose that, but I'll tell you, there's moments where I feel like taking [knocking] some heads together."

Debra Opri then said, "I'm telling you, Your Honor, you want the three of us [Birkhead, Stern and Virgie] to hold hands. It ain't ever going to happen. Your Honor that's naive, that's Camelot."Little did my friend Ms. Opri foresee, but in a few hours, the three antagonists in this play would be in front of the Fort Lauderdale Courthouse holding hands. This was one of the most photographed moments, and one of the most famous media slices in the history of a trial. There they were holding hands, and expressing their love for Anna Nicole and her daughter Dannielynn.

And at that point, Birkhead's testimony continued.

Seidlin: What college did you attend?
Birkhead: University of Louisville.
Seidlin: What did you major in?
Birkhead: Journalism and communication.
Seidlin: You graduated in four [years]?
Birkhead: It took me a little longer because I was paying my own way.
Milstein: What is your occupation?
Birkhead: I'm a freelance reporter and photographer.
Seidlin: Would you, if you were the father of little Dannielynn, let mom, grandma, visit that little girl?
Birkhead: Yes, I'd let anybody that had Anna's best interest and loved Anna ...
Seidlin: So you would give her [Virgie] visitation rights?
Birkhead Yes, sir. I think it's only fair for family and I think that that's just the appropriate thing to do ...

We came to an amazing juncture. The vast majority of the states in the United States do not give grandparents the rights of visitation. I was able to elicit from Larry Birkhead, who I believed was the father of Dannielynn, a willingness to allow Virgie visitation rights for her granddaughter. This opened up the door.

174

Seidlin: Why did you make her pregnant when you knew she was over-medicated?

Birkhead: When she came back from South Carolina, she was not medicated as much and she cleared herself up. . .at one point during the stay in the hospital, she asked me to go get some personal belongings out of the closet in the hospital. And when I went into the closet, she asked me to bring the bag out and she kept pushing the button for the drugs to come out . . . when I brought the bag back to her, she pulled the bottle out. Mr. Stern was in the room and they were waiting to see who came in and they opened the bottle.

Barth: Did Anna open the bottle or did Mr. Stern open the bottle?

Birkhead: It happened multiple times, so I guess he did and she did, and I witnessed both.

Barth: What did you do next, if anything?

Birkhead: I told them not to and I repeatedly told her not to and I watched and I stayed up for almost 24 hours a day to make sure that she didn't.

Seidlin: Do you think he [Stern] provided some kind of support system for her?

Birkhead: Support system in enabling or support system. . .

Seidlin: We all come with some broken suitcases and I'm saying this, was he providing some support system for her outside the medicated drugs?

Birkhead: Yes.

Seidlin: In your eyes, he's not pure bad, is he?

Birkhead: No.

Seidlin: There's some decent qualities in the man too, isn't there?

Birkhead: Yes, sir.

Seidlin: Not everyone here is the devil, are they?

Birkhead: No, sir.

At this point, I'm still trying to get a feel, an understanding of what makes Stern tick. He's a complex soul. But is he the destructive force that contributes or directly results in the death of Anna Nicole Smith and Daniel? Isn't this really a cold case that isn't cold yet, that will take years? What a web the human mind can create. And I have to enter the minds of these characters and try to unravel their intent. Because intent is what defines culpability in the law. It can take a murder one case down to an involuntary manslaughter case. It can take you from the death penalty to a couple of years in the can. So *mens rea*, Latin for "intent," is of the utmost importance for a prosecutor in deciding what charges, if any, to file against the prime suspect.

Seidlin: What could you have done to pull her out of her pain?

Birkhead: I guess just take all the drugs away, but I was told she needed them to live so I didn't know if I took them, would she die. What path to choose, because Howard told me she could die.

Seidlin: Forget Howard, there's other people at that house?

Birkhead: She told me and Howard also told me.

Seidlin: You know, as a judge, you stick your neck out, doing all this talking, trying to be proactive. I could have sat here, too, quietly and just let it go, but I'm trying to resolve it, at the end of the day, giving you a little curbside philosophy along the way.

Birkhead: They [the hospital] had her on a plan that they felt it was a plan for recovery. And they also told her primary doctors to stop prescribing her and they were taking over the plan from there.

I know Birkhead is getting tired and his nerves are getting frayed, but I am not happy with his last answer to such an innocuous question. So I warned him, "Don't get slippery with me. Just stay frank and candid. We are just searching. We are searching, my friend. We are searching to get up that mountain. Search with me, get me the truth ... "

It's ten minutes to twelve. It's the last day of the hearing and I slip in the following question to Birkhead, who would have a primary voice if he were declared the father, which I at this moment believe him to be. When I asked him the all-important question of where he would place Anna Nicole's body for burial, Birkhead replied, "I'm still having a hard time with that Your Honor ... but on the same token splitting them [Anna Nicole and Daniel] up is hard for me."

Seidlin: So you are telling me that Danny was [an] essential, integral part of her life?
Birkhead: Yes sir.

We are getting close to sandwich time, and I state in open court "these three parties have come to probate court, a court of equity ... We assume that they come with clean hands. Now, if I was to vividly describe my impression of all three parties, it would cause grief to the child ... Anna Nicole Smith was one complicated individual. Shakespeare, she could have filled maybe the character in Shakespeare's *Hamlet*, Ophelia, thinking about these moments of death and plots and Marilyn Monroe and all these other things that are going on and yet she is strong, she is successful. She's got TV shows and wealth ... she just needed more or better handlers. We'd all agree to that. She needed better handlers."

> **Seidlin:** When would she say she loved her mother, what type of day was that?
> **Birkhead:** When something, really, really bad was going on in her life or if there was something that should be a joyous occasion, like I said, she had her pregnancy, or just when she'd see people with other families, she'd say, I wish I had my mommy.
> **Seidlin:** So nature came in to play when there is a crisis in her life, she said mama.

I didn't want to go too far afield, so I said to Birkhead, "We're getting into Freud. I don't know how far we are going to go. We all have these memories." I then decided to have a little fun with my New York/California Opri. She said, "I'm proud to tell the world I have one of the best agents in the world. I am also in media."

> **Seidlin:** This isn't TV commercial time here.
> **Opri:** This has been the Krista Barth show.

Seidlin: There's nobody's show here.

I finally stop the banter, and say something that I can't say in my own home, "Counsel, when I speak, I'm the only voice I want to hear."

I don't like boredom. In any of my trials, and I literally had thousands of trials and hearings, I enjoyed when there was a little entertainment, when there was some fun, gives and takes. Otherwise, I would be like the caricature of the judge with gray hair and a belly, half asleep in his courtroom chair. Lawyers knew when they came in front of me, it was lively, it was full of action, and a lot got accomplished. For this trial, some judges, and some lawyers who had appeared in front of me, got passes. They knew, with this cast of characters and my personality driving it, this would be explosive and they wanted to watch the fireworks.

We conducted this trial in front of the conscience of America. We enabled our country to look into the bowels of unlawful distribution of prescription medication. And now this country is closing doors on some of these pharmacies and pill mills and doctors, and law enforcement authorities are charging these reckless individuals. I brought out the whole kitchen sink. I made us look in the mirror and ask ourselves is this what we want to do as a society? To close our eyes? Turn our heads away from the enablers, the pharmacies that fill these prescriptions, the fictitious names used by doctors on the prescriptions, and all the other criminal activities that took place in the past against our heroes, our stars—Marilyn Monroe, Elvis Presley, Heath Ledger and Michael Jackson?

FOURTEEN

MANY MOVES DOWN THE ROAD

The argument again arose that I should have the Bahamian government take a DNA test of Dannielynn, and I stated, "The court is not anointed king here, this court was appointed in '89 as a circuit judge. It's way, way beyond the court's jurisdiction."

In any good chess game, you must look many moves down the road. The master looks at the ultimate or final move. Opri asked me, "Can you let us brief you?" I responded, "I briefed myself already on this issue, because I knew you were coming out with it. I'm not going to be blindsided and not that you did, but I knew why you were sitting here and I knew you would be asking me this . . . "

Attorneys sometimes attempt to challenge the court, and they state, *Your Honor, will you explain your ruling.* As an old judge told me, however, when you are sitting in the king's throne, you don't need to explain yourself just because an attorney asks you to. You want your ruling to be reasonable and fair, but the voters put you in office and you don't have to jump through every hoop at the carnival. I've been through enough tests and I will decide. I must have the confidence to decide when it's right, when I need to give an explanation. And of course the appellate judges will need to look at the record as a whole to decide whether or not you made the right decision. If you give a narrow answer to a question, you might be wrong, so let the whole record speak for itself.

Opri tried again to corner the court, and I told her, "I don't want to hear anymore from that corner. I'm done." But Opri came at me again. She'd make a hell of a tennis player—I could use her as a doubles partner. So I rebuked her and said, "I just spoke . . . I'll give you a chance but I have to move on. I just have to keep moving." I knew I wasn't coming back to her argument and she knew it too. But she has good courtroom presence. She knew when to hold and when to fold.

But here we go again; the drums are banging loudly, as Houston asked Larry Birkhead, "Are you willing to take any test, do anything to establish you are Dannielynn's father?" I didn't want all hell to break loose again, so I said in open court, "We're not going to have drama here. I know, everyone wants to get their shot in." I felt like I was in a shooting gallery, and each attorney was a marksman, ready to fire when an opening occurred.

Never one to mince words, Opri then approached Birkhead, "Finally, Larry, I get to ask you a few questions." Opri cuts right to the chase. Like when I go into a fine restaurant, but I still want to be able to eat dinner in forty minutes. I can't take a three-hour meal. I'm ordering as I walk in the door. I give the server all the courses at once, and Belinda turns to me and asks me if we're at Wendy's or Subway.

Opri: Are you the biological father of Dannielynn?
Birkhead: Yes.

Seidlin: (to Opri) I like your style. I think you speak beautifully. You conduct yourself well, but I don't want flames here. I don't have a jury trial. You are trying a case in front of me, a good ole southern boy. I'm teasing you. You can do it outside my room. In my courtroom I just want to hear the facts.

Opri: As concerns the burial, correct.

Seidlin: If you are going to inflame him, it's going to get everyone moving like steam.

Opri: Are you basically telling me you don't want to hear anything on the paternity order out of California; is that correct?

Seidlin: My friend—we've gone down this road.

Barth: Like about a hundred times.

Seidlin: Ask him some questions.

Opri: I just want to clarify.

I thought it was time to rein in Opri. I had to let her know that the black robe was the boss here, so I told her, "I'm not here to answer questions. . .you're here to ask questions."

Opri really had her client's interest at heart, and felt rightfully so that I was entertaining the issue of paternity. Opri was on the right course and proceeded accordingly, but I wanted that answered only through the consent of Stern. I didn't want to enter that terrain if I had to order Stern to give up the DNA.

Opri: If you're deferring, I just want to know so I can put that on the record.

Seidlin: The record speaks for itself. I've been here too long to fall into a trap and I don't mean you are setting me up for a trap.

My Opri has a sense of humor and a beautiful smile and responded, "I am, but that's beside the point." Opri the litigator, the warrior, continued to march on. She now questioned whether Stern even had any standing to be in the courtroom.

Seidlin: Listen to me. You're good. You've been so good. You set a nice tone at the beginning. California, listen to me. California, remember the song "California Dreamin'?"
Opri: I always consider myself a New Yorker.
Seidlin: I want peace on Earth here. I don't want you to cloud me up.
Opri: I'm not trying to, Your Honor.
Seidlin: I'm serious. You want to prevail with your positions. I'm the ruler. You're going to have to be following my instructions. Don't let my smile. . .know the inside is tough.

Milstein, the loyal general, wanted to come to my aid and said, " . . . you've already ruled on the standing of Mr. Stern previously and any issues regarding that, so we don't need to muddy the water again today."

I've seen some lawyers that are awful. They are half asleep in hearings, in a semi coma. They should be home watering plants and having tea and cookies on the patio. They have no right defending person and property. So deep down I respected lawyers who fought hard for their clients, if when the point was reasonable they were willing to capitulate and allow the court to proceed with its hearing.

The other attorneys could smell blood in the water and I didn't want a free-for-all. They had to know I was holding the reins of this case, tight. I was physically and mentally up to the challenge, and they knew it and I knew it. Nevertheless, you are going to be challenged, so you have to kick ass and take names.

Seidlin: *Don't test me anymore. Don't test me. I've been tested by the best so don't test me. . .I can fight a ten-round fight so don't test me.* (To Opri) I'll allow you. I like it when you ask it that way.
Opri: I'm really a very nice person, Your Honor. Under different circumstances, we'd have a glass of wine together.
Seidlin: We would have tea.

Actually, I really like beer, a cold beer, the kind they pour for you in a German pub, but I didn't want to state that in a courtroom. I was trained that when I went to political and social functions I should never hold a glass when a picture was being taken. I was a kid from the Bronx who, throughout his career, sat and had dinner with presidential candidates, Florida Supreme Court judges, congressmen, senators, governors, the most powerful and the most prestigious personalities around. I enjoyed it all. And I always enjoyed the embrace of the person on the street. The ordinary person was my polestar.

Right before lunch, O'Quinn looked like a boxer in the tenth round. His legs were getting rubbery. I didn't know at the time he was diabetic. I didn't take enough recesses to allow him to get juice and other foods that would keep him balanced. I turned to Texas and said, "You have to eat. I am going to take a break. I'm working everyone too hard. Give him some water. My Texas friend, you didn't eat. You didn't eat. Let's get you some food."

Houston: He's a diabetic.
Seidlin: I figured he's a diabetic and he didn't eat anything. Let him sit down. This has been…everyone have a seat. Stay with me, Texas. What do you need as a diabetic right now?
Texas: Orange juice.
Seidlin: Here is my credit card. Buy him an orange juice . . . we're going to take a break. Get him orange juice right now. Have a seat, my friend. I want to keep you a long time from now. We're going to take a recess. You should have let me know. I would have taken breaks. I would have taken more breaks.

Texas stumbled and the courtroom shook. It was dramatic and it summed up the emotions that everybody was feeling. Again, Anna Nicole touched us. It was obvious her presence was in that courtroom. His stumbling sent shock waves through the media outlets. Texas had fallen. As if we were back at the Alamo. It sent shockwaves throughout the country, really the world. Everyone had embraced Texas. He became a folk hero. Everybody was rooting for Texas to come back on his feet, and in the afternoon he came out like a bull in a rodeo. His juices were flowing again and I was happy he was in good health.

Fifteen

And I Hope To God You Guys Give The Kid The Right Shot

Ford Shelley now takes the stand and is duly sworn in by the madam clerk. Shelley was a wealthy friend of Anna Nicole. His father-in-law is G. Ben Thompson. Houston wants to begin by showing a 51-second video clip of Anna Nicole that was recorded in the Bahamas when she was nine months pregnant. Barth interjects at this point.

Barth: This was stolen evidence out of her house. It's a film that this man stole.

Seidlin: Play. (As he's playing the tape) Who made this tape?

Houston: It was made by Mr. Stern. It also has the voice and pictures of his daughter. . .Stop. Stop. Mr. Shelley, wait until we ask questions.

Seidlin: You make a good traffic cop.

Houston: Sorry for doing your job. . .Mr. Shelley, will you please introduce yourself to the court?

Shelley: Shelley, I reside in South Carolina.

Houston: Do you have various residences around the United

States and in the Bahamas?

Shelley: Yes, sir.

Houston: Quickly, will you tell His Honor your relationship and how you know both Anna Nicole Smith as well as Mr. Stern?

Shelley: Anna came to Myrtle Beach with Larry Birkhead on vacation in the year 2005, in the summer, she and Larry got into an argument. And my father-in-law which she became friends and then subsequently after that, became more than friends.

Charlie Chan is coming out in me. I now have the three potential fathers: Stern, Birkhead and Ford Shelley's father-in-law. This I want to hear.

Houston: Would you tell the court about your place in the Bahamas?

Shelley: Yes, sir. Anna had come to Myrtle Beach. She called me in May of '06, sent us an email, told us she was pregnant and told us that she needed to leave California. That the press was getting really stressful. And she sent an email to us and asked us, would we come pick her up and take her home. So we agreed and we went—I went and took her and picked her up and brought her to Myrtle Beach and we stayed in one of the houses that we owned along the oceanfront. As she was there, she stressed to us the urgency of wanting to move. And asked us—asked me—to talk with my attorney in Myrtle Beach, what the laws were to unwed mothers and what the father's rights were. She told us that she was pregnant with Larry Birkhead's child and that she did not want him to have any rights to the child. Anna was our friend, still is, and we love her and we, of course, called the attorney but we found out she had no protection. So Howard was not there yet but Howard came and Howard had talked to my attorney . . . and found out that South Carolina would not be beneficial. I suggested the Bahamas, because I had heard about the laws to unwed mothers. . .so, therefore, we called there and found out what the laws were to unwed mothers. . .so we helped facilitate her going to the Bahamas.

An argument ensued about the issue of being a resident in the Bahamas. The question was, in order to be a resident, do you need to own property? Therefore, was the purchase—or the alleged purchase—by Anna Nicole of the house in the Bahamas really a hoax to fulfill the residency requirements? I didn't want to get into that, because it opened up another can of worms, which was trying to figure out Bahamian law and how it pertains to American law, and they then would bring in a line-up of Bahamian legal experts But it does touch upon the issue of whether or not Anna Nicole was seeking a permanent residency. Was she buying a house to establish residency? Or was it to evade Birkhead and the paternity lawsuit? I am ready to turn to the video, and as it is playing in open court, the following line of questioning takes place.

Seidlin: Who is asking her the questions?

189

Houston: Mr. Stern. (To Shelley) Sir, will you identify approximately for the court what date and time that was and tell him why you know it?

Shelley: It was in the last part of August [2006].

Houston: Why do you know that, sir?

Shelley: Because my child was on that video and asked to call me and she wasn't allowed by you [Stern] to call me to come home. It's on the full tape and they can get a copy of it, Howard. I'll never forgive you for it.

Smoke was coming out of Shelley's ears. He can't stand Stern and it was obvious. He was directing his answers and was staring at Stern.

Houston: You're familiar, by the ... with Anna Nicole Smith's state of mind when she was sober?

Shelley: She's an awesome person. Whether she was sober or not, she was awesome.

Houston: Quite frankly, and I'm just going to lead with this, she was impaired on that tape?

Shelley: She seemed to be.

Houston: And Mr. Stern asked, is this a mushroom trip? ... By the way, she was pregnant when this tape was made, correct?

Shelley: Yes, sir.

Houston: With Dannielynn?

Shelley: Yes, sir.

Houston: I have a couple of other areas [to ask questions].

Seidlin: No. I got Texas sick. I got to keep moving. Other people are not feeling so well. I have to keep going, plus I have a candle burning.

Barth: So your father-in-law was in litigation with Anna Nicole over this house?

Shelley: Yes.

Barth: In fact, that house isn't yours?

Shelley: Actually, it was my money.

Barth: How did you come into possession of the tape that you just showed this court, sir?

Shelley: Because on the day after Anna Nicole Smith passed away, which Howard and I had a two-hour conversation last Saturday on the phone, whereas Howard called me and asked me, would I get all parties together and call Virgie for him and ask her, could. . .he asked me to get in touch with Virgie, that they would not allow him to, so that we could settle this. And I said, Howard, I said, I will do everything I can because I'm with you. I'd love to settle it, settle this thing so that we can bury her and we can all get this thing resolved.

Barth: Did you have any chance to observe, through your friendship with Anna, her relationship with Daniel?

Shelley: I did . . . she loved him more than life and so did Howard.

Houston: Where did Anna want to be buried?

Shelley: Anna, at the time that she made the decision where he was to be buried, she told us too. She wanted to be buried, first of all in California, but she told us that she could not go back to California at that time to bury Daniel because she was afraid that she would be served with a paternity suit against

191

Larry Birkhead. And she made the decision to bury him there because of that and that's where she was going to make her domicile and she made that decision. And she told us that she, if something ever happened to her, she looked at me and said, Ford if something ever happens to me and Howard is not around, I want you take my stuff. . .

Brown: Did you ever see her using drugs, legal or illegal?

Shelley: I never saw her take medication except one time in my house at Christmas, where Howard did come out and he did give her medicine, but that's the only time. I didn't know what it was.

Milstein: Do you have any writings of Anna Nicole Smith, diaries, journals or emails of her within the last year of her life?

Shelley: Yes, sir.

Milstein: Is there a way that we can have those [documents] proffered to the court to see if within any of those documents, she has made a contemporaneous writing as to her last wishes?

Shelley: No, sir. But if Your Honor would allow me, on October 10 and the 11 [2006] she wrote emails to us at that time and threatened to sue my father-in-law for DNA and child support because he was the father of the child and we knew he couldn't because he had a vasectomy.

Seidlin: That's the third man then?

At this point I thought I had all three suspects. But Milstein pointed out, "That's one of [the] third men. I have several other phone calls."

What is this. . .spin the bottle? Where ever it lands that's the father? Let's not forget we also have Zsa Zsa Gabor's hubby.

Houston: After the death of Daniel, do you believe that Anna Nicole, based on your experience in dealing with her, was in such distress and was having issues with drugs so as to cloud her judgment as to where she wanted to be?

Shelley: Your Honor, Anna was a person who made her own decisions. And I think that Anna was emotional at the time, but Anna said where she wanted to be buried and that was beside her son.

Houston: I'm going to call Daniel's father, Mr. Smith. Over the phone from Texas.

Barth: I don't know if it's him. I never met this man. He had no relationship with his son. . .he hasn't seen him since he was an infant, Your Honor.

Seidlin: That is your last witness and that wraps it all up, all the live witnesses.

Texas says that he has Billy Smith, Daniel's father, on the speaker phone, and then we proceed to duly swear him in for his testimony.

We've seen everything in this hearing, we have live witnesses, we have people fainting, we have the judge wanting to buy juice for everybody, and then we have a witness, Daniel's father, live via the telephone, with no one in his home, like a commissioner to verify that he is Smith. I guess, upon reflection, I may have stretched the rules of evidence a little bit, but it did allow everybody an opportunity to present their witnesses in a frugal and expedited fashion. I allowed it in all my past hearings, and people would comment that I even allowed the dogs in.

You have to remember I came from humble beginnings. That is part of reading this judge—the guy who drove a taxi, taught tennis, was a school teacher. I reflected and represented the person on the street. I guess that is what allowed me to run for office six times and win six times, the last five times with no opposition. I was a county court judge for my first ten years and part of the jurisdiction was small claims court, like the judge shows on TV. But I wasn't limited to a thirty-minute spot. Small claims court was the people's court and you gave the people their day in court, because for many this was their first and only experience with the American judicial system, and I wanted them to be left with a good taste in their mouth.

Seidlin: How do I know you're Billy Smith?

Smith: Pardon me?

Seidlin: How do I know who you are?

Smith: Well, I'm Billy Smith, believe me.

Seidlin: Are you wearing boots today?

Smith: I didn't understand you.

Seidlin: I was just trying to be. . .take the tension out for a minute. Where do you live in Texas?

Smith: LaBahia.

Seidlin: How old are you?

Smith: I'm 38.

Seidlin: What kind of work do you do?

Smith: I run a farm.

Seidlin: What work do you do when you're working it?

Smith: Labor.

Seidlin: (To Barth) Now, you object to the identity of the father?

Barth: I object to everything, on every possible ground under the sun that he's not here in person.

Barth always had my confidence in the courtroom and I know she would be well respected in any courtroom in this nation. And I couldn't blame her for her objection.

Seidlin: I'm with you.

Barth: No opportunity to cross-examine him in person and he hasn't seen this child since he's been an infant.

Texas: Mr. Smith, may I call you Billy?

Smith: Yes.

Texas: This is John O'Quinn, sir. Billy, were you ever married to a woman named Anna Nicole Smith?

Smith: Yes, I was. We got married in '84, April 3rd.

Seidlin: What kind of work were you doing in those days?

Smith: I was a cook at a kitchen place.

Seidlin: Is it still in business?

Smith: Yes.

Seidlin: What's the name of it?

Smith: Krispy Fried Chicken.

Texas: Billy, did you and Anna Nicole have a boy child

together?

Smith: Yes, we did.

Texas: What did you all name that boy child?

Smith: Daniel Wayne Smith.

Seidlin: When was the last time you saw him, what year?

Smith: '88.

Seidlin: Why haven't you seen him since?

Smith: . . . She got in the movies and stuff and we didn't really communicate.

Seidlin: Did you speak to him on the phone at all from that year forward?

Smith: I called him.

Seidlin: Did you have a conversation with him?

Smith: Yes.

Seidlin: How long did it last?

Smith: About 20 minutes.

Seidlin: (To Texas) You want to ask him the ultimate question?

Texas: Getting right to it. . .Billy, do you know if your boy is presently buried in the country of the Bahamas?

Smith: Yes, I do. I wish that he was buried in Texas.

Texas: You wish that he was buried in Texas?

Seidlin: Are you prepared to have a court somewhere in this world exhume his body and bring him to Texas?

Smith: No. No.

Seidlin: So what should I do with his body? If I was a judge who had jurisdiction over that—over this boy's body—what's that?

Smith: I just wish that they'd be buried side by side.

Seidlin: The mother and the son?

Smith: Yes.

That sort of blew the wheels off the truck. And now Texas wants to rehabilitate his own witness. Texas rushed for time and not having an opportunity for face contact with Billy Smith, and maybe having these broken cell phone connections, this guy being on a farm, and you know how cell phones work on the wide open swats of land. Was this an analogy to the O.J. Simpson case, where the prosecutor had O.J. put the glove on and it didn't fit? Texas: Billy, you and I talked at the lunch hour didn't we?

Smith: Pardon me?

Texas: You and I, John O'Quinn, talked at the lunch hour, didn't we?

Smith: Yes.

Texas: If you had the money to do it, didn't you say you'd have your son brought back to Texas?

Smith: Yes.

Texas: Is that where you'd want him to ultimately be?

Rale: Leading.

Seidlin: Allright. We had enough. Thank you, Billy Smith . . . You know I feel for the parties here. I mean, I suffer with this case day and night and you could be one of the most misunderstood people, too, ma'am, mother [Virgie] . . . I had Milstein helping me work through this case. He took a lot of pressure off the court, but I still feel heavy. I feel the burden to be very heavy. I gave little anecdotes during this case to try to take the pressure off you all, to try to keep it moving, to try to make it a little softer because this was a heavy. This was a heavy burden … with a candlelight. . .the flame is going out. I want to preserve the beauty of your daughter. I want to preserve the respect, the beauty that she wanted. You played with her as a child and you knew what she wanted. She went for her dream and apparently from what I hear, she achieved it. She just, unfortunately, didn't have the strength that some of us have to fight through this. Because you all feel the pressure just from a few days' hearing. It's unbelievable. It's unbelievable. They try to put a negative hat on everybody here. Everyone they try to put a negative hat on, the parties especially, they tried to put a hat on and I saw you all here. I don't think anyone is so bad, so to speak, so bad. There's shades of grey. I think if you all one day get it together. . .I mean, I, as a court, would absolutely submit to you that you should resolve a lot of this, that you have enough brain power at each table here to have a global remedy.. . .I have suffered with this. I have struggled with this. I have shed tears for your little girl and your grandchild, but I hope. . .because I'll tell you something, *in the old days I'd be banging some heads together.* I mean it.

We had many hearings in chambers or in the jury room, and these hearings were outside the presence of the public and the media. And I tried so hard, using all the power of the court and all my experience as a human being and a judge, to resolve all the pending issues among these warring parties. But when the media are creating momentum, it's hard to put the brakes on, and get these parties to sit down and try to settle the issues. But I gave it a hell of a dance.

The tears that I shed in open court and in front of the world were just a continuation of tears that I had shed in the privacy of my home and in the closed door sessions that we had. Never be ashamed of expressing your emotions, but make sure they're always delivered in a calm, deliberate manner. I still have not shed my last tear for anyone in this case.

I continued to address the open court. *"You all really should do the right thing by this Dannielynn.* You should get into a jurisdiction immediately and you two are the primary potentials here to submit to a DNA and find who the father is. *It's enough baloney here. It's enough baloney . . .* I walked into this building really at age twenty-six as a kid. I was a stranger in a strange land and I always thought I'd leave at fifty-six. You stay thirty years and I wanted to walk out of here. . .standing up, standing erect. I kid around with my friends and family. I didn't want to be carried out of here like what happened to you, Texas, for a minute. No, no, I wanted to walk out of here healthy. I wanted to walk out of here healthy, you understand? I wanted to feel good. This thing wore me out. I'm going to take a while to regenerate. We all cried for her.

"You know, we were in the chambers and you all had me crying. I got to look tough, mama [Virgie] but this gets to me, too, and we cried for her. We had a service here. We did everything here. We had a service for her, all of us here today, and all the other days, and I run away from services. I can't stand going to a funeral. I can't stand talking about death. Even though in probate, we do contested wills and trusts and guardianships. I don't get into the death part of it. I'm trying to stay alive, but that's another subject. I was supposed to leave here July '06. I don't think my wife wants me to come home. I've got a little baby. I did a lot of talking. The more you talk in this business, the worse off you are, really. The less you say, the better. I knew that from the beginning. Let the truth be known, I wanted you all to know, you three parties, because that's the only ones I'm really interested in. I mean, I want to always treat the lawyers well, but I wanted you to know the way I was thinking. I even stopped at times to try each morning, I tried to bring us to where we are at. I may have bored you, but I wanted to at least let you know what I was thinking. I don't know if you all will ever be in the same room again. I don't know if you ever will be. But in the old days, I wouldn't have let you go. I really would never let you guys all go unless I wrapped this whole thing up, unless I had wrapped it all up, but I can't. I can't wrap it up ... I'm going to have a final resolution. I'm trying to cut it as equitably as I can, but what worries me, and I'm not letting the cat out of the bag, but what worries me is the boy. Danny already is in the grave. He's in the Bahamas. It could have been San Francisco. It could have been the Bronx. He's in the Bahamas ... I didn't come to any conclusions until now, until right now, but I'm trying to figure out how I can in a spiritual sense bring it all together. Now, the Supreme Court of Florida says justice is not perfect. It's what is reasonable and when you leave a court of law, you try to get a reasonable result. It's not perfect. It's what's reasonably equitable.

"I'm going to pronounce the disposition of this case and

I hope when you hear it, you handle with the respect and the dignity that Anna Nicole Smith would want. I hope when you hear it, you handle so that little Dannielynn can have this respect in the future because I think she'll look at these proceedings ... allright, you want a decision. You don't want anymore talk."

I called for a recess.

Immediately following the recess, I continued addressing the parties, this time giving the essence of my disposition concerning this case. "I wanted to be crystal clear for us that once this order is signed, you're all done with me ... I hope when it's read, we're dignified. I hope when it's read, we're dignified and we keep our cool ... I'm just reading the highlights of the conclusion ... the court and its participants in the matter before you have taken a long journey in a very compressed period of time. Although a whole host of matters have been touched on and a multitude of issues have been raised, there is only one issue before this court to decide: *Who is entitled to the custody of the remains of Anna Nicole Smith?* There could be only one proper and equitable answer to that question: *Dannielynn, Anna Nicole's only child and heir,* next of kin. Therefore, based on the court's review and analysis of argument, testimony and materials presented to it, the court orders and adjudges as follows. RICHARD MILSTEIN, ESQ AS THE GUARDIAN AD LITEM FOR DANNIELYNN HOPE MARSHALL STERN IS AWARDED CUSTODY OF THE REMAINS OF ANNA NICOLE SMITH. The Broward County medical examiner is ordered to release those remains in accordance with Milstein's directives. Milstein is directed to consult with Arthur, Birkhead, and Stern with respect to the disposition of Anna Nicole Smith's remains. However, the manner, means and all aspects of handling those remains from their release from the Broward medical examiner to their final interment are with Milstein's sole and absolute discretion as guided by the best interest of Dannielynn ... you'll read it, *but I want her buried. I want her buried with her son.* There is no shouting. This is not a happy moment. *I want her buried with her son in the Bahamas, I want them to be together.* You know, she had to live all of her years under this kind of exposure. I just get a week and a half of it and it's ready to flatten me down. She's going to be with her son. She's going to have her son next to her .. . I have no longer any jurisdiction. It's in Milstein's hands. He's charged. . .and Dr. Perper is going to help. Dr. Perper said he'd fly with him to the Bahamas and the Sheriff's Department indicated they're going to help ... *And I hope to God you guys give the kid the right shot.* I sign this order effective almost 4:00 p.m ... I've completed all my tasks and Godspeed to everyone."

The Appellate Court affirmed my conclusion, although not all my reasoning, but I was able, by taking my time, to show Anna Nicole's intent and where she wanted to be buried, and the Appellate Court reasoned that was the primary threshold. What was Anna Nicole's intent, and the evidence pointed to the Bahamas.

I didn't want to tear up during the final moments of the judgment, so I attempted to tap the pen on the courtroom desk. I too mourned Anna Nicole's death, her son Daniel's death, but most of all, I was celebrating the birth of a new human being on the face of this planet: Dannielynn.

This was one more child that I was attempting to steer right on life's journey. That tapping of the pen, spoofing that on *Saturday Night Live* twice, erased the tears and gave me a good belly laugh. The line, "and I hope to God you guys give the kid the right shot," that line with my dramatic tears burned an image of the scales of justice, being held by lady justice, letting a tear roll down her cheek. Was a court supposed to remain detached and neutral and not express any love and emotion for the matter before it? Do you want a surgeon out there doing the cutting in a detached and neutral manner? Don't the rich and powerful attempt to create a bond between them and the surgeon? Don't they want a relationship with the doctor holding their organs, their testicles, in his or her hands? You want some doctor coming off the street, not knowing who the hell you are, performing life threatening surgery? It's only in an emergency room setting that you get doctors and surgeons whom you are unfamiliar with. Don't the very elite around this world fly in their own planes and get the doctor they so choose? Should that ability—to handpick your surgeon, who will perform your surgery at the time and in the place you choose—be only for the elite? No matter what your background was, this judge gave you VIP treatment, and everybody had an equal chance, an equal opportunity to receive the court's justice.

Let the public decide. But the public has come back, the jury has come back, the public deliberated, the jury deliberated, and I feel it everyday on every street I walk. In every store I enter, the public says you're him, you're the judge, God bless you. And they kid around and they tell me I'm better looking in person, and I think, well what do they think I look like on TV? And then I kid my daughter and I tell her I'm going to buy a rug and put it on my head.

But it is interesting to note that all over the United States there are courses now for judges to give them sensitivity training; to train them to show empathy, sympathy and compassion for those that appear before them. Because, really, in the early days of our court system, the U.S. Supreme Court and some of the state Supreme Courts have shown approval and tolerance towards intolerance—meaning discrimination against gender, race, color and creed.

This country and American jurisprudence continue to evolve. The centerpiece of the law only functions when the population respects the courts. We have seen in countries around this world that respect for government only happens when the government and the court system reflect the population, which comprises every ethnic background, gender, religion and race. And the judicial system of any nation should reflect the makeup of its citizens. Only in 2009 was the first Hispanic American appointed to the U.S. Supreme Court, and only with the election of Barack Obama as president did the United States get, also in 2009, its first black Attorney General.

Sixteen

The Bahamian Inquest

In March 2010, I managed to obtain a set of legal documents that only a handful of people in this world possessed: the transcript of the Bahamian inquest into the death of Daniel Wayne Smith, son of Anna Nicole Smith and Billy Wayne Smith, grandson of Virgie Arthur, and brother to Dannielynn.

The witnesses in the Bahamas were under oath, and their testimony is important for several reasons. You need to compare the testimony in my courtroom with the testimony presented in the Bahamas. I believe that California Attorney General Jerry Brown and his staff reviewed the testimony from the Bahamas. I believe, furthermore, that this additional testimony contributed to the charges against Howard K. Stern, Dr. Kapoor and Dr. Erosevich. So, as good investigators, let's look at the transcript, because in the law, the best evidence is the document, which speaks for itself.

What better way to understand Daniel's death than with actual testimony that was given to the judge and the seven-member jury in the Bahamas. We will take the liberty of analyzing and interpreting what was stated and, in turn, allow you, the reader and juror, to draw a conclusion.

I am requesting that a thorough examination and investigation be made into the circumstances surrounding Daniel's death. This operation by the Bahamian authorities was slipshod. They didn't have the capabilities to conduct a first class investigation into potential foul play and, secondly, the government authorities had no desire to portray Daniel's death as anything but accidental: they abhorred bad publicity. Like the Seminole Police Department in Florida, they did not want the negative press that a potential murder investigation would garner.

When I served as a legal adviser to the Sheriff's Department in Broward County, we had twenty-six little fiefdoms, municipalities, police departments. It was the Sheriff's policy, and this policy is still reflected in most jurisdictions in America, that a serious, sophisticated, high-end police agency will not investigate unless it is invited by the local police agency. We need the FBI, Scotland Yard, the Deuxième Bureau, the Carabinieri or Royal Canadian Mounted Police. You can't have a police department that isn't properly funded, that lacks the resources and experts to undertake a proper investigation.

The Bahamian inquest includes the testimony of Larry Birkhead, and his statement given to the Royal Bahamian Police Force marked January 24, 2006.

Do you remember in my trial, when we were looking at the will that Anna Nicole signed, and it had that clause about her leaving out future children from her estate, and I said the whole document smelled at that point? Well, I'm holding this police report in my hot little hand, and right at the beginning, the captions are completely incorrect. How do you go on reading this police report when its credibility is immediately brought into question? For starters, the date that's indicated on the document—January 24, 2006—is impossible, unless they used a time machine to go back in time. And they list Larry's age as 23; he hasn't seen 23 for at least 14 years. When I sat in traffic court, date and age on a police report could get a traffic ticket thrown out, let alone a possible murder investigation, and these officers would have to take the witness stand and have their notes and testimony dissected like a frog in a biology class.

This raises many red flags for me. But I knew this going in . . . that this was going to be a sloppy and inept operation. Can you imagine that this is the best that the Bahamians could produce, when they fully knew that everybody would at some point be able to review their work?

This is Birkhead's verbatim summarizing, and in his own writing, of many of the events in question.

"My name is Larry Birkhead. I was in a 2 and 1/2 year relationship with Anna Nicole Smith. During that time I lived with her at Studio City, CA home. During that time Anna's attorney Howard K. Stern was also present frequently at her home and Anna's son Daniel lived there as well. During our relationship, Anna has become pregnant twice. One pregnancy resulted in a miscarriage, the other in the birth of my daughter Danniel [note that the name Dannielynn is spelled wrong] that was born in the Bahamas. During the relationship I witnessed drug abuse by Anna Nicole and those around her. Anna was/is addicted to *methadone.* She also takes Klonopin, Topamax, Ambien, Xanax, Soma and other drugs through doctors. She *"doctor hops,"* getting *multiple prescriptions from several doctors at once."*

I interject here to tell you that I believe this line and the next couple of lines, with the help of what was stated in my courtroom, changed the world's opinion and perception about pharmaceutical death.

Birkhead continues, *"one doctor, her primary doctor Sandeep Kapoor, another doctor (and a neighbor in California) Christine Esroinch* [this doctor's name is spelled incorrectly] *and other doctors as well.* In February 2006, Anna informed me that she was once again pregnant. I immediately became alarmed due to her last miscarriage. I became very concerned about the drugs she was taking under prescribed alias names and her own name. Names included Michelle Chase, Jane Brown, Vickie Marshall, Anna N. Smith and other names. *Anna always ignored the pill bottle labels and doubled dosages. She would hide and take the drugs while pregnant because I would tell her she was going to kill our baby.* In May 2006 Anna entered Cedars Sinai Hospital to detox from drugs. During that time Anna's attorney Howard K. Stern came to the hospital during her 2 week stay and slept on the cot in the room. I slept in the hospital bed with Anna. Anna was on methadone I.V. in her arm in decreased dosages from her regular prescription in an effort to wean her off of drugs. While at the hospital Howard brought a duffle bag into the room containing methadone and was administering the drug to Anna when she complained of pain and was not allowed more of the drug by the hospital officials. I explained to Anna the danger of this. Her continued drug problem became a major source of tension causing her to flee to the Bahamas after I confronted both her and Mr. Stern about Anna's drug problem and the effect it would have on my unborn child. [May 2006] Mr. Stern and Ms. Smith inform me that I would never see my child and Anna told me she would move where I would never get the baby or see it. Before she came to the Bahamas and during our relationship, Anna started seeing a change in Daniel's behavior. She told me he was using drugs and asked me to talk to him. During Easter weekend 2006, Anna and myself had to stay in a hotel down the street from Anna's California home because Mr. *Stern told her to choose him or me.* Anna told Mr. Stern it was my child and she wanted to be with me. Anna was in tears because of Mr. Stern's negated attempts to keep me away from her and interfere in our relationship. When we returned home that weekend (Easter 2006), Anna and I noticed a bottle of methadone was missing from her bedroom. Anna confronted Daniel, who had friends at her home, and Daniel said he didn't take the medicine. We later reviewed home security tapes to reveal he did take the pills. Anna's home is on 24 hour security tapes in every room that are archived by a company called Maximum Security. Also during my relationship with Anna that spanned from August 2004 to May 2006, she wanted me to do recreational and prescription drugs with her. One time she gave me a pill for back pain which she later told me was methadone. She also gave me ecstasy as well as her son Daniel. I reportedly turned her down on offers of medicine and drugs. *Howard K. Stern frequently purchased drugs by prescription in large quantities from Key Pharmacy in North Hollywood, California.* Anna would abuse the drugs and ignore doctor's instructions to lower her doses for her health. After Anna Nicole became pregnant (4 months later) and after she and Howard and myself got into multiple arguments over drugs, Anna attempted to tell a man from South Carolina named Ben Thompson he was the father. Howard and Anna went to South Carolina in May 2006. When she got there she told him he was the dad, he said I couldn't be, (so) I had a vasectomy. Anna persisted to tell him via email (which I have personally seen and obtained a copy of) that she wanted child support and DNA from him (Ben). When Mr. Thomson (who I personally verified this with and this was told to me) refused to sign the birth certificate, Anna refused to pay him for the home he helped her buy known as Horizons on Eastern Road. After that, Mr. Stern who was never romantically involved with Ms. Smith, came forward on TV to say he was the father of Anna's newborn baby. I have maintained contact with Anna through phone, instant messages "AOL" via computer and have discussed with her our child where *she has urged me to drop my custody fight and she might let me see my baby.* Going back to the time at Anna's home I personally observed Daniel use ecstasy and smoke marijuana with Mr. Stern and Anna Nicole. I also observed a drastic weight loss and mood change in Daniel.

I discussed his drug use that his mother expected away from the home [,] which he denied to me, but was obvious in my opinion from his behavior. Daniel expressed a desire to move out on his own and get a job, that was met with resistance from his mother. At times she wouldn't speak to him because of it. Anna Nicole urged Daniel in my presence to experiment at home with drugs and alcohol. She (Anna) said it was safer if she could watch him while he was under the influence of drugs and alcohol."

Turning back to the Bahamian inquest of Daniel Smith's death, my aim is to compare the testimony by the key witnesses in my case with the testimony at the inquest and look at the consistencies and inconsistencies. There are also additional sworn statements from other proceedings that may change your conclusions, and my conclusions. Remember, the inquest happened after my trial, and after Anna Nicole's death, and, as I stated during my trial, we won't know the complete truth, or have the complete pieces to the puzzle, until much later. Therefore, you are the jury for a super trial. You're not only the jury for the Anna Nicole case, which I presided over, you're also a juror for the Bahamian inquest and all additional documents and evidence that I will submit to you.

My trial was earlier in the game, even though Daniel died a few months before his mother. And the Bahamian inquest took about a year to complete, and my sources tell me there was political interference. On March 17, 2008, Birkhead was questioned about the death of Daniel by Mr. Braithwaite, the Bahamian chief examiner.

Question. Sir, will you state your full name for the record please?
Answer. Larry Birkhead
Q. And sir, do you know Anna Nicole Smith?
A. Yes, I did.
Q. During your relationship with her, did you come to know her son?
A. Yes I did.
Q. That was Daniel Smith?

A. Yes.

Q. During your relationship with Anna, did you and she have any discussion about Daniel's behavior?

A. . . . I will say, between January and May of 2006 she started having problems with him and his behavior.

Q. What sort of problems were those sir?

A. He returned to community college in California, and some of the friends he was hanging out with she didn't care for too much . . . and he started to break those curfews and the rules of the house.

Q. Did you at any point sir observe Daniel Smith using any drugs?

A. Yes, I did.

Q. So she [Anna] give it to Daniel, did he receive it?

A. I can say I know he put something in his mouth, like I said earlier, and I don't know what it was. I got into an argument and I left, but I can't tell you—I can only tell you what I was told.

Q. You said in your statement; I personally observed Daniel use Ecstasy and smoke marijuana with Mr. Stern and Anna Nicole. I personally observed.

A. I think what I meant to say was present, but since I can't recall the situation. I am not going to speculate on what I meant to say. I cannot recall.

Q. Mr. Birkhead, I just want to draw something to your attention. You read the statement at the time you gave it, right?

212   **A.** Well, at the time that I gave it that was in a room, and

they said write it all out, and they will go back and say—cause there was an interview, a pre-interview, and then there was me writing the statement. So when I was in the room they tell me I had to write everything which I just told them upstairs. That I didn't understand why I am going to repeat it again, so I had to put it in writing at that time.

Q. You signed that statement?

A. Right. And if I said it at the time I believed it to be true. But now I can't recall every single thing.

Your Lord, Your Worship. . .that is how they refer to the judge in the Bahamas, and he seemed as flabbergasted and frustrated as I would have been, but I would have kicked some more ass. We have a death inquest, and the purpose of the death inquest is to determine whether Daniel died accidentally, by suicide, or some form of homicide. And you have the Bahamian police interviewing a key witness, Larry Birkhead, and they tell him to go downstairs and fill out his statement. Where is the videotaped transcript? At the minimum there should be a tape recorder and it should contain questions and answers. I gave you his whole statement, written by Larry Birkhead, which in turn has been submitted by the Bahamian Police to the inquest. It's a narrative, like some police officer directing a witness to reduce to writing the facts surrounding a car accident, a fender bender.

We have the high profile death of a celebrity's son that drew a great deal of attention throughout the world. I'm thinking next that the Bahamian authorities will call in the Aruba police to help them with this investigation. This is a tragic set of facts and I see

213

why Virgie, her family, and Anna Nicole's fans are disappointed, not to mention anybody who really wants to seek justice.

Q. So you have no evidence that Daniel was on drugs?

A. No. I saw a bottle being taken.

Q. You saw a bottle being taken on a tape, but you never saw him put any in his mouth?

A. That's correct.

Q. ... and you were concerned about Anna taking methadone ... it wouldn't have been unreasonable for you to remove it out of her presence so she wouldn't be able to take it?

A. Actually one time I did.

Q. Is it that Daniel was doing the same thing, took the methadone so she can't have access to it?

A. I think that will be an opinion what goes on in Daniel's head.

I spoke to people very close to Daniel, as well as several experts who examined his drug usage. And they all said he complained bitterly to Anna not to do drugs, especially methadone, and he was not a drug user. As the toxicology report will indicate, Daniel was prescribed Lexapro, which is an antidepressant. Therefore, there is a likelihood that Daniel wanted to hide the methadone from his mother.

The Court then warned Birkhead: "I am telling you the consequences that may happen if you don't answer. I have a discretion that I can detain you in custody for seven days. Not [just] you, any witness who does not answer, you see. Once the question does not incriminate you, you have to answer it."

The witness, Birkhead, replied, "Okay." Attorney Evans then asked:

Q. . . . would it be unreasonable for Daniel to remove the methadone so she will not have access to it?

A. Since I never spoke to Daniel about his mother's drug usage, I can't answer that properly.

Attorney Evans then states in open court: "one of the important things is this, where did Daniel get access to the methadone which the pathologist would have found to be responsible for his death. There is a small window of doubt over the opportunity. One of the witnesses speak of the duffle bag prior."

Mr. Evans: Yes, Your Worship. You see, Your Worship, when we are dealing with an inquiry, we are looking at all possibilities. My learned friend is looking after Mr. Stern's position. The item of methadone could have come from anyone in the room except Dannielynn.

The Court: Anyone including the deceased herself.

Mr. Evans: . . . So we cannot be close minded to evidence.

The Court: And therefore why are you pursuing so relentlessly the question of the drugs?

Mr. Evans: Because in his statement he was quite clear and categorical where it came from, who dispensed it. My opinion, he has spoken about it in a number of occasions in

Broward County, talked to the press, *but this is the first time that he has developed a difficulty with his memory.*

It's interesting to note that the statement that Larry Birkhead gave to the Royal Bahamian Police was in January of 2007, just days before Anna Nicole's death. And now Birkhead faces cross-examination by Mr. Munroe.

Q. In January 2007 when you were giving this statement and Vickie Lyn[n] Marshall, Anna Nicole, was still alive?
A. Yes, sir.
Q. When you gave your statement to the Bahamian police did they probe you and ask you questions like how did you know things?
A. No, sir.
Q. Did you ever see Howard and Daniel together?
A. Yes, quite a bit.
Q. What was the nature of their relationship?
A. Well, I thought—he actually, to me, it seemed more like sometimes a father, sometimes, a brother, because he will spend so much time with him and take him places. And Anna couldn't always go out in public and do all the things that everybody can do, so they will go to the movies, they will go, you know, out to eat, different activities, things of that nature that most friends wouldn't do with other people's children. I thought it was, you know, different.

We now have an opportunity to look at a third sworn statement by Larry Birkhead about his life with Anna Nicole and how he dealt with her drug use. This time, it was a videotaped deposition that he gave on July 22, 2008 for the United States Southern District of New York, in the civil action lawsuit launched by Howard K. Stern against author Rita Cosby, who authored the first book about the Anna Nicole case, *Blonde Ambition*, and her publisher, Hachette Book Group USA. The questions are from Mr. Maynard, attorney for Hachette. Let's cut to the chase.

Q. Before Dannielynn was born, did Howard ever tell you that he was the father of Dannielynn?

A. No.

Q. When did you first learn that he claimed to be the father?

A. On the Larry King Show.

Q. You saw it on television?

A. Yes.

Q. During the period between November 2005 and February of 2006, did Mr. Stern have a sexual relationship with Anna Nicole Smith?

A. I never saw one.

Q. Never?

A. I never saw any sexual relationship.

Q. She never told you about that?

A. No, she denied that she did.

Q. Did you ask her about Howard being the father?

A. No, no. I had conversations in the past about whether she and Howard ever had sex and she said no.

Q. She said no. Did Howard ever tell you that he had sex with

Anna Nicole Smith?

A. No.

The attorney later asked Birkhead about Anna's hospital stay. Here's the meat of that issue.

Q. What was the purpose of the drip, as you understood it?

A. It was a methadone drip and even though she was trying to get off of it, I understood it to be they were weaning her down in regulated doses that were acceptable because if she were to just flat out get off of it, then it could kill her and the baby . . .

Q. During the time you were in that hospital room, did you ever see a duffle bag?

A. Yes.

Q. What was in the duffle bag?

A. Personal items and medication.

Q. What kind of medication?

A. The only one that I observed the label on was methadone.

Q. During the time you were in the hospital, did you ever see Mr. Stern give Anna Nicole Smith any medications?

A. I saw him give her the duffle bag that contained the medications, but I didn't see him dispense medications.

Q. Did you see her take drugs out of the bag when he gave it to her?

A. Yes and I saw her take them on her own when the bag was next to her.

Larry Birkhead admitted during this deposition that he and

Howard K. Stern had a conversation prior to her leaving for South Carolina.

A. I talked to him about the medications and said something to the effect that if she can't get off of them, then maybe I will raise the baby. And he said something back to me like 'we knew you were going to do this,' and later on she took off.

Q. When did Anna then go to the Bahamas?

A. I'm not 100% sure when she actually went to the Bahamas. It seems like the way I was finding out information is I paid a subscription to go on Anna's website to get updates about how the baby was doing and also she was making a journal about where she was and she said she was going to an island to have her baby. And then at the same time my website that I had, because I didn't have a publicist or anything and I was overwhelmed with all these people bugging me about the paternity and stuff. I just responded to certain things on a statement on my site. I didn't really know how to do it. I just kind of put it up. And I found out how to monitor the traffic to see where the hits were coming from and I kept getting a lot of hits from the Bahamas. So I kind of figured that was where she was.

Q. During the time that she was in the Bahamas, did Daniel Smith ever try to smooth out the relationship?

A. I'm not exactly sure where she was located at the time but Daniel called me around July of 2006 and basically it was kind of a familiar thing. It was not so much for him but it was like she was having someone be a go-between and basically, why are you fighting with mom and why don't you shape up, like everything was my fault and aren't you happy about this whole thing and the baby and all this stuff. So it was a conversation I had where I would say something to Daniel and he would repeat it to his mother and go back and forth and then finally Anna got on the telephone. She started crying and she would hand the phone back to Daniel, a back and forth thing. And the last time I talked to Daniel was that day.

Q. After Anna Nicole left to go to the Bahamas, did you believe that she was under the control of Mr. Stern?

A. Well, I had conversations with Anna where she told me that she couldn't talk at some point because Howard was coming in the room so she had to hang up. I was also told that Howard was in on the part. . .I was told by Ford Shelley that he was at least on the part of the South Carolina attorneys looking at the laws there for Anna and whatever. So I could only assume but I'm not privileged to the conversations they had with each other, but I felt like because Anna wasn't clear on the laws and different things that I don't think she would have the knowledge. I felt like she was being directed in some fashion.

Q. By Mr. Stern?

A. And others.

There were a lot of questions and confusion about why Larry Birkhead pursued a paternity cause of action against Anna Nicole. And about his timing of this lawsuit and his aggressively pursuing the DNA testing while Anna was grieving for her son. Birkhead knew that she was fragile and completely over-medicated. I remember sitting in my courtroom thinking his approach was harsh, knowing that she was as shaky as a three-dollar bill, that Anna was one unstable person, and this paternity suit could push her over the edge. These additional facts that are now coming out into the open enhance and illuminate my understanding of his strategy.

Q. . . . did you see Mr. Stern's appearance on Larry King sometime after that?

A. Yes.

Q. And that was the one where he claimed that he was the father, is that right?

A. Yes.

Q. What was your reaction when you saw Mr. Stern say that?

A. I had two reactions. One, I laughed because I thought she could have said anybody. I was thinking that they were going on there and say Ben [Thompson] because I'd already heard rumblings that they were trying to get him to do that. But when he said it was him, then I laughed about it and then I got angry about it and then I left and went to a party and brushed it off. But I was still angry. And then I think shortly thereafter I might have filed my paternity case.

Q. Did you think Mr. Stern was lying when he said he was the father?

A. Yes.

Q. Mr. Birkhead, did you travel to the Bahamas in January of 2007?

A. Yes.

Q. Was that in part to get a DNA test completed?

A. Yes.

Now we—you, the reader and jury, and I—know that part of the reason for Birkhead's journey to the Bahamas was for DNA. And, lo and behold, the other part appears to be that he was giving a statement to the Royal Bahamian Police—the statement that has the wrong date, January 24, 2006, instead of the correct date, 2007.

Q. And you are living in the Studio City house now?

A. Yes.

Q. Do you pay rent to stay there?

A. I have paid expenses. I pay expenses there every month. I paid around thirty thousand in house payments, but the estate pays the payment every month after I bailed it out of arrears or whatever.

Q. Have you been confirmed as Dannielynn's guardian?

A. Yes.

Q. Has Mr. Stern been confirmed as the executor of Anna Nicole's estate?

A. Yes.

Q. Did you oppose his confirmation?

A. No.

Do you remember during my trial, I suggested the three

parties work together and try to do what was in the best interest of Dannielynn? From this deposition, we see that two of the parties, Stern and Birkhead, are apparently working together in most instances.

Q. Are you familiar with something called the Dannielynn Hope Irrevocable Trust?

A. Yes.

Q. What is that?

A. It is a trust that was set up with the monies from *Entertainment Tonight* and the Splash News pictures that was set up.

Q. From the funeral?

A. Yes.

Q. Is there money in the trust now?

A. Yes.

Q. Tell me.

A. I think net like a hundred and something thousand dollars.

And here, in my trial, the court was led to believe by some of the parties that poor Virgie called the media outlets during the viewing of Anna Nicole's body at the Broward medical examiner's office.

SEVENTEEN

THE GHOSTS KEEP KNOCKING

On March 18, 2008, Howard K. Stern faced the Bahamian inquest. At the outset, when he was asked by Chief Examiner Braithwaite where he currently resided, Stern answered, "Where do I live at present? I live in Los Angeles, CA, in [a] suburb called Sherman Oaks."

This disappointed me. Anna Nicole and Daniel are alone in the Bahamas. He wasted no time in relocating to Los Angeles. This further convinced me that Anna Nicole and Stern going to the Bahamas was just a ruse, an effort to avoid all the issues concerning the paternity of Dannielynn, with no intent to live in the Bahamas permanently. Is fame and fortune calling everyone away from the Bahamas? Wouldn't this call have been heard by Anna Nicole if she were alive? It's obvious that her intent was to return to Hollywood. She was born to be a star and there is no way in hell she would have avoided the limelight for any extended period of time. No wonder the ghosts keep knocking at my door.

Her soul and Danny's soul need to be placed on sacred ground in the Lone Star state with people who grew up with her and loved her in her simpler days. Every child is a star for the parents, family and friends. The Hollywood star just has a bigger stage. In Anna Nicole's case, like Michael Jackson's, there are still great sums of money to be made from her work, from her image and her likeness. And in Anna Nicole's case, there is a lot of dough still cooking in the J. Howard Marshall estate. Anna was originally awarded hundreds of millions of dollars from the estate by a Los Angeles federal court, and that was later reduced to zero by a federal appeals court.

Anna Nicole, like Michael Jackson, could be worth more dead than alive. Dead stars no longer spend any money, plus no one has to deal with their eccentricities. All that's left is the goose laying the golden eggs. Money, money, money and more money. Look at the executors for Michael Jackson's estate. They control great power and money and are rewarded handsomely in fees and expenses. People don't realize that you don't have to be named in a will as a beneficiary in order to receive money from an estate. You are entitled to a percentage of the estate as the executor, and you may be additionally compensated if you are the attorney overseeing the estate. You can also apply for extraordinary expenses when and if there is litigation. You can also be compensated for any and all work that is done for any contracts and deals that are consummated.

The questioning regarding Stern's former whereabouts continued.

Q. And did you also, sir, know her son, Daniel Smith?

A. I knew him very well.

Q. Now, sir, in September of 2006, where were you residing?

A. I was back and forth between Los Angeles and Nassau, Bahamas.

Q. When did Anna initially move to the Bahamas?

A. She flew out here on July 18 [2006] with Ben Thompson and Ford Shelley.

Q. And did you at some point join them?

A. I did. I flew out separately, also on July 18 of 2006.

Q. Could you describe Danny's demeanor at that time, that was June of 2006, you say?

A. In South Carolina.

Q. Yes.

A. He was very thin. Again, we had known that he wasn't quite being himself that year, but in South Carolina, he seemed okay. He slept a lot. He slept a lot, but he seemed like he was okay to me. There was a concern that we thought actually that Daniel might be anorexic because he was so thin ...

Q. Were you ever present at the home in Studio City when any drugs were present?

A. In terms of prescription medication or...

Q. Well, yes, prescription medication.

A. Anna did have prescription medication ... and I had been prescribed prescription medications at times myself.

Q. Was there any methadone in the home in Studio City, CA?

A. Yes. Anna has been prescribed methadone for pain for a number of years.

Howard Stern went on to say, "I had never seen Daniel take a

227

bottle of methadone or do any type of illegal drugs. I never saw Anna smoke marijuana. I never saw Daniel smoke marijuana."

Q. Did you ever, in California, see Daniel use any type of illicit drugs?
A. No. I never seen him use any type of illicit drugs. I have seen him drunk on three occasions.

Howard K. Stern is like a fly on the wall in Anna Nicole's house and in her life. Therefore, he is the only one, or maybe the best witness, to address the issue of Daniel's demise. Stern is with Anna Nicole 24/7. He is always at her side; he knows when she sneezes or has a bowel movement. So we are back to square one. How did Daniel have this large quantity of methadone in his system?

Q. Did Daniel at some point come to the Bahamas sir?
A. He did.
Q. Are you aware of what time he arrived in the Bahamas?
A. I am.... [Daniel] landed in the Bahamas at approximately 10:30 p.m. that night, the night of September 9 [2006].
Q. How did Daniel get from the airport?
A. I picked Daniel up at the airport and we drove directly to Doctor's Hospital.
Q. What was his demeanor during that ride, sir?
A. He seemed like he was in a good mood. We talked. . .he said, "I can't believe I have a baby sister. I just can't believe it." And I was trying to tell him some of the things there are

to do in the Bahamas. And he seemed to me like he was in a good mood ...

Q. Okay. Now, you said that he appeared well during this journey from the airport to the hospital?

A. He did. You know, he was still very thin and he was still very pale. And, you know, I was aware that he was hospitalized in July for depression and so we knew that it was actually the same day that I flew out to the Bahamas is when I learned that Daniel was hospitalized and he was hospitalized for a week in ICU.

Q. Did you ever speak with Daniel?

A. I spoke with Daniel afterwards after his hospitalization ... he said he was hospitalized and he was having severe back pains and he was very depressed ...

Q. And what happened when you got to the hospital, sir?

A. We went up the elevator to Anna Nicole's room and Daniel went and picked up Dannielynn—her name wasn't Dannielynn at the time—but picked up the baby and held her in his arms and hugged his mom. We took some pictures.

Howard K. Stern then states, "we talked a little bit more and Daniel said that he was hungry, so Anna sent me to go get food and I didn't know too many things that were open ... so I went to Esso on the Run and I picked up food. I thought that Daniel said that he would want chicken strips. I got him chicken strips. I thought he would want to try a beef patty, because it's not something that we had in the States. He always drinks Coke, so I got him a Coke. So I also got tuna sandwiches for myself and

Anna and I drove back up to the hospital and went back up to the room."

> **Q.** I see. After you got back to the hospital with the food, what happened, sir?
>
> **A.** I went back up to the room, and Daniel and Anna and I ate. And at the time Daniel ate, I was toward Anna, you know, there were two beds in the room, one is closer to the door and the other was closer to the window. Daniel was eating his food, sitting on the bed closest to the window and I was sitting at the front of Anna's bed eating next [to] her.
>
> **Q.** You are saying Anna was in which bed now?
>
> **A.** Anna was in the bed closest to the window. From the time that Dannielynn was born, I stayed in the hospital with Anna, except to go out and pick up food. I stayed with her. One bed was by the door and one was by the window and Anna was in the bed by the window throughout.

This is like musical beds. I understand why Braithwaite is scratching his head, because Stern's testimony is inconsistent regarding the bed. This would place Stern in the bed by the door, which was facing Daniel and his mother Anna.

> **Q.** You just said that Danny was sitting on the bed by window or door?
>
> **A.** In terms of eating the food, Daniel was sitting on the bed by the door.
>
> **Q.** And you were with Anna on the bed by the window?

A. Correct.

Q. After Daniel finished eating what happened, sir?

A. We were going to try and go to sleep and I was going to sleep on the floor in between the two beds, and we started out that way where I was on the floor and Anna was on the bed by the window and Daniel was in the bed by the door and that's why we called for pillows and blankets and stuff like that and I was sleeping actually in front of the baby. The baby's cart was in between the bed that Anna was in and the bed that Daniel was in, so I was in front, closer to the door where the baby's cart was. And you know, that didn't last very long, I would say maybe 15 or 20 minutes. And Daniel said that he wasn't tired and why don't I just take the bed by the window, so I did that and I like I said, I had been pretty tired just because I was awake for—neither Anna nor I slept that much since Dannielynn was born, just through the excitement. And I went to sleep in the bed by the door and Anna tried to go to sleep in the bed by the window. And Daniel, I believe he had at that point was maybe sitting on the foot of the bed that Anna was on watching TV...

It doesn't add up. Daniel comes to the hospital to visit Anna Nicole. Why doesn't Howard K. Stern take a powder, let this child reacquaint himself with his mother and new baby sister? They can have a special moment together. And Howard should go put his head on the bed at their home at the Horizons. Why does he need to be sticking his nose up her rear every moment of the day? Did Stern want to inhibit or chill Daniel's ability to convince

Anna Nicole to come back home to California? I mean what man after he has been with a woman a few months doesn't want space, doesn't want his own time to walk around? The honeymoon is not a continuous saga. And we're led to believe there is no romance between Stern and Anna Nicole anyway. So assuming this is strictly a friendship, overlapped with their common business endeavors—the Marshall estate—who would want to spend all this time together? Unless, you are in the palace and you think that a coup d'état is going to occur at any moment. But how can you live your life with someone, when you always think you are about to enter quicksand. . .or was Stern's intent to stop Anna Nicole from departing the Bahamas?

I remember when my little girl was born. I remember sitting on a fake leather chair and spending the night in the hospital room. On the second day, however, when Belinda's parents arrived to spend time with her, I took off like I was shot in the ass. I wanted relief. I went home and took a nap, took a shower, took a shave and a jog. Why doesn't Stern react normally and exit to regain his strength and tend to his hygiene?

Q. Immediately prior to your going to sleep, where was Daniel?

A. . . . I think he was at the foot of Anna's bed. Now, there were a number of times in the night that Anna would wake up and have to go to the bathroom and she had just had a c-section a couple of days earlier, so Daniel and even myself would help Anna to the bathroom and that happened, you know, I would wake up and sort of a groggy sleep and help

Anna to the bathroom and that happened a few times through the night . . .

Q. You have any idea how many times you got up during that night, sir?

A. It was maybe 3 or 4, 3 or 4. And the last occasion Daniel said to me *"I don't know why I'm so tired."* He said that and I didn't think anything of it . . . it was the middle of the night. But I don't know what time.

Q. On the occasions when you did get up, where exactly was Daniel?

A. Well, when I would get woken up, Daniel was already helping his mom. He was, you know, standing by the bed to help his mom out of the bed.

Q. When was the last time you saw Daniel awake, sir?

A. The last time that I saw him awake was when he said to me, "I don't know why I'm so tired."

Here's the next red flag. The question before a court or an inquest would be: if Daniel voluntarily ingested the toxic cocktail—methadone—was he asking a rhetorical question, one that he doesn't expect the answer to? Why would anyone who knowingly took this death mix ponder and be inquisitive to a third party about its result? This doesn't fit neatly into a logical package. My professor at Hunter College would take back his A+ from my report card if I accepted such a line of questioning.

Q. And when he said that to you, where exactly were you?

A. That was the time when I didn't get out of the bed. So I

233

was actually in the bed closest to the door and I was just sort of sitting up as Anna was using the restroom. I was sitting up in the bed.

Q. And what time did you finally get up that morning, sir?

A. At the time I didn't know what time it was. I was woken up by Anna saying, "Howard, Howard, Daniel's not breathing," and I sort of just shook awake, went to the other bed, touched Daniel's neck. I didn't feel anything, and we immediately called the nurses.

Q. When you said you were awakened by Anna, what exactly did you say she said?

A. I think she said, "Howard, Howard, Daniel's not breathing," or words to that effect. And it was it was a pretty loud voice. It was a panic voice from Anna.

Q. And where was Daniel at that time, sir?

A. At that time Daniel was next to Anna in her bed, in the bed closest to the window.

Q. And was he moving at all, sir?

A. No.

Q. How did he appear to you at that time?

A. I was really scared. He didn't look good. It was horrible.

Q. What happened after you pressed the emergency buzzer, sir?

A. . . . Anna said, "you've got to get in here immediately." And within a matter of seconds people began rushing into the room. And at this point Anna was hugging Daniel and they were trying to move her away and they were like trying to pull her off of him and she wouldn't go. She stayed on the bed and just more people began rushing in the room and I was sitting behind Anna, kind of with my arms around her and Anna was screaming, she was praying to Jesus, "Please don't take Daniel, take me instead."

Q. What was happening in respect of Daniel at that time, sir?

A. People were working on him, people were trying to revive him.

Q. When you say people?

A. The doctors and nurses . . . they came in pretty quickly.

Q. After these efforts to resuscitate Daniel, what happened, sir?

A. Anna screamed, "No, No," and didn't accept that Daniel died. So she told me to go to the head of the bed and at this point there was like a bag that you put that the doctors were pushing to get air into Daniel and I was pushing that and Anna was pressing on Daniel's chest over and over and screaming, *saying she didn't want to trade out children.*

Stern tells us that a Dr. Minnes came in, "and told us that Anna should check out because once the U.S. embassy was notified that media would come and descend very quickly on the hospital, so Anna—so we had to check out. But Anna wouldn't leave, she wouldn't go home without Daniel. She said Daniel was not dead. She wanted to take Daniel home. She literally wanted to take Daniel home. She refused to leave the room."

Q. So, at some point you checked out of the hospital?

A. Well, what happened was we were trying to get Anna to get ready to leave. She refused. She was holding on to Daniel and she was trying to lift Daniel and then—incidentally, that's how the picture—there's one picture, *one picture that's taken of Anna and Daniel together, one after Daniel died.* Not a series. It's one. And it's because Anna wanted to take Daniel home. She didn't believe he was dead. She wanted proof. So I took that picture. I would do it again. Just like I would have done anything for her at that time. That's why the picture was taken . . .

This is macabre. Go back in time to my trial, when Anna is eight or nine months pregnant and appearing drugged out, and looking like Bozo the Clown. And Stern is videotaping her and inquiring is this a mushroom trip? Then fast forward to the moments after Daniel's demise and the pattern continues. Who would photograph a dead son being held by the faithful mother? How do you rationalize this away? What explanation will you, the reader and juror, accept? Are you still buying the Brooklyn Bridge? Does Anna Nicole want a photograph of her deceased son?

Q. Were you aware at any point, sir, of Daniel being on any medication?
A. . . . I was told that he [was] prescribed Lexapro, an antidepressant.
Q. Did you at any point, sir, give Daniel any medication?
A. Never.
Q. Did you give Daniel methadone?

A. Never. I would never do that. Daniel was never I did not think he would want methadone.

Q. At any point while Daniel was in your presence in that hospital room, sir, did you see him take any medication?

A. No, I didn't ...

Q. Are you aware, sir, whether or not any methadone was in that hospital room?

A. There would not have been methadone in the hospital. There was not. Not to my knowledge. And I was the one that brought the two bags that were there, so, no. Let me describe this or explain this for one second. Anna had been taking methadone for pain for a number of years. When we learned that she was pregnant, the doctor said that—I was there for this—that she couldn't stop taking it immediately all together or she would lose the baby. So there was a gradual reduction of the dose that she had been on up until maybe a week before Dannielynn's birth when she was entirely off methadone. And that's why she originally had only been prescribed methadone in pill form.

Q. You said there was a time when she was entirely off methadone?

A. Right before the birth, yes. And that's why there was no methadone in that hospital.

Q. How close to the birth was she completely off methadone?

A. It was pretty close. It was a matter of days. It was a matter of days.

237

Stern then goes on to say, "When she would try and stop all together with the 5 milligram pills, she would have effects like she might be going into a withdrawal. So because of that the doctor prescribed *methadone in a liquid form* that could be taken in less than 5 milligram increments, so that's why she was prescribed a *liquid methadone.* And that's what we did have at the Horizons house [Bahamas] prior to her giving birth. But it would not have been in the hospital."

Q. How did she get the methadone?

A. From a doctor. It was a doctor's prescription.

Q. The Attorney General wants to know if it was a doctor in the Bahamas?

A. No.

Q. What type of methadone was at the house?

A. Well, I know at that point there would have been liquid methadone there and there was probably still.

The Court. Don't say "probably." You knew for a fact that there was liquid methadone?

A. I know there was liquid at the house. I don't know for sure whether there was pills at the house. I knew for sure that there was still pills in Anna's house in Studio City.

It seems like everything is justified, excessive drugs, even violating the prescription dosages, but the response is always a doctor prescribed the medicine. We're being told by the witness Howard K. Stern that she is being weaned off methadone. Was she weaned off for about 12 minutes right before the birth? Or was it about three seconds, as the baby Dannielynn gasped for her first breath? Anna Nicole is a known addict. The California Attorney General charged Stern and Dr. Erosevich and Dr. Kapoor for giving excessive drugs to a known addict. You have Larry Birkhead telling us that when the hospital was making a good faith effort to wean Anna Nicole off methadone with the IV drip, Stern and Anna Nicole bring in their own duffle bag with methadone. Birkhead states that he saw Stern hand Anna Nicole the duffle bag with this prescribed methadone that was brought from outside the hospital, because she wouldn't accept the doses of medication recommended by her health care experts. Additionally, we have Anna Nicole with her face painted like a clown, during her pregnancy, appearing to be high as a kite. A court would instruct a jury in evaluating a case to use common sense. It's everyday knowledge and judgment to determine what is reasonable. So I leave it to you, my reader, my juror, to tell me if this is reasonable. Did Anna Nicole come to the hospital with a bag of goodies?

During this inquest, an issue arises that there were methadone pills on the bed closest to the door. The Bahamian Attorney General asked Stern, "So you were not present when any pills were removed from that bed?" Stern succinctly replied, "Absolutely not. Didn't know anything about it."

The question is: where did the methadone come from? We know that Daniel came from California and as he landed in the Bahamas, he went directly to the hospital. Would he bring a drug like methadone, which was not prescribed to him, through all these airports and then through customs at the Bahamian airport?

> **The Court:** But you have never seen him take any form of illegal drugs?
> **A.** Never.

Stern then states, "that Anna said that if he wants to drink or if he does want to experiment with things that she would want that done in her presence because she was always very protective of Daniel and didn't want him out with people whom she didn't know and that was one of her concerns with a group of friends that he met."

It's not unreasonable for a parent to tell their child, if you want to have a beer or a glass of wine, do it in my presence, in the comfort of our home. And many parents that I have had conversations with believe it takes away the excitement of an unknown mystery.

> **The Court:** Now, you would have also heard evidence that she had some form of problems to the use of methadone?
> **A.** I heard Larry [Birkhead] say that. I disagree.
> **The Court:** You disagree with that too?
> **A.** Yes.
> **The Court:** Was she using methadone?
> A. She was prescribed methadone by a doctor.
> **The Court:** Did you personally ever give her methadone out of her medication?
> **A.** In terms of if I handed over a bottle to her?

The Court: Not just the bottle. Did you ever take up the medication and give it to her yourself?

A. It's possible.

The Attorney General, I visualize, has smoke coming out of his ears, like the locomotive from the old Lionel train set that my father purchased for me one Christmas. I can hear the choo choo sound coming from the Bahamian Attorney General as well.

The Court: It's possible. Now, you would have also heard Mr. Birkhead say yesterday that there were occasions when she abused the use of methadone by using as much as 10 tablets or some other medication; are you aware of that?

A. That's not the testimony I heard. He asked how many total pills of anything, what is the most he has heard her take he has seen her take ten pills.

The Court: Have you ever seen her take ten pills?

A. I never seen her take ten pills of methadone.

The Court: Of any type.

A. Sure. She took supplements where she would take six supplements of a kind to help her go to the bathroom. There were numerous types of stuff she would take like that.

Stern has an answer for everything. Some questions would be better left unanswered. Was he the sounding board for Anna Nicole? Was it the blind leading the blind? When does brain power come into play? Attorney Evans now begins to question Stern.

The Court: Now, were you at any point concerned at the amount of medication that she was taking?

A. Are you talking about before or after Daniel's death?

The Court: During pregnancy.

A. We went to a doctor and the doctor talked about the safest way to reduce the medication she was on.

The Court: I think the question, Mr. Stern, was were you at any point concerned?

A. During her pregnancy?

The Court: Yes.

A. No, because I knew she was going to a doctor, talking to a doctor about reducing the medications she was on in the safest way possible.

The Court: . . . She [Anna Nicole] was very upset . . .

A. It was horrible. Horrible.

The Court: Did she in that state make any accusations about you?

A. No. That was falsely reported in the media here.

The Court: You know nothing about that?

A. Absolutely nothing. There were a lot of lies that were reported in the media.

The Court: And to your knowledge there were no other occasions when she would have made any accusations against you relative to what happened to Daniel?

A. Never, never. When Daniel died she didn't believe he died. She thought he was going to come back. She thought he was going to be like Jesus.

Evans went on to question Stern about the photo he took of Daniel shortly after he died, at Anna Nicole's side in her hospital bed.

The Court: You never benefitted in any way from this picture?

A. Never. That picture would never have seen the light of day if it was up to me. Never. And I think that it is sick that it got released.

The Court: And you had nothing to do with its release?

A. Absolutely not. You should subpoena Geraldo Rivera to see who did it.

It figures. Geraldo Rivera, whom I spent the summer with as a judicial analyst, has a strong belief in the conspiracy theories. The investigative journalist that he is, it is an odd twist that the photo ended up with him for a moment.

EIGHTEEN

A Complete And Thorough Investigation?

And then it was Ford Shelley's turn to testify before the inquest. After Chief Examiner Braithwaite asked about his occupation (real estate developer), place of residence (Myrtle Beach, South Carolina), and if his father-in-law owned a house in the Bahamas (which he still did at the time of the inquest), he then tackled the issue of Shelley's relationship with Anna Nicole and why she wanted to go to the Bahamas.

Q. Did you, at any point, sir, come to meet a Ms. Vickie Lynn Marshall, also known as Anna Nicole Smith?

A. Yes, sir.

Q. When was that?

A. The first time I actually met her was at the Hard Rock Casino, in July of '05.

Q. That is Hard Rock Casino where?

A. In Hollywood [Florida].

Q. Did you ever come to meet her son Daniel?

A. Yes, sir.

Q. When did you meet him?

A. I actually met him the first time in July of '05, I met he and Howard Stern in the casino.

Q. Did your family ever come to form a relationship with Ms. Marshall [Anna Nicole]?

A. Yes, sir.

Q. Did you know the purpose for Ms. Smith coming to the Bahamas?

A. Yes, sir.

Q. What was the purpose for her coming here?

A. To what Anna represented to me was that Anna wanted to get away from the media. She was a high-risk pregnancy and she wanted to have her daughter in a beautiful country, and she wanted to get away from Larry Birkhead. She didn't want him to exert any parental rights, is what she told us.

Ford Shelley told the inquest that his father-in-law and his entire family took a plane to the Bahamas to visit Anna Nicole after the birth of Dannielynn. Shelley said that they saw Dannielynn and took the plane back to South Carolina. Shelley states "we pulled up in the driveway . . . and I got a phone call from a very hysterical Ben Thompson, said we needed to go there [the Bahamas]. I asked him what was wrong. He said that Daniel was dead and he said, get here. So I called our pilots, . . . and we were here within four hours."

Q. What, if anything, happened when you got to the Horizons, sir?

A. When we got there, of course, the first thing we did was

I greeted Howard and Anna and expressed our condolences. Howard wanted us to try and help with the baby and Anna was sleeping.

Q. While at Horizons that evening, did anything unusual happen?

A. ... We were trying to get something to put on the website, as far as a picture, to let everybody know what happened to Daniel.

This is a crazy world, completely crazy. We think we are sophisticated? But our minds are completely absorbed in the world of Facebook, Twitter and blogging. Who really gives a damn about outside opinion at that moment when your loved one just died? People are worried about sending out a picture of Daniel on the internet? Or are they worried and preoccupied with his death and this is just a distraction? Another addiction that we all have, to distract us from the subject at hand. A gruesome subject, the mysterious death of Daniel.

Shelley proceeds to tell the inquest: "We took a picture that they had taken on a raft of ours, at home in the Cays, and posted it on the website. We were back and forth checking on Anna; and Anna wanted us to get Daniel's suitcase out of the car. So we got it, and the suitcase was in the room, in the master bedroom. Someone had already gotten it, and Howard opened it up and went through it, and there was...he had just a few pieces of clothing in there. I wanted to say there was a Zantac or something like for heartburn, and that was it."

Shelley stated that his brother-in-law saw that the van door was open and there were some clothes in the back seat. And Shelley stated, "Well bring them up and Howard said those are Daniel's ... my brother-in-law came in and brought the clothes up ... Howard set them on the bed, and when Howard set them there, he had his shirt, there was a ball cap, and a pair of jeans. And Howard was going through the pockets, then he pulled this thing out, like this [*he indicates*]; there were two white tablets that fell out on the bed, and Howard picked them up. And I said, what is that? Howard picked the pills up and walked in the bathroom. I said, Howard, what are you doing? He walks in that bathroom and closes the door, and when he walks in and closes the door he comes out, I hear the toilet flush. I said, what happened? He said I took care of the problem. I said what did you do? He said, don't worry about it. It was odd ... "

There is a death at Doctor's Hospital in the Bahamas, the death of a young person who was a visitor, just twenty years old, and under strange and suspicious circumstances. Why is it that the Bahamian police aren't immediately on the scene, performing a potential crime scene investigation? How did the chain of custody for evidence—Daniel's clothes and all other items are potential evidence—break down? There was no one at the helm, no one steering this ship. Where are the crime scene investigators? Were there pills in his pocket? How were they acquired? Did someone place those pills in his pocket?

The FBI would be able to get answers to these questions. It is interesting that one of the FBI services listed on its website involves Legal Attaches, called "Legats." If an American citizen dies on foreign soil, these Legats will make an inquiry. The FBI have Legal Attache offices in 200 countries around the world; and one of their Legat suboffices for the Americas region is located in Nassau.

Another curious note is that Ford Shelley tells us "she [Anna Nicole] wanted to call her mama, and she wanted to call Larry. And Howard went on the left side of the bed, sat down beside her and said, 'Why you want to call Larry? He was the one that said you were an unfit mother.'"

As Shelley's testimony continues, the assistant Attorney General wants to delve into the subject of Anna's drug use.

Shelley states "in California, in May, I brought her to South Carolina. You asked if I had seen drugs in the room. There was a duffle bag that she carried medication in ... in the Bahamas that bag was there too ..."

Q. Around the time of Daniel's death, were you aware of any specific types of medication that were present?
A. No, other than in the refrigerator, in the kitchen, there was a bottle of methadone in the kitchen.
Q. How do you know it was methadone?
A. Because it was written in the name of Michelle Chase.
Q. On it written methadone?
A. Yes, sir. This is the same bottle of methadone that she had on Myrtle Beach, that was sitting on the night stand by the bed.

After that, Shelley is cross-examined by Mr. Evans.

Q. Mr. Shelley, let me take you back to when Anna stayed with you in South Carolina. Are you able to say whether she was on medication at that point in time?

A. Yes, sir....She told us what she was taking. We were concerned because of her pregnancy. I was instructed by Howard, as far as her medication and what she was taking ...

Q. Are you able to tell us what Howard tells you with respect to the instructions?

A. He just said that Anna had her medication. They were there. She knew, of course, how to take them and he just said, just keep your eye on the bag because it had a lot of stuff in it.

Q. You looked in the bag?

A. When we unloaded the bag, the one thing that really stood out was the two-milligram bar, that we called Howard about and was concerned about, and he explained it. We, at this time, hid it. And when he did not find it, Howard Federal Expressed it in the name of Michelle Chase. He explained to us it was an alias.

Q. How well did you get to know Daniel?

A. Pretty good, top chef.

Q. How would you describe him?

A. He was brilliant.

Q. Seemingly a happy kid?

A. Happy?

Q. Yes.

A. No, he was miserable. He was miserable living in a shell. He was tired of his mother being attacked; tired of having to be homeschooled and not being free. He wanted to break free. He didn't want to be known as Anna's son. He loved his mother but wanted to have a good time.

Q. Now, in your time of knowing Daniel, did you ever know him to be involved with drugs?

A. No, sir. He can't even hold his liquor. . . .

Q. And during the time that you knew him, did he display any behavioral characteristics that may have led you to think that he might have killed himself?

A. Danny was afraid of his own shadow. No, sir. No, sir. . . . He never displayed a sign of strong depression at all. He was with me a whole month at Christmas. . . .

The Court then states out loud: "The cause of death? I am trying to find out the cause of death."

Remember my trial. How many times did I say I have to remain with the issue of where to bury Anna Nicole? In any trial or hearing there are all kinds of side issues, or even primary issues, that throw up road blocks on the way to resolving the case. The Lord, His Worship, in this case also known as the Court, seems to share the same frustration I had in my case.

Mr. Munroe asked Shelley about arriving November 16 and giving a statement to the Royal Bahamian Police Force on November 17.

Q. You gave it [the statement] right after you came to Anna Nicole Smith's house and tried to kick her out; is that about right?

A. You know, you are so good. I wish I had hired you first.

Q. Trying to kick her out? I am trying to find out. . .I am trying to hold an inquest into the cause of death.

There is a controversy concerning who owns the house. Is it Anna Nicole, or Shelley's father-in-law, G. Ben Thompson? So Shelley states "you know what, sir, this is going back to the house and I refuse to answer any more questions. I am a witness and I have rights. I refuse to answer."

The Court supported his position.

Evans, the attorney, attempted to make a closing statement to the court. "You have an individual die in a room, from a substance that was ingested in a room with only four persons present, if you count the baby. So the question is, did he [Daniel] take the substance himself? Did he get it from his mother? Or did he get it from Howard?"

The Court states: "What I am saying, there are certain questions that the court and the jury will ask: (A) Did he take it himself?; (B) Did he get it from one of the other occupants? If he took it, why take it? If it was accidental or intentional? If someone else gave it to him, were they intentionally or accidentally? . . . an inquest should be thorough."

Mr. Evans stated: "If the reason we are doing this is to be thorough either the police would carry out the investigations or we have to."

The Court replied, rather oddly, I thought, "What investigation?"

I appreciate the hard work and effort of these players in the

Bahamian inquest. But when you read the transcript, you feel like you are going back in time, to Samuel Beckett's *Waiting for Godot*. Two guys sitting on a park bench reflecting on the day. Is this the complete and thorough investigation into Daniel's death, this Bahamian inquest?

Nineteen

No More Closing Your Eyes

Let's now look at the testimony of pathologist Dr. Lee Hern at the inquest. The questioning began with the subject of the potent drug methadone.

Q. . . . if you can start with methadone and the levels you spoke to, sir.

A. The concentration of methadone that we found in the postmortem and perimortem blood are consistent with a fatal intoxication by methadone, especially in a person who is not a habitual user and lacks tolerance to the effects of methadone.

Q. What is [the] methadone drug used for?

A. A synthetic narcotic developed by the Germans in the Second World War as a painkiller, because they couldn't get morphine. It is much longer-acting than morphine. Otherwise its effects are identical to morphine.

Dr.Hern continued, "It [methadone] is a prescription medication. Under U.S. law it is what is called a schedule II substance, which is a high abuse potential, but valid medical use. It requires a doctor's prescription. Who is prescribing it has to have a license from the Drug Enforcement Administration, because it is so addictive you have to have a license to legally prescribe it. It is illegal to possess it without a valid prescription, and it is now prescribed for two general purposes. One, is for heroin addicts, to prevent them from needing heroin. It provides a long-acting relief from the cravings associated with heroin addiction, so they don't have to engage in criminal activity to get money. They are given it on a long-term period, and they don't get the high on it, if they should use it. In the last seven or eight years, methadone has been prescribed for pain relief as well; and probably more frequently. When we see it now, it is being issued as a pain medication as a narcotic just like morphine. . . .In the stomach, depending on the size of the pill, it comes in 5 milligram and 10 milligram pills, so we have a quantity in the stomach after, enough was absorbed to cause death, equivalent to 4 and 1/2, and little more than 2 pills; that, in addition to having a line concentration in the blood tells me that a lot was ingested."

Q. What do you have in mind?

A. It comes in 5 milligrams and we had 22 milligrams left in the stomach after he absorbed what killed him. That is 2 and 1/2 or 4 tablets at 5 milligrams. Two 10 milligrams would equal 20, and he had a little more than that. That is my basis for saying that after he absorbed enough to cause his death, he still had remaining in his stomach that amount of drugs.

Q. What would be the normal prescription for methadone for pain relief?

A. It varies. Generally 5 to 10 milligrams for a person who is not tolerant to it would be a sufficient dose to relieve pain. People who are addicted to it because of long term use can survive much larger dosage. They have a tolerance, and it doesn't act on them as strongly.

Q. Is it known in your work whether methadone is a drug which is abused as in the sense of being used for purposes other than being prescribed by a doctor for the mentioned purposes?

A. Yes, we are seeing more and more cases. In Miami, where methadone is being used, diverted from legitimate reasons, and taken to get a high, and because the people taking it are not tolerant to it they end up dying and coming into our office.

Recently, a Palm Beach pediatrician was indicted on three counts of first degree murder for prescribing painkillers to known drug addicts. The grand jury that heard the evidence decided that the doctor was legally liable for the deaths of these individuals. Police investigators in Florida concluded that a number of individuals have died from overdoses from oxycontin and methadone and anti-anxiety medicine. California Attorney General Jerry Brown charged Dr. Conrad Murray with homicide in the death of Michael Jackson, but with the lesser included offense under the statute of reckless disregard of human life, a charge that carries a maximum penalty of four years in jail. Here, the Florida authorities have put more chips into the pot. They charged the pediatrician with first degree murder. This is an area of the law that is evolving, but the skeleton is taking on more meat and we're beginning to see an enormous response by law enforcement, the media and the public.

There is no more willful blindness, no more closing your eyes to all that is around you. The leading legal authorities are stepping up and throwing charges at those responsible for violating the Hippocratic Oath, as well as the pill factories and the enablers. Everyone associated with the angels of death. Anybody who is in the chain of custody of those pills or drugs. The excuse that *I'm using a prescription that is drawn by a doctor* is lame.

The questioning of Dr. Hern continues, this time with the effects of methadone.

Q. Now sir, if any, what are the physical manifestations of methadone use . . . ?

A. First of all, they become very sedated. Their eyelids droop. At that stage it is what you call pinpoint pupils. That is what is reported. Their respiration slows and becomes more shallow, and they will, as their intoxication progresses, they would go to sleep, become comatose, their breathing becomes slower and slower, they are not getting enough oxygen, they begin to die. They stop breathing.

Q. It would have taken the pills within 2 to 3 hours before his death?

A. Yes.

Q. Does methadone use have any physical manifestations, in terms of any irritations on the body?

A. Irritations?

Q. In the sense of wanting to scratch oneself?

A. That is a phenomenon that is related to narcotics. It is oral histamine release. It is like a substance that manifests in allergies, so that when a person is under the influence of narcotics they would itch all over, and scratch themselves; yes.

Dr. Hern discussed the other drugs that were detected in Daniel's body, namely, Sertraline, Citalopram, Norcitalopram, Amitriptyline and Topiramate. "This is consistent with the therapeutic uses of the drugs," Dr. Hern told the inquest. These are very safe drugs. A toxic concentration would be much higher.

Q. . . . is there any significance to that finding of methadone metabolites?

A. Yes. That is because methadone produces so much tolerance over a period of time, it is recommended to look at the metabolite because if a person is depending, and taking over large doses they would build up more of the metabolites in their blood. In this case, we did not indicate any in the sample near the death and only a trace in the postmortem. *That tells me he was not a habitual user of methadone.*

Hern then stated "with a dose as large as what we have, leaving as much in his stomach after he died, he would become lethargic and go to sleep in a matter of 20 minutes, half an hour, and sleep would become deeper over a period of time." Dr. Hern stated unequivocally "clearly the methadone was the key to understanding his death. But for the methadone he would not have died."

Q. Can you say, sir, whether having regard to the quantity, ingestion would have been deliberate or accidental? Are you able to proffer an opinion in that regard, intentional as opposed to accidental?

A. One of ways that we attempt to arrive at such an opinion is based upon the amount in the stomach; and based on the amount in the stomach it indicates that this was not an attempt to get high. In other words, it would have been a smaller dose. I can't say with absolute certainty, but in high degree of probability it is intentional ingestion.

What does Hern's testimony really add up to? It's not worth a can of beans. All it tells you is that Daniel died from methadone, but you need to put that in context with the circumstances surrounding the death. Specifically, you need a real investigative team examining all the details surrounding his death. Was the methadone placed in his food or drink by a third party? Or did he intentionally take his own life? And there is no way one could draw a conclusion without hard evidence *and* Dr. Hern's testimony. You need both.

When you order in a Chinese restaurant, you take one from column A and one from column B. Here, however, we are missing column B. We have the toxicology report, we have some factors that raise red flags, but we need serious, highly trained investigators to examine this mystery. Maybe an imperfect crime was committed upon Daniel? When I read the transcript of the Bahamian inquest, I went through it with a fine tooth comb. This Bahamian court, they're polite, they're respectful to one another and to the witnesses, but they are feather dusting. They don't do the windows. Given the delays, this case was destined for the "Bahamian Triangle." It was a ship sinking with a lot of buried treasure and unknown tales to tell. The inquest consisted of jurors who would decide whether a crime has taken place. If they decided there was a crime, their recommendation would be sent to the Attorney General's office for possible criminal charges. But when you speak to ordinary Bahamians, they are suspicious of their Royal Bahamian Police Force, and have no faith in their work.

Q. Now, the other drugs you found in the system, other than the methadone, was there any significance to the interaction?

A. No, not in my opinion. The antidepressants don't interact strongly with the methadone and the amounts of those in his blood were not sufficient, even if they interacted with each other, to cause his death. They are very safe drugs.

Q. Is it usual to find that spread of [different] antidepressant medication to treat the self same condition?

A. It is common, in my experience, to see more than one, because they all work a little differently. So, it is common for a physician to prescribe one, and if it is not enough to alleviate the symptoms they may add on a second one, or even a third one. I've seen cases where that occurred.

261

Wouldn't it be helpful at this point to interview the doctors whom Danny was seeing? Wouldn't it be helpful to know if he had any prescriptions filled during this period of time? Also, someone should have visited the pharmacy to see if he actually filled those prescriptions. Wouldn't it be helpful to interview witnesses to see how he acquired these prescribed drugs? Maybe it would help us find out how the methadone was acquired. The how, where, why, who, what—a team of analysts trained in the smell and grit of an investigation would be able to bring everything to light. Where is Sherlock Holmes when you need him?

Q. Now methadone has been used sometimes when other painkillers would have proven ineffective?

A. It is more frequently now used as a substitute, because it is long acting. They used to give OxyContin, which is a time-release narcotic. OxyContin, because of a rash of overdoses and bad publicity it generated in the States, many pain specialists started giving methadone instead. That may or may not be a good idea.

The candle is burning and I am wearing glasses again. I have upgraded from my flea market version and, low and behold, Dr. Hern unknowingly agrees with me. He stated, "In order to determine whether or not a suicide has occurred, just the findings in the toxicology don't usually resolve that issue. *You need to look at other things like statements, behavior, things like that we don't have the luxury of having access to.*" Dr. Hern is diplomatic. I would have been more blunt. But we both reached the same conclusion: you can't solve this cold case with only a toxicologist.

Q. . . . could he have taken that without being aware?
A. Possible. It would have been bitter, but bitterness could have been camouflaged.

The *Tribune*, the most reliable gatherer of neutral, detached information in the Bahamas, reported that the coroner was dismissed, the coroner's inquest was cancelled, and, according to my interpretation, the inquest we just reviewed didn't take place until there was enough political pressure applied. In New York State, in part because of a scandal that was dubbed "Troopergate," past governors ordered an overhaul of the state police to insulate the agency from political interference. This is like separating a stripper from a pole. Politics permeate every organization, every agency. The United States Supreme Court manifests politics in some of its decisions; Gore *vs.* Bush is just one example. People come to their positions with preconceived ideas and notions and it's very difficult to sever that political bent from their decision process.

In an article about Troopergate that appeared in the March 1, 2010 edition of *The New York Times*, reporters Nicholas Confessore and Serge F. Kovaleski wrote, " . . . all police departments are to some degree political institutions, insular organizations accustomed to concealing their short comings and even wrongdoing." State senator Eric Adams—who was also a former captain in the New York City police department—said

" ... these guys [the state police] are put in precarious situations where they want to do their job, but at the same time are told to do things that are not within their duties." Senator Adams asks, "How can you say no to the person who your livelihood depends on? The top echelons of the department are political."

I agree with the assessments of many experts who analyze law enforcement. I'm not saying that there is outright corruption, or that there is a culture of deceit and fraud. But as a former legal adviser to the Sheriff's Office, I witnessed on a first-hand basis so many bad decisions that were based upon political considerations. The sheriff used to tell me that politics permeates every institution, but politics is good, politics is the art of getting things done. Michael A. L. Baloni, who was a top public safety aide to two former governors of New York State, with oversight of the state police, stated in the article, "I never saw a culture of corruption. I have seen bad judgment and mistakes."

Meanwhile, in the Bahamian inquest, there are more red flags flying than there were in Moscow at the height of the Cold War. What happened to the global media? Why didn't they ask for an open-to-the-media inquest? Even in America, we suffer from the power behind the curtain, the wizard that pulls the strings. We're still trying to get full details in the deaths of Marilyn Monroe and Elvis Presley. What happened to the old fashioned news reporters who would roll up their sleeves, get a good reading light, put on a soft pair of shoes, hit the pavement and get all sides of the story, with no prior agenda but to seek the truth?

Granted, sometimes there is no conclusion. Sometimes there is just not enough evidence to persuade a jury. Remember, this is not a movie, where you need a result at the end; this is real life. There were two suspicious deaths within a few months of one another. There were some common denominators, but too many unanswered questions. When I sit on a park bench feeding the pigeons, I take pride in the fact that I tried to find out the truth.

The original coroner authorized Anna Nicole's Bahamian lawyer to hire Dr. Cyril Wecht as a private pathologist to perform a second autopsy on Daniel's body. Dr. Wecht concluded it was a drug related death of an accidental nature.

On page 54 of Dr. Wecht's book, *The Question of Murder*, he says, "The toxicology and histological results came back, allowing me to advise Dr. Raju to term Daniel's official manner of death an *accident*. National Medical Services lab, which has more sophisticated testing than was available to the Bahamian Coroner, found a total of seven prescriptions drugs in Daniel's body." Dr. Wecht goes on to say, "the methadone was at a relatively high level for someone unaccustomed to taking the drug, although we really don't know what his experience was with that medicine. The Lexapro was at a high therapeutic level and the Zoloft somewhat higher, in the toxic, but non-lethal range. But again, it was the combination of these three drugs that caused the problem."

Dr. Wecht's conclusion is completely contrary to that of Dr. Hern, who was hired by the Bahamian authorities to perform the pathology tests. Both these doctors, like Broward County's Dr. Perper, are among the most highly respected medical examiners in the world. But both doctors, as much as I respect them, are concluding accidental death by overdose without having the other half of the puzzle. The other half would be a thorough investigation into the circumstances surrounding the deaths. You need to know what's behind door number one—what drugs, if any, caused the deaths—and what's behind door number two— what motives, what witnesses and what other factors would lead to accidental vs. intentional death.

TWENTY

THE NEW EPIDEMIC

The Anna Nicole Smith case revealed to the world the problem of stars, hangers-on, enablers, multiple doctors writing multiple prescriptions, fictitious names, and pharmacies providing excessive drugs. What's to be done about it?

In California, Attorney General Jerry Brown was able to implement voluntary policies to combat prescription drug addicts who visit multiple doctors for prescriptions. Brown said, "We have so much [drugs] moving on the streets and we have so much moving in doctor suites, and we have to attack both." As a result, a new secure website has been established to monitor prescription drug use. Doctors can log on and analyze what other prescriptions their patients are utilizing. Law enforcement will review the site to spot any type of drug abuse.

Brown pointed out, "Somebody died here," referring to Anna Nicole Smith's death from a drug overdose. "People think those drug dealers on the street corner are the only threat. People in white smocks in pharmacies and with their medical degrees are a growing threat."

In the United States, around thirty-eight states have some system to monitor prescription drug use. Many other states are responding to provide doctors and pharmacists with quick internet access to patient prescription drug histories in order to reduce doctor shopping and other pharmaceutical abuses. But prescription monitoring in the United States is still in the Dark Ages. It can take health professionals weeks to obtain information on drug use by patients. This delay can allow some patients to get large quantities of drugs from multiple doctors for personal use or sale.

Could it be any more ironic that Florida's Broward County, the county where Anna Nicole died, has become the pain killer capital of the United States? Just recently, three pain clinics were raided in neighboring Palm Beach County. These clinics brought in $14 million in cash in one year. Florida's Gold Coast—so named because of the vast wealth of its residents and consisting of Miami, Fort Lauderdale (Broward) and Palm Beach County— houses hundreds of pain killer clinics.

According to Broward County Sheriff Al Lamberti, "It's a business of great cash. This is worse than the cocaine cowboy days and the marijuana days." Hollywood (Florida) police captain Alan Siegel added that "Broward County has become the Columbia for pharmaceutically diverted drugs. We're supplying everywhere." And to compound the problem, according to Mark Trouville, special agent in charge of the Drug Enforcement Agency (DEA) in Miami, "just 45 South Florida doctors dispensed nearly 9 million pills of oxycodone." According to the DEA, Broward County is home to thirty-three of the fifty doctors who dispense the most oxycodone in the United States.

My law enforcement friends support the view that Florida

should have a prescription drug database to allow doctors, pharmacists and police to monitor for doctor shopping. I believe we should take it many steps further. I am urging Congress and the President of the United States to establish a *national* registry, whereby there is an instant computerized database of the real names of patients and what prescription drugs they possess. All of my doctor friends, all the pharmacies that I have visited are in favor of this program, because, in effect, it safeguards the law-abiding dispensers of drugs. Certainly, ninety-nine percent of the doctors and pharmacists in the country are legitimate, hard working citizens. There are only a few rotten apples in the barrel. Unfortunately, many laws have to be created to attack the evil-doer, the exploiter, and above all, the enabler/murderer.

Of course, some will argue that we are invading the right of privacy of the individuals who would be targeted by such laws. But, in controlling any human activity, we have to find a balance between regulations and freedom. And people believe, as Anna Nicole did, that a *prescription* legitimizes their overconsumption. They use their prescriptions as a shield and justification. I take them because a *doctor* prescribed them. It's a poor and weak rationalization for their addiction and need for drugs.

NBC's *Today* show recently recognized that the entertainment scene has become the nucleus of a prescription drug ring. Actors and celebrities who are using stolen prescription pads or buying off doctors at a rate of $30,000-$50,000 a month are a "new epidemic." For a special investigative report that aired on *Today*, a former Hollywood actor went undercover to visit a doctor's office to get prescriptions. He left the office with a bag filled with pharmaceutical samples and prescription slips for several medications, all completed and signed by the doctor in question. And all of this with *no physical examination* conducted by the doctor. The transaction was so easy, the undercover decoy said, "it was almost like buying a pizza."

Jimi Hendrix, Janis Joplin, Elvis Presley, John Phillips, Heath Ledger, and Brittany Murphy—the list goes on. The sheer volume of drugs administered, prescribed to and ingested by Anna Nicole and Michael Jackson shocked the ordinary citizens of America.

These doctors are feeding on greed, selling their power as medical doctors for a brush with fame. And, in turn, these celebrities are getting any prescription they want, with no questions asked. What makes it more frightening, and more frustrating, is that as a result of a legal loophole, the police and many law enforcement agencies are having a difficult time proving that these greedy, star struck doctors are showing malice and gross negligence when they freely prescribe "suicide cocktails" to Hollywood's rich and famous.

This prescription drug epidemic reaches beyond the glitz and glamor of show business. It has a very tight grip on our military personnel. In an article that appeared in the March 16, 2010 edition of *USA Today*, the Pentagon health office stated that in 2009 its military doctors wrote nearly 3.8 million painkiller prescriptions for members of the U.S. armed services. This was more than four times the number of prescriptions given to service men and women nearly a decade ago, in 2001.

"One in four soldiers admitted abusing prescribed drugs, mostly pain relievers. . . fifteen percent said they had abused

drugs in the 30 days before the [Pentagon] survey [in 2008]," the article added. Assistant Army Secretary Thomas Lamont told *USA Today* that the Pentagon is going to take steps to control this growing problem in the military by establishing a multiservice task force, whose goal is to "outline how to limit prescription medication use and ensure that Army hospitals all use the same procedure for dispensing medicine."

I believe that my six-day ordeal, which was televised globally, served its purpose as a warning to the world of the dangers of prescription drug addiction and the ease with which these drugs can be obtained. We in law enforcement know that publicity really gets the attention of those in charge. When a food critic walks into a restaurant, the kitchen will do everything in its power to make sure the meal is cooked properly. Jerry Brown served two terms as California's governor, and he is a heavyweight in understanding the political makeup and structure of the government. This extremely talented individual has brought great change to the laws and great improvements to the court system in California. The charging document that his office drew up against Howard K. Stern, Doctor Sandeep Kapoor and Doctor Khristine Erosevich speaks for itself.

Superior Court of the state of California
for the county of Los Angeles

The People of the state of California

vs

Sandeep Kapoor d/o/b 5/20/68
Khristine Erosevich d/o/b 11/08/47
Howard Kevin Stern d/o/b 11/29/68

The undersigned is informed and believes that:

Count 1   On or between September 11, 2006 and February 8, 2007, in the county of Los Angeles, the crime of conspiracy to commit a crime . . . a felony, was committed by the above mentioned . . . commit the crimes of PRESCRIBING, ADMINISTERING, AND DISPENSING CONTROLLED SUBSTANCES TO AN ADDICT, . . . unlawfully prescribing a controlled substance . . .

Jerry Brown jumped into action. Prosecutors filed charges not only to prevent those charged from committing further wrongful acts, but also to chill the rest of society from partaking in these illegal activities. But California had no jurisdiction over the death of Anna Nicole Smith, no jurisdiction over whether or not to file homicide charges against any individuals for the reckless conduct that led to her death. That jurisdiction lies exclusively in the hands of the Broward prosecutor. But the Broward prosecutor's hands are tied. A Mack truck is holding him back from filing any criminal charges. Because the medical examiner who would be the prosecutor's key witness in any homicide trial has declared that this was an accidental overdose.

Brown stated in no ambiguous terms, "What we have in this case is a conspiracy among three individuals." Brown said of Stern and doctors Kapoor and Erosevich, that the trio was being charged in total with 23 felonies for their roles in the lead up to Anna Nicole Smith's drug induced death, that this was done knowingly, and with tragic consequences. Brown referred to Stern as the "principal enabler" and stated the lawyer "funneled highly addictive drugs to Ms. Smith; we're not talking a few dozen, we're talking hundreds and hundreds of pills. The law's been violated, it's a conspiracy, this is bad business."

Brown criticized the two doctors charged for having "violated their ethical obligations as physicians. . .these three individuals repeatedly and excessively furnished thousands of prescription pills to Anna Nicole Smith, often for no legitimate medical purpose." He added that "doctors are licensed to avoid those pressures. . .probing into motives is always a speculative undertaking, but certainly there is a . . . gain here to be part of the celebrity glitz and glamor. . . these people were caught up with being in a relationship with and being around Anna Nicole Smith . . . . This is serious stuff. Our goal is to prepare the evidence as well as possible. Now it's up to the district attorney and his discretion to handle it the best way possible."

Neil McCabe, Virgie Arthur's attorney, said in reference to the charging documents that, "as always Virgie wants justice for the death of her daughter and her grandson."

Twenty-One

Full Circle

We have a second home in Middleburg, Pennsylvania, which is a farm town. My daughter Dax and her cousin Raya spend part of the summer there learning to horseback ride at a camp, the R.E.D. Farm, whose owner volunteers her time and horses for the specially challenged. Abigail too wants to improve the quality of life for one child at a time.

I spend my days walking to little towns, visiting quaint bookstores and antique shops, always on the hunt for good food. In Mifflinburg, the owner of a little antique store brought a book to my attention. *The Addiction of Mary Todd Lincoln* by Anne E. Beidler, she felt, illuminated many similarities to Anna Nicole Smith's case.

In the introduction, Beidler writes, "The destruction began in Mary Todd Lincoln, wife of Abraham, long before she became our nation's first lady. You probably know a Mary Todd Lincoln. A person in pain. A person in pain who goes to the Doctor and then goes home and takes the prescribed medication whenever necessary to relieve the pain. And at first it works wonderfully. After a while, however, the dosage must be increased. And increased again."

I read that first paragraph and I reflected on the history of our country, that prescribed medicine leading to addiction has been with us almost from the beginning. And we have a duty to ameliorate the proliferation of these drugs. Through our collective consciousness and active participation, we can cause our governing bodies in this country, and throughout the world, to specify that a certain conduct is prohibited and to provide the resources to regulate and enforce those laws.

Beidler says that the doctors of Mrs. Lincoln's era were prescribing morphine for pain. "At first both doctors and patients called this new form of opium the wonder drug. . . . It was not long however before they began to call morphine the demon drug . . . over a century ago . . . many other men and women . . . , were victims of a devastating American epidemic, drug addiction."

It's amazing that back in the 1870s, this problem was evident. Beidler states "all these opiates were available from the doctor himself (many doctors had their own drug cupboards), from the druggist by prescription (the prescription could be renewed indefinitely, and pharmacists often delivered), over the counter in patent medicines (many people could not afford to see a doctor), and by mail (which was cheap and handy for rural America)."

A more recent First Lady, as a result of her emergence from drug abuse and alcoholism, established and lent her name to the clinic where Virgie Arthur took Anna Nicole to get help with her drug dependency problem: the internationally famous Betty Ford Clinic. One of my favorite American presidents was Ulysses S. Grant, whom I first read about when I was a student in the 6th grade. I went to the adult library for his biography, and my Father

Dave was upset that I got the adult version of his life story, because it was replete with stories of his drunken days, especially when he commanded the Union Army during the Civil War.

But now there are forces in motion. Our good society is responding to the drug epidemic. We started with Elvis Presley back in the 1970s, when his "Doctor Nick" was charged, but was found not guilty by a jury. Some 30 years later, the three parties in the Anna Nicole Smith case are charged with felonies. In between, there were many celebrity deaths, but the coverage of Anna Nicole's case wasn't confined to newspapers. It was blasted all over the world. You could not avoid it. It repulsed Americans everywhere to see a pregnant woman with these duffle bags of drugs. She entered the Hard Rock Casino, couldn't even stand up, never left the room and died in bed in her own feces in room 607.

Then we have Michael Jackson, what I call "Anna Nicole II," who died under some similar circumstances: overprescribed medication, drugs in other people's names, enablers, and the abuse of potent and dangerous drugs—in Jackson's case, propophyl— that should have been administered only in a hospital setting. Michael Jackson's case raised the price of admission. This defendant, Dr. Conrad Murray, was charged with a form of murder. . .involuntary manslaughter. Now, we see—with the doctor in Palm Beach county who was charged with first degree murder for prescribing prescription drugs to known addicts—that the price for admission or wrong doing by these medical professionals is murder 1, the ultimate price for the taking of someone else's life. The penalty for that is life in prison, or in some states, the death penalty.

We have come full circle. Once, we closed our eyes and allowed the consumption of massive quantities of prescribed drugs by our stars with no criminal liability to those involved. Now we've reached the other end of the spectrum and, in some areas of this country, are reaching for the full power of the court, the ultimate sentence.

Twenty-Two

The Apple of My Eye

At some point the thought occurs to most parents that they may predecease their children. Who takes care of Jack and Jill if both parents suddenly die? I had my first and only child at the ripe old age of fifty. I wonder sometimes if I will be with my daughter Dax through all her important phases of life? Will Belinda and I be on this planet when she graduates high school? When she attends college? If and when she gives birth to her first child? The sudden death of Anna Nicole Smith illuminated how important it is for parents to make provisions for their minor children.

When the mother and father simultaneously pass away, minor children can be swimming against the current. I know many parents who, when they travel without their children, will not travel together. These parents are educated, have dough and if a plane goes down, for example, they want one parent alive to care for the children.

In Anna Nicole's case, there was a period of time when her surviving child was in limbo. Howard K. Stern had physical custody of Dannielynn and, for all intents and purposes, acted as the father. But there was a major question of who should really care for Dannielynn. Anna Nicole, when she was physically and mentally well enough, could have created documents appointing a caretaker or guardian for Dannielynn. Of course, at the end of the day, those documents would have been trumped by the biological father. Subsequently, this did occur, and Larry Birkhead was proven through paternity tests to be the father. But what would have happened if the actual father never did come forward? At that point, Howard K. Stern would have been the father because his name was on the birth certificate in the Bahamas.

I was a late bloomer. I had a child when I had almost no hair left. And when I finish this book, I plan to visit one of my fine lawyers to update documents that appoint a guardian or individual who will care for, supervise and raise the apple of my eye. You can appoint a separate, independent person to manage your assets and income for your loved one. With all the criticism thrown at Michael Jackson notwithstanding, he had the foresight to appoint his mother and Diana Ross as the successor guardian. Children are not chattel or property. They are the most important thing on the face of the earth for parents, their next of kin, their blood. Sometimes I say that Dax is my twin.

One time, I was in a restaurant in L.A., and a producer was recruiting me to host a TV show. We had dinner upstairs in a private dining room and the only other customers were Danny DeVito and his wife Rhea Perlman, along with their small entourage. After dinner, I walked over with Dax to Danny's table, and I said to him, "Do you remember the movie *Twins*? I always say to Dax, you are my twin." Danny turned to my daughter and asked her, "What is your response to *Twins*?" Dax replied, "I'm not bald like my father." Danny and Rhea and the rest of the people at their table had a laugh, and we left. Then my agent ran back upstairs to thank Danny for being so gracious to the judge and his family. And Danny slaps his hand on his head, like he did thousands of times in *Taxi*, and said, "I knew it was him," and Rhea said, "I knew it was the judge."

This is an essential and necessary subject to discuss with your significant other. But thinking won't make it so. As depressing as it is, parents must specify in writing who will be in charge of their loved ones in case of premature death. They must sign this document and review and update it on a regular basis.

We have contracts to purchase a car, to sell a house, contracts with partners and for business investments. For anything significant in life and business, we have documents to indicate the essential terms of the agreement. How can we not have documents to specify the terms of our children's welfare? I don't intend to be a pitchman for the probate lawyers of the world, but I think their business should increase dramatically.

TWENTY-THREE

MONDAY MORNING QUARTERBACKS

Since the six-day Anna Nicole Smith trial concluded in February 2007, many of my fellow judges and lawyers, along with many media outlets, have commented on how I conducted myself in court during the trial. Many of those comments were positive.

Fox News senior judicial analyst Judge Andrew Napolitano, for example, said, "Judge Larry Seidlin's behavior in a courtroom without a jury is perfectly normal." Judge Napolitano told Foxnews.com that needling the attorneys and acting folksy weren't out of the ordinary in a non-jury hearing.

Judge Napolitano went on to say, "It was natural that the lay person would be shocked by Seidlin's words and actions, because judges act differently in front of juries—and in fictional dramas on TV and in the movies. But appellate courts and attorneys are used to bawdy bench behavior like Seidlin's. People are saying, my God, this guy is a clown. It's a circus or a zoo in there. And I'm saying no it's not. That's who he is. He's very down to earth ... there's no right or wrong here ... it's a little bit shocking, but when there is no jury, judges frequently let down their guard. We're not seeing anything unethical."

Judge Napolitano disagreed with those who said that I was callous. "I don't find him to be insensitive. He is the way judges are in the courtroom. He has said unusual things, but not so unusual that they would make me question his thinking or believability."

I thought that lawyer Tom Mesereau's comments about one of his own cases applied perfectly to my conduct in the Anna Nicole case. "I thought we were winning all along. But the media reported the very opposite. And, of course, jealous, shallow legal pundits had a field day criticizing my performance. To them, God help any lawyer who engaged in unconventional trial behavior. Such hearsay merited capital punishment."

Christopher Francescani, editorial producer of ABC News' Law and Justice Unit, sent me the following note: "I think the most telling moment of the Anna Nicole Smith hearing came last night when it was over—when, after days of diffusing all these bickering parties, they walked out hand in hand! You have been a cult hero in this case—a common judge with an uncommon touch for taking the fight out of wounded, angry people. Others have called this a circus, a spectacle, but it seemed to me to be genuinely human experience—one that certainly drew you in, heart and head."

The dust has settled. The following interviews with well known legal professionals whose judgment I trust and respect were conducted February/March, 2010. They give you, the reader and juror, a more complete picture of some of the issues.

Yale Galanter is a criminal defense attorney based in Miami, Florida and Aspen, Colorado. Galanter initially wanted to become a professional golfer, but he studied law and worked as a state prosecutor under former U.S. Attorney General Janet Reno. He is best known for representing O.J. Simpson since 2000.

Judge Larry: In the death of Anna Nicole Smith in Broward County, why was someone not charged with homicide?

Galanter: Well, I think nobody was charged with homicide because I don't think the medical examiner's office was looking at it as a homicide. I think they were looking at an overdose. I don't think they had enough facts to develop a homicide case.

Judge Larry: Is it your belief that the medical examiner, Dr. Perper, when he stated in my courtroom that it was an overdose—an accidental overdose of drugs—did that tie the state attorney's arms?

Galanter: Well, I don't think that when Dr. Perper gave that opinion, that he had enough information or had done a thorough enough investigation. That's really the problem. I mean, you know, because when the M.E. gives an opinion, most of the time they have tunnel vision. They autopsy the body, but they don't look at any of the underlying facts and they don't direct the police department to investigate the underlying facts. And I think if that would have been done, that Howard may have been charged.

Judge Larry: Dr. Perper may have been premature in his conclusions on the cause of her death?

Galanter: He was definitely premature in that he ruled it an accidental overdose without looking at any of the underlying facts, what they call lifestyle facts.

There's no doubt about that, because subsequent information would tell us that Howard and her doctors were all enabling her. Somebody gave her too much medicine, and somebody was either negligent or criminally liable. So it was definitely not an accidental overdose. There was more to it.

Judge Larry: And what charge do you think would fit the facts?

Galanter: I think definitely one of the manslaughter charges. I don't think any of the intentional homicide charges can fit. You know, I mean, it could be any of the reckless, willful, wanton, homicide charges that we have in Florida could definitely fit.

Judge Larry: And who would have been slammed with that charge?

Galanter: Well, it depends. I mean, it depends on how far the state attorney's office wanted to go. You know, but definitely Howard because he was involved, and possibly one of her other physicians.

Judge Larry: And can the state attorney still open up the case?

Galanter: I don't think they can open it now, because I think California already leveled charges.

Judge Larry: They leveled charges. They had jurisdiction against Stern and the two doctors. They charged them with enabling, with giving drugs to a known addict.

Galanter: Right. I don't think Broward County would recharge. I don't think that would happen.

Judge Larry: Well, Broward County has the jurisdiction . . .

Galanter: Larry, it's not a jurisdictional issue. It's a criminal issue. I mean, criminally speaking, you know, prosecutors will not take two shots. In California they decided to do that, so I think that usurps Florida. I mean, technically, they can do it, but just as a matter of manpower and money, they're not going to do it.

Judge Larry: And what else? Tell me more.

Galanter: I mean, Anna Nicole's death was an incredible tragedy. You know, you were the perfect judge to decide these issues. Look what you got. I mean, you had loved ones fighting over where to bury the body. . . . you were in court for like a whole week on that one issue. It was just a tragedy all the way around. The fact that her son predeceased her. The fact that the people who loved her, ostensibly cared about her, didn't care enough about her to say, listen, you need rehabilitation or you need help or you need treatment. You know, just the fact that they let this go, and they couldn't say no to her is a tragedy.

Judge Larry: Give me the highlights of your career.

Galanter: The highlight of my career is—honestly, you are going to think this is very corny. But the highlight of my career is that I've always considered myself to be a loyal, devoted son to my parents, a great husband to my wife, and try to be a caring, responsible lawyer to all of my clients.

Judge Larry: And what are some of the highlight cases you've had?

Galanter: Well, you know, of course I represented O.J.

287

Simpson. I'm currently representing Charlie and Brook Sheen. You know, I was involved with Michael Jackson for a while. I mean, I've certainly had my share of celebrities along the way. But, my real claim to fame is the fact that I just really enjoy helping people who are in trouble. Because people who come to me have problems. And I'm fortunate enough to have the skills to be able to help them.

Judge Larry: Why do you feel I was the perfect judge for the Anna Nicole case?

Galanter: Because you are—you know—you are beyond the technical law. You're very good at figuring out the whole picture and what's going on. You don't look at the minutia, and that's why lawyers always liked practicing in front of you because it's not always black and white. You get a good handle on things. You spend the time, and then you make a decision, it might not be a decision that everybody agrees with, but at least you make a decision that you truly believe is the right decision. And a lot of judges don't do that, Larry. You know, you should be commended for that.

* * *

Thomas Mesereau, Jr. is a criminal defense lawyer who successfully defended Michael Jackson against charges of child abuse. In November 2005, Mesereau was chosen by Barbara Walters as one of the 10 most fascinating people of 2005.

Judge Larry: In the death of Anna Nicole, why in Broward

County was someone not charged with homicide?

Mesereau: Nobody was charged with homicide because I don't think the M.E.'s office looked at this as a homicide. I think they were looking at it as an overdose. I don't think they had enough facts to call it a homicide case.

Judge Larry: So it's your belief the M.E., Dr. Perper, when he stated in my courtroom it was an overdose—an accidental overdose in drugs—did that tie the state attorney's arms?

Mesereau: Well. I don't think that he had enough information or had done enough of an investigation.

Judge Larry: No one charged in Broward County about Anna Nicole's death?

Mesereau: I'm not a member of the Florida Bar, and I have not been involved in the case. But I have to assume that in a situation like this, any prosecutor is going to pause because the medications were prescribed by physicians, and a prosecutor knows that one of the first things the defense is going to say is that, we were just the messenger, and we picked it up at the pharmacy, and we delivered it to the patient. It was the doctor who prescribed it. We don't prescribe medications; we don't know much about medications; we know nothing about how they interact with one another; we know nothing about what quantities are appropriate, and if a doctor prescribes a certain medication we have to assume like almost everyone else, that the doctor knows what they are doing. Don't point a finger at us; point a finger at the doctor. And because of that fact, I think that any prosecutor is going to be a little hesitant to go after someone who appears to be just the delivery person.

Judge Larry: And did you know that Dr. Perper is our Broward County Medical Examiner?

Mesereau: I do know he is, yes.

Judge Larry: And he came out and said that Anna Nicole's death was through accidental overdose. Would that also hamper the prosecutor's decision?

Mesereau: I think it would have to because, you know any crime requires a certain mental state, a certain form of intent. In law school, you learn about general intent and specific intent, but regardless what term you use, it does require one to have a criminal state of mind to be guilty of almost any crime. And the problem here is that a doctor prescribes the medication, presumably a pharmacy then at the doctor's request prepares the medication, and someone like Mr. Stern, I assume, will take the position he simply delivered it. And I also think Mr. Stern will say why aren't you going after the pharmacy if they made the medications? Why are they less culpable than I am for simply picking it up and delivering it? And that is a problem because doctors with medical licenses who are presumably experienced and trained in the prescription of medications sanctioned it. And they basically said do it. So that's going to cause a problem, because you got to prove a case beyond a reasonable doubt. You got to prove there was criminal intent. It's not like purchasing drugs from a non-legal source on the street. Then you know it's wrong. But if you're getting them from a physician who told the pharmacy to prepare them and you're simply delivering them, you know, are you guilty of a crime? That's the question.

Judge Larry: Do you think that Dr. Perper was premature in announcing immediately that it was an accidental overdose?

Mesereau: . . . I assume he just did what he thought was right. He looked at the facts as they were presented to him and came to his own conclusion. . . . He's obviously a very distinguished pathologist with tremendous experience. Did he look at enough evidence to come to that conclusion? I don't know. Did he simply look at the report [toxicology]? Did he look at some of the underlying documents that went into making the report? Did he actually look at Anna Nicole? I don't know.

Judge Larry: Wouldn't he need to examine the witnesses around Anna Nicole and the evidence around Anna Nicole to determine whether it's accidental or somebody may be causing the death of Anna Nicole?

Mesereau: I would think so. I would think before you can say something is an accident as opposed to something that's intentional, you do have to know what witnesses were doing and who were at the scene, what their intentions were with Anna Nicole . . . I think there's a lot more to look at, not just an autopsy report.

Judge Larry: Based upon your experience, and you are one of the finest lawyers in the United States, what do you think is going to happen to Howard K. Stern?

Mesereau: You know, I really don't know. I haven't been to any of the court proceedings and I haven't looked at the evidence. I have to assume that the prosecutors think there's a lot more to what he did than simply delivering a package. I think they looked at his history with Anna Nicole. I think they looked at what exactly he gave her and why. I think they looked at his behavior when she was apparently under the influence of medication. I do recall turning on the television and seeing him videotaping her when she appeared to be acting very strangely. I think they probably thoroughly investigated it. I have to assume they looked thoroughly at how packages of medications he was picking up and from what sources. I think they probably investigated as to whether or not he was involved in prescription drugs allegedly being prescribed in someone else's name. I don't know the facts, but I would have to assume that the Los Angeles County district attorney's office and the Attorney General's office looked into all these issues.

Judge Larry: Do you think my trial set the precedent where other stars would now begin to be examined concerning the enablers, the prescriptions, the drugs, the doctors and the pharmacies? Do you think I opened up the door? It was my case and the Michael Jackson case also, and when I was on the major networks, I called Michael Jackson's death "Anna Nicole II." Did I open up the door to the California Attorney General to start looking at this stuff?

Mesereau: I think the facts that your hearing was televised and all these issues were examined, at times very emotionally, definitely made other law enforcement agencies think carefully about whether or not this is criminal conduct. But remember, the physician who was prescribing Elvis Presley inordinate amounts of medication was charged with manslaughter and acquitted years ago. So juries, in my opinion, don't like to convict doctors unless there's a tremendous pattern of abuse and criminal conduct. And I do think your hearing did make the world think a lot more carefully about, you know, who should be responsible. And these enormous amounts of medications are being prescribed to an addict. I do believe that.

Judge Larry: Have you ever seen enablers, doctors or pharmacies connected to stars be criminally charged?

Mesereau: Again, Elvis Presley's doctor was charged with manslaughter and defended by an outstanding criminal defense lawyer in Tennessee, James Neal. Even though there was proof that Elvis was being prescribed an enormous quantity of medications that probably had a lot to do with his demise. Again, I wasn't in the case. I wasn't in the courtroom. I didn't see the evidence as it was being unfolded and examined. But I do believe that the medical doctor prescribes medication to someone, most of the public wants to believe that that's appropriate. Now if the doctor committed malpractice, maybe that belongs in a civil trial, maybe it belongs in an administrative hearing on his license. But I think a lot of people are reluctant to bring it to [the] level of a crime. But that may be changing because of Michael Jackson, because of Anna Nicole Smith. Because we are now seeing almost an epidemic of young entertainers are dying because of prescription drug abuse.

I then got into the subject of the media coverage of Michael

Jackson.

Mesereau: . . . An acquittal was going to end the story for them and they [the media] did everything they could to spin a guilty verdict, and having been in the middle of a hurricane like that, you know, I'm very skeptical of the media in general.

So when I see the media spinning Anna Nicole, or spinning some other case a certain way, I'm a little bit skeptical because I've been in the middle of, I think, the worst media onslaught probably ever in a criminal trial.

* * *

Don Clark is a former FBI agent who reached the highest pinnacles of power and authority in that agency, and who formerly worked for the O'Quinn Law Firm on behalf of their client Virgie Arthur.

Judge Larry: Are there any statements that you are willing to go on the record with concerning the death of Anna Nicole and Danny?
Don Clark: No confidence with the Judiciary in the Bahamas for their inquest. Danny, he was a kid that never took drugs. He was upset with his mom Anna Nicole because she was involved in drug use. Here is a kid that was healthy and he was in the hospital, but it had nothing to do with drugs [stomach ailment]. As far as I know, he never had a drug problem,

no drugs at all. Danny, many of the family and friends that knew him well, said he was disgusted with his mother doing drugs. I am saying that justice was not served in the Bahamas regarding the death of Danny. Who killed Danny? I can't say a hundred percent who killed Daniel. There is evidence in the American courts that her live-in Howard K. Stern contributed to her drug use.

Howard K. Stern picked Danny up at the airport. He brings him to the hospital. This kid is joyous, excited to see his newborn sister. So the concept is he is healthy, he gets there and goes to the hospital to see his sister, he is excited to see his mom and yet a few hours after midnight, he is dead. This makes no sense to any decent legal enforcement body. That this is a kid with no record of drug use and had total disdain for anyone using drugs. Just the two of them from the airport to the hospital.

From my sitting in the inquest in the Bahamas for over a year, it appears that Danny's consumptions of a large quantity of drugs [methadone] came through food and drink at the hospital. This food and drink at the inquest showed Howard K. Stern bought it in the grocery store and purchased the food and drinks. It stands to reason that the person that procured the food and drinks and brings it to the hospital and presents it to the person who was eating it and drinking it in the hospital. This is the same person that said he controlled Anna Nicole's prescription drugs.

The Bahamas fails to do an in depth investigation into how these drugs got into Danny's body. They also committed a grave error in getting rid of their crime scene. They never talked to the store. Not detailed enough to find who put the drugs in the food and the drinks. The inquest actually said he died of a possible accident or overdose; it was not suicide. Both police agencies, the Bahamas and the Seminole Police Department, were inept. They didn't want negative publicity. Dr. Perper ruled it was an accidental overdose based on an autopsy without the benefit of the surrounding facts.

I can't read Stern's mind, but it would appear, it could have been a plot to get rid of Daniel and subsequently to get rid of Anna, that leaves the baby who has a guardian and the baby would inherit the Marshall estate.

* * *

Richard Milstein is a prominent Miami lawyer and civic activist, whom I appointed guardian ad litem for Anna Nicole's daughter, Dannielynn, during the trial. I've spoken to Milstein many times subsequent to the trial.

Judge Larry: What was your impression of the will Anna signed?

Milstein: The will is badly or poorly drafted. The will did not protect Anna Nicole because it disinherits future children. Normally that paragraph is included for a man who may have had a child out of wedlock.

Milstein has a more elegant appreciation for the King's English than I do. This clause would be for a Tiger Woods or any man who has a large appetite for women. And is sexually active and has a large wallet, too.

Milstein: It is an odd situation for a woman like Anna Nicole, because a woman knows when she has a baby, because she is carrying the baby, now a man may not know, maybe like Senator John Edwards, and that is open for debate. Therefore, when you read the phraseology in the will it's just strange. Of course there is an exception; if a woman was an egg donor at some point, then there would be some reason to have a statement like that.

Judge Larry: Did Anna Nicole want to have the Bahamas as her domicile?

Milstein: In the video that I witnessed, there's a question whether she is on drugs or not; therefore, the issue of her domicile, whether she wants to remain in the Bahamas or not, is clouded. But from interviewing witnesses inside and outside the courtroom, I believe she wanted to be out of the limelight and her actual intent was to remain in the Bahamas. Even though there is conflicting testimony and Anna Nicole's personal thinking on this issue may have not been clear. But she made a decision to have a house in the Bahamas and I believe the privacy issue and having enough limelight, she wanted privacy. Additionally, she bought a plot and that was where Danny was buried, in the plot next door.

Judge Larry: Richard, as you know I had no jurisdiction over Danny's body, no authority to exhume Danny's body. This would have taken time and money which we had no luxury of during our trial. On February 5, 2010, knowing what you know now, where would you bury Anna Nicole's body today?

Milstein: The same place.

Judge Larry: Did Howard K. Stern, through reckless conduct, kill Anna Nicole?

Milstein: I just think Howard K. Stern was an enabler. She had lots of people around that were enablers and most stars surround themselves with enablers. I spoke to him outside the court and inside the court and had telephone conversations with him. I think he loved her and was infatuated with her. My analogy is Joe DiMaggio and Marilyn Monroe; no matter what she did, he was there for her.

Judge Larry: How do you feel about the fact that I appointed you to the Anna Nicole case?

Milstein: What I liked about the case was the fact that I had to use my wits. There were no pleadings. I knew nothing about Anna Nicole, nothing about any of the parties, no reality TV, no personal matters about her.

Judge Larry: Were you pleased that the Appellate Court affirmed my decision?

Milstein: The Appellate Court ultimately affirmed your decision through looking at Anna Nicole's intent, which we covered thoroughly.

Judge Larry: I made you do everything. We even requested that you go to the Bahamas.

Milstein: I was glad that I managed her burial.

Judge Larry: Have you had any conversations with the parties subsequent to the trial?

Milstein: After the trial, I had a conversation with all three parties. I told them to respect the court's decision. I believe all three—Stern, Birkhead and Virgie—loved Anna Nicole in different ways; each one loved her in their own way.

* * *

Sue Brown is a distinguished family trial lawyer who represented Larry Birkhead for the family matters in Florida.

Judge Larry: We covered the waterfront in this case. We tried to examine all the issues related to Anna Nicole and Dannielynn, would you say?

Brown: Yes. Yes. You definitely were trying to do the right thing for the baby.

Judge Larry: The x-rays, there was media attention concerning x-rays that were found in the building that I reside in. Do you ever recall x-rays being admitted into the trial?

Brown: No. Actually not. *Obviously, somebody planted that.* That's what it sounds like to me.

Judge Larry: When you say planted, was there someone just trying to get themselves in the media, or was it a plan to place negative publicity upon me?

Brown: I guess so. Plus, how do we even know they were her x-rays and not somebody else's?

Judge Larry: I called up the administrative clerk of the probate division, and I said to her, were there any x-rays admitted into the trial? And she said "absolutely not."

Brown: Her medical records had nothing to do with the issues that you heard.

Judge Larry: Do you have any regrets?

Brown: I only wish the court would have been able to have jurisdiction over the baby. That would have short-circuited a lot of matters.

Judge Larry: Why would you have wanted Judge Larry to have the issues of Dannielynn?

Brown: I think you would have figured out a way to order the DNA test, and it might have short-circuited a lot, even if it got reversed, they would have needed some extraordinary writ, but it would have short-circuited a lot of trouble in the Bahamas.

Judge Larry: How long did it take for the DNA testing? How long did it actually take after you left my courtroom?

Brown: I was in your courtroom in February and I think it got resolved, if I remember correctly, in mid April.

Judge Larry: Even though my style was a little bit out of the box, do you find the way I run a courtroom to be effective?

Brown: It certainly was effective. That was one of my few experiences with you, but it certainly was effective. I had a few others after, but it was effective.

Judge Larry: I somehow get to the bottom line in an expedited fashion?

Brown: Yes. You certainly got to the bottom line on that one, and you got upheld on appeal.

Judge Larry: Have you had any contact with your client since?

Brown: I've seen him [Birkhead] since. I went to the baby's birthday party, but it's been a while now. He's got his own life now.

Judge Larry: You went to the little girl's birthday party?

Brown: Yes. Her first birthday party, yes.

Judge Larry: Was it nice and was it in Los Angeles?

Brown: No. It was in Kentucky.

Judge Larry: You had fun over there? And the little girl looked good?

Brown: Oh, she looks just like her mother. She was beautiful.

Judge Larry: Does she seem to be prospering, the little girl, living a good life?

Brown: Yes. Yes. And it's a happy, happy. A very, very happy ending, I think.

Judge Larry: Tell me about that happy ending?

Brown: Well, here you are dealing with the father and all the hoops he had to jump through, and the whole jurisdiction thing, clearly troubles me. I just had another case where there were jurisdictional issues, and I thought of that one [Anna Nicole], the way someone can move and really throw the cog in the wheel, so to speak.

Judge Larry: Who threw the cog in the wheel?

Brown: I'd rather not say. For Anna, initially I believe. I don't want to place any blame. I ended up liking Howard at the end. I don't want to say anything negative.

* * *

Neil C. McCabe was a full time law professor for nearly twenty years before joining the O'Quinn Law Firm. McCabe has appeared as a legal expert on many television and radio broadcasts, in the print media, and on worldwide webcasts. I immediately developed a respect and admiration for him. I told him if he was in my courtroom in the old days, I would nickname him the professor.

Judge Larry: Virgie has a right to visitation as a grandparent?
Professor: In California, a grandparent such as Virgie has a right to go and petition for that. But we're positioned right now in such a way with the defamation that promulgated against Virgie. [The O'Quinn Law Firm represents Virgie Arthur in a lawsuit she brought against Howard K. Stern, his sister Bonnie Stern, Larry Birkhead and other parties, claiming defamatory statements and a conspiracy to defame her with the intention of injuring her reputation.] We think we need to bring the lawsuit that we brought and vindicate her reputation before we go to a family court and try and get, over Birkhead's objection, some kind of visitation rights with the child.
Judge Larry: How does she afford to pay you?
Professor: We're on a contingency fee basis, Judge. She's not paying me. The idea is that whatever recovery down the road, we'll take a percentage of that. Originally, when John [O'Quinn] was in your court, trying to help Virgie, he was doing it on a pro bono basis. But then later came out with

a defamation case against various people, and we could sign up Virgie on a contingency basis. So that's the basis we're operating on now. We're footing the bill with the hope of a future recovery.

Judge Larry: Does Birkhead have any money?

Professor: Oh yeah. He has testified in a preliminary hearing in the criminal case in California against Stern and the doctors, that he's made a couple of million dollars for trotting this baby out in front of the media.

Judge Larry: Does Virgie, on a personal note, does she miss not seeing Dannielynn?

Professor: Of course she does. You know, she's got other grandchildren. She loves her grandchildren. I think she's raising one of them right now. And yes, of course, she misses Dannielynn. Dannielynn is going to get older. At some point, she's going to make her own decision about what relationship she has to have with her grandmother, and Birkhead won't have anything to say about it.

Judge Larry: Tell me the relationship between Birkhead and Stern?

Professor: They're on good terms, apparently. Birkhead appeared in the preliminary hearing in California on the criminal case against Stern, and from what I can tell from the reported testimony, he did whatever he could to help Stern rather than help the prosecution. The prosecution was the one who called Birkhead to the stand, and as a matter of fact, the report was that Birkhead and the prosecution got kind of crosswise at more than one point. So I think they're working together. Birkhead has been interviewed publicly saying that whatever Stern tried to do to him before, it's water under the bridge. They publicly portrayed themselves as working together for the benefit of the baby.

Judge Larry: What was your opinion of the Bahamian inquest?

Professor: I was there at the inquest every day. So was Virgie and so was our investigative strategist Don Clark. And we had counsel hired in the Bahamas being active in the inquest, spent a lot of money, and we think it was a pretty unfair proceeding in the end. They would not even let the jury decide whether it was a homicide, Judge. But we liked the fact they wouldn't let the jury decide whether it was a suicide. But if that's the trade off, then we have to just have accidental death when nothing to indicate to me this boy ingested the stuff, the methadone that killed him, willfully. And, you know, Judge, he did die of a massive overdose of methadone. The rest of the drugs in his system had no part in his death.

Judge Larry: Tell me about Birkhead's testimony at the inquest.

Professor: They have the testimony of Birkhead, and it shows how he changes his testimony. He says oh, I don't remember telling the police what I told them about watching Anna Nicole and Stern do drugs together. By that time, they're clearly working together instead of against each other.

Judge Larry: What was your impression of the testimony of Dr. Hern, the toxicologist from Miami?

Professor: Dr. Hern, who said the boy died from a massive administration of methadone, [which was] enough to kill more than one person, and he was not a methadone user. There were no metabolites in his system.

Judge Larry: Who hired Dr. Hern?

Professor: The Bahamian authorities asked him to come in. We had nothing to do with that whatsoever. We were there and we heard his testimony.

Judge Larry: As you recall in my courtroom, Stern said that Daniel said to him, why am I so tired?

Professor: That's telling testimony actually against Stern a lot of the time. If he is knowingly taking methadone, why is he asking why he's so tired?

Judge Larry: Was that line on your radar screen also?

Professor: Yes. Not at the time, because I did not know I would be involved in the case in your court. I was only brought—John O'Quinn said that the judge is about to come out and rule against us, so get over here.

Judge Larry: It's too bad you didn't come. I had a nickname for you already . . . You would have been "the Professor."

Professor: They do call me that. We were in court the other day arguing on another case and one of the lawyers referred to me as Professor. He was telling the judge, I know more than you do.

Judge Larry: Tell me about Texas [O'Quinn].

Professor: I loved the guy. And you know what, I look out my window right now and I can see the scene of the accident everyday and to me, the best thing is, he didn't ask me to go with him that day. I was supposed to be there. He said, no, you have too much work to do back at the office, you stay. And I wound up going and taking care of the matter later after it [the accident] was done. It was a bad accident.

Judge Larry: O'Quinn, was he a heavy hitter in Texas?

Professor: He was one of the most successful trial lawyers in all of Texas history. He was one of the five lawyers who represented the state of Texas against the tobacco companies.

Judge Larry: What was the result?

Professor: Those five lawyers split amongst them $33 billion in fees and that was coming in every year as an annuity.

Judge Larry: You took Virgie's case. That wasn't a money maker. You guys spent so much time and money on that.

Professor: It was not a money maker. John [O'Quinn] took that with the concept it's pro bono, and that included not just representing her in your court and the appeal from that. We hired outside counsel to do the appeal, obviously to oversee it, but we ended up as Florida counsel and then, in the Bahamas too. That's me and Don Clark and Virgie, and usually her husband or another relative and then the Bahamian lawyers and they're very expensive. We were there for a long time, off and on. We didn't expect any money out of any of that. We just did it.

Judge Larry: How many days did you spend in the Bahamas?

Professor: I got to say, Judge, I just can't tell you. We were there, then and again, over, you know, months. Because they dismiss it or take recesses and they come back, and they work around everybody's schedules, so we were there a lot. I'd love to be in the Bahamas just having fun. But we were working, sitting in the little un-airconditioned courtroom. I'm not happy with the outcome, for a variety of reasons.

Judge Larry: Tell me about Anna's death.

Professor: I will say that the view of the California authorities, prosecuting him has been made clear in court, that they believe that Stern is certainly responsible for providing Anna Nicole Smith with drugs that led to her death. So in that sense, they seem to be taking the position publicly; that they believe Stern's responsible for that.

Judge Larry: What about Daniel's death?

Professor: They [California] haven't taken a position on Daniel, because obviously, that's not something that they have focused on. We took the position in the Bahamas on behalf of Virgie, that we believed that Stern was involved; that we cannot believe that Daniel knowingly took a massive overdose of methadone; and therefore, we pursued a course of inquiry that he could have unknowingly ingested the drug because it was dissolved in a sweet drink, and we elicited testimony, counsel and I, that the boy could have unknowingly ingested the drug, dissolved in a sweet drink and Dr. Hern, from Miami, on the stand, agreed that that was a possibility.

Judge Larry: What was Stern's motive?

Professor: Let's see. Suppose that the—just suppose that—what's his name, the private eye in California that the boy talked to before going to the Bahamas. Let's suppose that what he has said is true. That the boy was concerned about Stern's influence over his mother, and he went. . .and the boy went to the Bahamas trying to get his mother to come back to the States instead of hiding out from Birkhead in the Bahamas. He may see that as threatening. It seems incredible for me. But let's put it another way. The baby's been born. Stern is engineering it so that on the birth certificate he's going to appear as the father. In the Bahamas, that's pretty much it. You know, you're the father. Especially since he's cohabitating with the mother, and other factors, and if they're going to put on a fake marriage ceremony, well, that's a third factor. So he, then, can pose as the father. They stay in the Bahamas because the boy doesn't get to talk his mother into coming home. They're insulated from Birkhead; that is their plan. They're doing everything in the meantime to try to defame Birkhead, you know. And therefore, Stern keeps control of the baby. And if you have control of the baby, you have a shot at the Marshall money that they're suing over in California. And Stern had a six percent interest off the top, before expenses, in whatever recovery there was, and Anna Nicole sued against Pierce Marshall.

Judge Larry: And the motive—his motive for Anna Nicole's death?

Professor: Well, one theory, and I'm not saying it's not it, I'm not saying it's fact. The one theory is that Anna Nicole was accusing Howard of being responsible for her son's death. Am I making this up? No. It's in the record in Stern *versus* Cosby. Two witnesses, Paul and Patrick, friends and hangers-on of Anna Nicole, both testified that before the funeral of Daniel and at the funeral of Daniel, Anna Nicole was accusing

Howard of being responsible for the death of Daniel, to which Howard responded with silence. Now, you remember the maxim, *qui tacet consenti're*—"silence is consent." If you do not protest in the face of an accusation, it's the same as admitting it. It's a great scene in *A Man For All Seasons*, where Thomas More makes that point. *Qui tacet consenti're*. So it got Anna Nicole accusing Howard publicly of being responsible for her son's death and you have an inquest coming up.

* * *

Shane Kelley is a distinguished attorney, who concentrates his practice in probate, trust, and guardianship and litigation. As in the trial, I have Shane as my clean up hitter.

Judge Larry: Does Anna Nicole's estate have an opportunity to have this heard by the Supreme Court of the United States?

Kelley: The Supreme Court is usually interested in issues that have national significance. It is unusual for the Supreme Court to accept jurisdiction of a case simply to determine whether an appellate court acted properly based on the specific facts of the case.

Judge Larry: You knew this question was coming. What's the likelihood of Anna Nicole's estate prevailing and Dannielynn ultimately receiving part of Howard Marshall's estate?

Kelley: I believe that there are issues that are important enough that still remain in the case, which may convince the

Supreme Court to once again accept jurisdiction.

Judge Larry: If the Supreme Court accepts jurisdiction, and I understand that it is a rare instance, when they do accept jurisdiction, and what's the odds of Anna Nicole's estate winning?

Kelley: If the Supreme Court does accept jurisdiction, the remaining issues are subject to valid arguments by both sides, *that it would be a coin toss as to how this case is resolved.*

Here you have one of the most brilliant minds in probate law. And, just like in Las Vegas, a roulette table, or a pair of dice will decide the issue. Doesn't this case reflect Anna Nicole's lifestyle of always being on the edge? Everything she did was a gamble and even her legal proceeding is a crap shoot. Dannielynn still has the opportunity of receiving a huge portion of the Marshall estate.

TWENTY-FOUR

WHAT I NOW KNOW TO BE THE TRUTH

The Anna Nicole Smith trial had an enormous impact on everyone involved, including law enforcement and its measures towards enablers, pharmacies, doctors and any other individuals that may have conducted themselves recklessly. Michael Jackson was really Anna Nicole II in many respects and this messy affair has implications for all celebrities, not to mention everyday citizens.

The message is clear: overdosing on drugs may not be an exclusive and sole act by the addict. Sometimes those addicts—whether celebrity or private citizen—have the devil's workers around them, contributing directly to their demise.

Based upon my research and analysis, I believe that Anna Nicole went to the Bahamas to avoid the paternity contest in California. It's possible that her transaction with her friend G. Ben Thompson and Ford Shelley might have been a sham, that she did not own that house and the money was lent to her by Ford Shelley and his family. This would cause her residency to *not* meet the requirements of Bahamian law, and I don't believe her intent was to make the Bahamas her home. I think that she was just too affected by drugs, that her mind could not form a legal intent to where she wanted to live.

She buried her son Daniel in the Bahamas under the same clouded circumstances. Her anxiety, her state of mind, and the drugs did not allow her to form a healthy impression of what to do with Daniel's body. We needed more time, but time was no friend to my court, especially while Anna Nicole's body was decaying at a rapid pace. Remember that Anna Nicole treasured her beauty and wanted to be with her son. But when you look at this case slowly and dwell on the facts, what connection does Danny have to the Bahamas? What bond, if any, exists between him and that foreign land? He was on the island for just a few hours, and the evidence indicates that his goal was to return Anna Nicole, his mother, back to Los Angeles. Therefore, Anna Nicole's intentions, if they were actually hers, were just a subterfuge to remain legally sealed off from one of her lovers and the father of her child, Larry Birkhead.

If I had one wish, if I had a single regret—to answer the question I asked Virgie on a previous occasion—that regret would be that I didn't have jurisdiction over Daniel. I don't like messing with bodies, but justice would have been better served. And justice still would be better served if someone with the financial wherewithal and legal standing now exhumes both bodies and brings them home.

Clearly, Anna Nicole's home and Daniel's home was on American soil. And there is an equitable argument to be made for those two bodies to be buried, together, in either Texas or California. I might be inclined, if I was sitting on the bench, to place their bodies in her home state of Texas. Anna Nicole and

312

Daniel have a right to be surrounded by their friends and family, and Dannielynn should be able to visit them.

I understand that those two gravesites have very few, if any, family and friends visiting, and it would be sensible to accommodate the living with convenient access to the gravesite. Let's bring them home! They were warriors, these two. Anna Nicole fought to make a mark in show business, and Daniel, who loved and idolized his mother, fought to get her off drugs.

Based on my interviews with top law enforcement officials, I believe that there should be a new and complete investigation into Daniel's death in the Bahamas and Anna Nicoles's death in Broward County, Florida.

All sources and witnesses state that Daniel came to the Bahamas in the evening and died during that night. He was enthusiastic to see both his mother and his new baby sister. I can't find anyone who said that Daniel had any form of drug problem, and all evidence points to the fact that he was against the drugs, even prescription drugs, that his mother was taking. Look at the time line from his arrival in the Bahamas to his death just a few hours later.

I believe that God, in his ultimate wisdom, has put us on this earth in an imperfect state. We all suffer with certain weaknesses. Celebrities and high profile dignitaries, those who often enjoy the most, sometimes also suffer the most, because their life is played out in the media for all the world to see. Every day for them is a reality TV show.

Many world leaders have admitted bad judgment based upon facts that came their way *after* the decision was made. But every decision can be reviewed under the evening sun. Most, if not all, of us make decisions while stimuli are coming at us like bullets out of a machine gun. You make the best decision you can, based upon the facts and evidence that are in front of you. It's ironic that some of our so-called experts thought I took too much time with my folksy monologues, but it was my custom, that was the pattern of how I conducted business in my courtroom for three decades. How much more time would we have needed to make the perfect decision? It's interesting to note that two weeks later, or two months later, it still would have brought us to the same conclusion.

This case, like a good French wine, needed time to ferment. It needed time to pull all the pieces of this labyrinth together. And oddly, the pieces still keep coming together. I'm still being contacted by "Deep Throats," experts in law enforcement who want to tell their tale, who want the truth to come out at all costs. I find it astounding that these people, who have no pecuniary or personal gain to achieve, just want to do it for the sake of pure justice.

I would like to be a movie producer for you, my reader and my juror, but I can't tidy up the package. There are still loose ends and I have a deadline with my publisher, just as I had in the trial, an artificial and arbitrary end. But I still need more time. I am not ducking the bullets. I think I bit quite a number along the way, but I don't know how much more time it will take, how much more evidence I need to see, before I come to a heavenly conclusion. Therefore, I am comfortable, as I was in my courtroom, to conclude with what I now know to be the truth.

And let the chips fall where they may.

The tragic death of Anna Nicole Smith and her son Daniel is a story that won't go away. It will haunt us until we get the answers, until mother and son find peace, at rest, at home.

APPENDIX A

I was an adjunct professor at our local university, and the students enjoyed my presentation of cases. I was known for being able to get to the essence of a complex matter and explain it so that people could understand it. I want to get to the essence of the news that came off the court wires on March 19, 2010, regarding Anna Nicole's interest in J. Howard Marshall's estate.

Circuit Judge Beezer wrote an excellent opinion consisting of thirty-two pages of deep legal analysis. That's where we'll start. For you, my reader and juror, I will, as usual, quote the pertinent parts of the opinion and then dissect them.

In Re: Vickie Marshall. Debtor

Elaine T. Marshall, Executrix of the Estate of E. Pierce Marshall, Plaintiff-Counter-Defendant/Appellant-Cross-Appellee.

v.

Howard K. Stern, Executor of the Estate of Vickie Lynn Marshall, Defendant-Counter-Claimant/Appelle-Cross-Appellant.

Nos. 02-56002, 02-56067

United States Court of Appeals, Ninth Circuit.

Filed March 19, 2010

Before: Robert R. Beezer, Andrew J. Kleinfeld and Richard A. Paez, Circuit Judges.

Opinion by Judge Beezer, Concurrence by Judge Kleinfeld.

Notice first that Howard K. Stern is the executor of the estate of Anna Nicole. And second, that this case has been languishing in the probate and bankruptcy divisions for a very long time. The attorney's fees for this case, I would bet, are in the millions and millions of dollars. Oddly enough, this case has outlived both J. Howard Marshall, and his son, E. Pierce Marshall, who was one of the primary moving parties.

Judge Beezer in his written opinion states: "This case involves a tort claim by Vickie Lynn Marshall against E. Pierce Marshall, the son of her late husband J. Howard Marshall II, for Pierce Marshall's purported interference with a substantial inter vivos gift (estimated to exceed $300,000,000) that her late husband intended to give to her. The claim comes to us in an unusual procedural posture. It was asserted as a state law counter claim to a nondischargeability complaint and proof of claim that Pierce Marshall filed in Vickie Lynn Marshall's bankruptcy proceedings in the Central District of California. Both the bankruptcy and district courts found that Pierce Marshall was liable for tortious interference and awarded Vickie Lynn Marshall millions of dollars in compensatory and punitive damages.

"While Vickie Lynn Marshall's tortious interference claim was pending in federal court in California, a probate court in

Texas was administering the estate of J. Howard Marshall II. Both Vickie Lynn Marshall and Pierce Marshall were actively engaged in this Texas litigation, participating fully in the five month jury trial held by the Texas probate court. To discern J. Howard Marshall II's true intentions regarding his will and assets held in trust, the Texas probate court had to resolve allegations that J. Howard Marshall II's estate plan and the transactions underlining it were tainted by illegality and that, contrary to his estate plan, J. Howard Marshall II intended to give Vickie Lynn Marshall a substantial inter vivos gift. In its judgment, which was issued after the bankruptcy courts judgment on Vickie Lynn Marshall's tortious interference claim but before the district court had adjudicated the appeal from the bankruptcy court, the Texas probate court upheld the validity of J. Howard Marshall's estate plan and estate planning documents, finding that J. Howard knowingly effected his estate plan free from the undue influence or coercion of his son Pierce Marshall. The Texas probate court further found that J. Howard Marshall II did not intend to give Vickie Lynn Marshall a gift from the assets that passed through his will or that were held in his living trust. These and other legal and factual determinations adverse to Vickie Lynn Marshall would be fatal to her tortious interference counterclaim, should they be afforded preclusive effect in this proceeding."

Probate court and guardianship are assignments given to senior judges. These cases can become very complicated and have a tortuous avenue of legal options, especially when there is a lot of money at stake. The body is dead and the parties are out for blood and money. Basically, what happened here is that

319

the Texas probate court, located in Houston, had a thorough jury trial concerning certain specified issues. Once these issues were resolved, and I'm going to review them for you, then these issues don't need to be litigated again (res judicata).

In the law, you don't get two bites of the apple in front of two separate courts. If you are displeased with the lower court ruling, your option is to appeal. Here we had two parallel tracks taking place. Many of the issues being litigated in the Texas probate court were also being duplicated in the California bankruptcy court.

We are disappointed that at this point, Dannielynn got a big goose egg in the Howard Marshall estate. And you may be wondering, why didn't some trial judge who presides in his chambers, someone with a bald head and dark complexion, for example, get out his easel and start to put numbers on that chalkboard and say "My friends, we are going to cut a deal today. We are going to give x number of dollars to the Anna Nicole estate and we are going to give y number of dollars to the Marshall estate."

Why are we going through this dance? Why are we spending all this time and money? One of the parties will pipe up and say it's principle. I say it's money. I know it's money and you know it's money, and if it was their money they would settle it. But they are working on someone else's money. But I know first hand—and you watched me first hand—try to mediate and try to settle, and you don't come away with the best bar poll ratings for trying to settle these cases early. Basically, you are taking food off somebody's table.

320   Judges should be proactive. That's what the statutes now state.

The law encourages judges to try to resolve these cases early. But it takes a heavy will and strong physical endurance for a court to truly embrace this technique. I would turn to the parties in a probate case, the folks directly affected by the distribution of the wealth, and tell them you can have the money in an hour or we can litigate this for the next few years. Then I would watch their mouths begin to water. I would look at my clock, that big round clock that sat in the back of my chambers, and if it said 10 a.m., I would turn to the lawyers with the parties present and say if we can resolve this case right now, can some checks be cut by noon? I knew the answer, because good trial lawyers only ask questions in an open court that they know the answer to. Boy, would I slice the fat off that corned beef sandwich.

But some cases are impossible to resolve, where the issues and the parties are just too diametrically opposed, where there is either black or white and no shades of grey, or where the administrator fees or attorney fees become the 600-pound gorilla in the room. The side issue of fees can dwarf the main cause of action. And there is just so much tail that you can kick. With all the power and prestige that the president of the United States wields, there are rogue nations that can't be tamed. In court, there are irrational parties or emotional parties that can't be toned down.

So that, my reader and juror, is the condensed version of this opinion. Next we'll look at the way Judge Beezer, himself a seasoned jurist, describes Anna Nicole, Howard Marshall, and the facts and circumstances surrounding their lives. His is a fascinating take, which he knows will be read by both legal scholars and the average Joe. The judge places a large human touch on this case. Here are the highlights.

"As detailed by the district court, J. Howard Marshall II was a self made entrepreneur who eventually found great success in the oil industry. Born in 1905, J. Howard Marshall II attended Haverford College and graduated Magna Cum Laude from Yale Law School before working during the 1930s for the Roosevelt administration on the proration of the oil industry. After continued involvement in the oil industry, J. Howard Marshall II became one of the founders of the Great Northern Oil and Gas Company in 1954. The wealth of the Marshall family is primarily based on the interests acquired by J. Howard Marshall II in Great Northern Capital Oil and Gas, which was the predecessor company to Koch Industries. In 1982, as an estate planning mechanism to reduce (or avoid) the cost of probate, J. Howard Marshall II placed almost all of his assets (including his interest in Marshall Associates, the family partnership that then held the Koch stock) in a revocable inter vivos trust, known as the J. Howard Marshall II living trust, or the living trust. From 1982 until his death, J. Howard Marshall II executed a series of amended and restated instruments governing the terms of the living trust.

"At the time J. Howard Marshall II met Vickie Lynn Marshall, essentially all his assets were held by the living trust. ... Marshall II modified his living trust for the last time on July 13, 1994, just a few days after his marriage. On that date, J. Howard Marshall II made the living trust irrevocable.

"J. Howard Marshall II met Vickie Lynn (Smith) Marshall in October 1991. At the time, Vickie Lynn was a 24 year old divorcee and single mother living in Houston, Texas. She worked as a waitress and dancer to provide for her son, but she aspired to become an international superstar like her idol Marilyn Monroe."

Judge Beezer continues: "After a courtship lasting more than two years, J. Howard Marshall II and Vickie Lynn Marshall married on June 27, 1994.

"Their union was short lived. J. Howard Marshall II died on August 4, 1995, of heart failure at the age of 90. Although he lavished gifts and significant sums of money on Vickie Lynn Marshall during their courtship and marriage, J. Howard Marshall II did not devise any real or personal property to her in his will, nor was a provision for distribution of income or principle of the living trust ever made in her favor. Similarly, J. Howard Marshall II did not give Vickie Lynn Marshall any interest in his business assets or stock holdings."

And here is an interesting part: "On March 7, 2001, the Texas jury returned its verdict. The jury unanimously answered a number of special verdict questions, making the following factual findings. 1. The living trust and will were valid and had not been forged or altered; 2. J. Howard Marshall II had not been the victim of fraud or undue influence; 3. He had the requisite mental capacity when he executed his living trust and will; and 4. He did not have an agreement with Vickie Lynn Marshall that he would give her one half of all his property. . . . Accordingly, the Texas probate entered judgment in favor of Pierce Marshall on all claims and held that Pierce Marshall was entitled to his inheritance, free from all claims by Vickie Marshall . . . "

My reader, this state decision by the Texas probate court trumped the federal court cases that had ruled in favor of Anna Nicole.

I don't believe we've heard the last of this probate case. There are issues that are ripe for appeal; there will be a rehearing before the federal appellate court "en banc" (in which all the appellate judges in that court may preside). If Anna Nicole's estate loses there, they will then appeal to the U.S. Supreme Court. As you can see, this case is far from over. As I said previously in open court, the wheels of justice are square, not round, and justice thus moves very slowly.

I believe that the three primary parties in my case—Howard K. Stern, Larry Birkhead and Virgie Arthur—will once again hold hands. Maybe not physically, but perhaps spiritually for this appeal, because I believe they would all be rooting for Dannielynn to receive some slice of the enormous estate of J. Howard Marshall. These three may not see eye to eye on many of the issues surrounding the deaths of Anna Nicole and Daniel, but they all have a clear and abiding commitment to make certain that Dannielynn enjoys what her mother fought so hard to achieve.

APPENDIX B

ORIGINAL
FILED
LOS ANGELES SUPERIOR COURT

SEP 2 3 2009

JOHN A. CLARKE, EXECUTIVE OFFICER/CLERK
_____, DEPUTY
G. ARMENTA

SUPERIOR COURT OF THE STATE OF CALIFORNIA

FOR THE COUNTY OF LOS ANGELES

THE PEOPLE OF THE STATE OF CALIFORNIA,

Plaintiff,

v.

01 SANDEEP KAPOOR (05/20/1968),
02 KHRISTINE EROSHEVICH (11/08/1947), and
03 HOWARD KEVIN STERN (11/29/1968)

Defendant(s).

CASE NO. BA353907

2ⁿᵈ AMENDED
FELONY COMPLAINT

The undersigned is informed and believes that:

COUNT 1

On or between September 11, 2006 and February 8, 2007, in the County of Los Angeles, the crime of CONSPIRACY TO COMMIT A CRIME, in violation of PENAL CODE SECTION 182(a)(1), a Felony, was committed by SANDEEP KAPOOR, KHRISTINE EROSHEVICH and HOWARD KEVIN STERN, who did unlawfully conspire together and with another person and persons whose identity is unknown to commit the crimes of PRESCRIBING, ADMINISTERING, AND DISPENSING CONTROLLED SUBSTANCES TO AN ADDICT, in violation of Section 11156(a) of the Health and Safety Code; UNLAWFULLY PRESCRIBING A CONTROLLED SUBSTANCE, in violation of Section 11153(a) of the Health and Safety Code; OBTAINING A CONTROLLED SUBSTANCE BY FRAUD, DECEIT, OR MISREPRESENTATION, in violation of Section 11173(a) & (b) of the Health and Safety Code; OBTAINING A CONTROLLED SUBSTANCE BY FALSE NAME OR ADDRESS, in violation of Section 11174 of the Health and Safety Code; ISSUING A PRESCRIPTION THAT IS FALSE OR FICTITIOUS, in violation of Section 11157 of the Health and Safety Code, and REPEATEDLY AND EXCESSSIVELY PRESCRIBING, FURNISHING, DISPENSING, OR ADMINISTERING DRUGS TO ANNA NICOLE SMITH, in violation of Section 725(a) of the Business and Professions Code, that pursuant to and for the purpose of carrying out the objectives and purposes of the aforesaid conspiracy, the said defendants committed the following overt act and acts at and in the County of Los Angeles: See Attached.

* * * * *

327

COUNT 2

On or between June 9, 2004 and September 10, 2006, in the County of Los Angeles, the crime of CONSPIRACY TO COMMIT A CRIME, in violation of PENAL CODE SECTION 182(a)(1), a Felony, was committed by SANDEEP KAPOOR and HOWARD KEVIN STERN, who did unlawfully conspire together and with another person and persons whose identity is unknown to commit the crime of PRESCRIBING, ADMINISTERING, AND DISPENSING A CONTROLLED SUBSTANCE TO AN ADDICT, in violation of Section 11156(a) of the Health and Safety Code; UNLAWFULLY PRESCRIBING A CONTROLLED SUBSTANCE, in violation of Section 11153(a) of the Health and Safety Code; PRESCRIBING, ADMINISTERING, DISPENSING, OR FURNISHING A CONTROLLED SUBSTANCE TO A PERSON NOT UNDER SANDEEP KAPOOR'S TREATMENT, in violation of Section 11154 (a)& (b) of the Health and Safety Code; OBTAINING A CONTROLLED SUBSTANCE BY FRAUD, DECEIT, OR MISREPRESENTATION, in violation of Section 11173(a) & (b) of the Health and Safety Code; OBTAINING A CONTROLLED SUBSTANCE BY FALSE NAME OR ADDRESS, in violation of Section 11174 of Health and Safety Code; ISSUING A PRESCRIPTION THAT IS FALSE OF FICTITIOUS, in violation of Section 11157 of the Health and Safety Code; AND REPEATEDLY AND EXCESSIVELY PRESCRIBING, FURNISHING, DISPENSING, OR ADMINISTERING DRUGS TO ANNA NICOLE SMITH in violation of Section 725(a) of the Business and Professions Code, that pursuant to and for the purpose of carrying out the objectives and purposes of the aforesaid conspiracy, the said defendants committed the following overt act and acts at and in the County of Los Angeles: See Attached.

* * * * *

COUNT 3

On or between June 5, 2004 and September 10, 2006, in the County of Los Angeles, the crime of CONSPIRACY TO COMMIT A CRIME, in violation of PENAL CODE SECTION 182(a)(1), a Felony, was committed by KHRISTINE EROSHEVICH and HOWARD KEVIN STERN, who did unlawfully conspire together and with another person and persons whose identity is unknown to commit the crime of PRESCRIBING, ADMINISTERING, AND DISPENSING A CONTROLLED SUBSTANCE TO AN ADDICT, in violation of Section 11156(a) of the Health and Safety Code; UNLAWFULLY PRESCRIBING A CONTROLLED SUBSTANCE, in violation of Section 11153(a) of the Health and Safety Code; PRESCRIBING, ADMINISTERING, DISPENSING, OR FURNISHING A CONTROLLED SUBSTANCE TO A PERSON NOT UNDER KHRISTINE EROSHEVICH'S TREATMENT, in violation of Section 11154 (a) & (b) of the Health and Safety Code; OBTAINING A CONTROLLED SUBSTANCE BY FRAUD, DECEIT, OR MISREPRESENTATION, in violation of Section 11173(a) & (b) of the Health and Safety Code; OBTAINING A CONTROLLED SUBSTANCE BY FALSE NAME OR ADDRESS, in violation of Section 11174 of Health and Safety Code; ISSUING A PRESCRIPTION THAT IS FALSE OF FICTITIOUS, in violation of Section 11157 of the Health and Safety Code; AND REPEATEDLY AND EXCESSIVELY PRESCRIBING, FURNISHING, DISPENSING, OR ADMINISTERING DRUGS TO ANNA NICOLE SMITH in violation of Section 725(a) of the Business and Professions Code, that pursuant to and for the purpose of carrying out the objectives and purposes of the aforesaid conspiracy, the said defendants committed the following overt act and acts at and in the County of Los Angeles: See Attached.

* * * * *

COUNT 4

On or between June 9, 2004 and September 22, 2006, in the County of Los Angeles, the crime of UNLAWFULLY PRESCRIBING A CONTROLLED SUBSTANCE, in violation of Section 11153(a), of the Health and Safety Code a Felony, was committed by SANDEEP KAPOOR and HOWARD KEVIN STERN, who did unlawfully issue a prescription for a controlled substance, to wit: AMBIEN, HYDROMORPHONE, DILAUDID, CLONAZEPAM, METHADONE, AND XANAX.

* * * * *

COUNT 5

On or between June 5, 2004 and January 26, 2007, in the County of Los Angeles, the crime of UNLAWFULLY PRESCRIBING A CONTROLLED SUBSTANCE, in violation of Section 11153(a), of the Health and Safety Code a Felony, was committed by KHRISTINE EROSHEVICH and HOWARD KEVIN STERN, who did unlawfully issue a prescription for a controlled substance, to wit: AMBIEN, CLONAZEPAN, DIAZEPAM, HYDROCODONE, PROMETHAZINE WITH CODEINE, CHLORALHYDRATE, et al.

* * * * *

COUNT 6

On or between August 18, 2006 and September 22, 2006, in the County of Los Angeles, the crime of OBTAINING A PRESCRIPTION FOR OPIATES BY FRAUD, DECEIT, OR MISREPRESENTATION, in violation of Section 11173(a) of the Health and Safety Code a Felony, was committed by SANDEEP KAPOOR and HOWARD KEVIN STERN, who did unlawfully obtain and attempt to obtain a controlled substance, to wit: OPIATES and did procure and attempt to procure the administration of and prescription for said controlled substance by fraud, deceit and misrepresentation .

* * * * *

COUNT 7

On or between October 17, 2006 and November 24, 2006, in the County of Los Angeles, the crime of OBTAINING A PRESCRIPTION FOR OPIATES BY FRAUD, DECEIT, OR MISREPRESENTATION, in violation of Section 11173(a) of the Health and Safety Code a Felony, was committed by KHRISTINE EROSHEVICH and HOWARD KEVIN STERN, who did unlawfully obtain and attempt to obtain a controlled substance, to wit: OPIATES
and did procure and attempt to procure the administration of and prescription for said controlled substance by fraud, deceit and misrepresentation .

* * * * *

COUNT 8

On or between August 18, 2006 and September 22, 2006, in the County of Los Angeles, the crime of OBTAINING A PRESCRIPTION FOR OPIATES BY GIVING A FALSE NAME OR ADDRESS, in violation of 11174 of the Health and Safety Code, a Felony, was committed by SANDEEP KAPOOR and HOWARD KEVIN STERN, who did unlawfully obtain and attempt to obtain a controlled substance, to wit: OPIATES and did procure and attempt to procure the administration of and prescription for said controlled substance by fraud, deceit and misrepresentation .

* * * * *

COUNT 9

On or between October 17, 2006 and November 24, 2006, in the County of Los Angeles, the crime of OBTAINING A PRESCRIPTION FOR OPIATES BY GIVING A FALSE NAME OR ADDRESS, in violation of 11174 of the Health and Safety Code, a Felony, was committed by KHRISTINE EROSHEVICH and HOWARD KEVIN STERN, who did unlawfully obtain and attempt to obtain a controlled substance, to wit: OPIATES and did procure and attempt to procure the administration of and prescription for said controlled substance by fraud, deceit and misrepresentation .

* * * * *

COUNT 10

On or between June 9, 2004 and September 22, 2006, in the County of Los Angeles, the crime of PRESCRIBING, ADMINISTERING, OR DISPENSING A CONTROLLED SUBSTANCE TO AN ADDICT, in violation of Section 11156 of the Health and Safety Code, a Felony, was committed by SANDEEP KAPOOR and HOWARD KEVIN STERN.

* * * * *

COUNT 11

On or between June 5, 2004 and January 26, 2007, in the County of Los Angeles, the crime of PRESCRIBING, ADMINISTERING, OR DISPENSING CONTROLLED SUBSTANCES TO ANNA NICOLE SMITH, AN ADDICT, in violation of Section 11156 of the Health and Safety Code, a Felony, was committed by KHRISTINE EROSHEVICH and HOWARD KEVIN STERN.

* * * * *

OVERT ACTS AS TO COUNT 1

Overt Act 1. On 9/11/06, KHRISTINE EROSHEVICH prescribed chloral hydrate and lorazepam, controlled substances, to ANNA NICOLE SMITH.

Overt Act 2. On 9/11/06, HOWARD K. STERN directed KHRISTINE EROSHEVICH to bring controlled substances for ANNA NICOLE SMITH to the Bahamas.

Overt Act 3. On 9/12/06, KHRISTINE EROSHEVICH arrived in the Bahamas with controlled substances for ANNA NICOLE SMITH.

Overt Act 4. On 9/12/06, SANDEEP KAPOOR prescribed a controlled substance to Michelle Chase, intended for ANNA NICOLE SMITH.

Overt Act 5. On 9/12/06, with knowledge of ANNA NICOLE SMITH's addiction, SANDEEP KAPOOR prescribed two (2) prescriptions for hydromorphone, a controlled substance, to Michelle Chase, intended for ANNA NICOLE SMITH.

Overt Act 6. On 9/12/06, with no legitimate medical purpose, SANDEEP KAPOOR prescribed two separate prescriptions for hydromorphone, a controlled substance, to Michelle Chase, intended for ANNA NICOLE SMITH

Overt Act 7. On 9/12/06, SANDEEP KAPOOR prescribed hydromorphone and Dilaudid to Michelle Chase, intended for ANNA NICOLE SMITH, for no legitimate medical purpose.

Overt Act 8. On 9/15/06, KHRISTINE EROSHEVICH faxed a prescription for controlled substances for Michelle Chase, intended for ANNA NICOLE SMITH, to SANDEEP KAPOOR.

Overt Act 9. On 9/15/06, SANDEEP KAPOOR forwarded KHRISTINE EROSHEVICH's requested prescription for controlled substances for Michelle Chase, intended for ANNA NICOLE SMITH, to a pharmacy in Los Angeles County.

Overt Act 10. On 9/15/06, HOWARD K. STERN was informed by a pharmacist that the requested prescription for Michelle Chase, intended for ANNA NICOLE SMITH and submitted by KHRISTINE EROSHEVICH through SANDEEP KAPOOR, would not be filled.

Overt Act 11. On 9/15/06, SANDEEP KAPOOR was warned of the dangers of submitting requests for prescriptions for Michelle Chase, intended for ANNA NICOLE SMITH.

Overt Act 12 On 9/15/06, a pharmacist informed SANDEEP KAPOOR that the submitted prescription request for Michelle Chase, intended for ANNA NICOLE SMITH, would not be filled.

Overt Act 13. On 9/15/06, KHRISTINE EROSHEVICH called another doctor to discuss the requested prescription for Michelle Chase, intended for ANNA NICOLE SMITH.

Overt Act 14. On or about 9/15/06, KHRISTINE EROSHEVICH was informed by another doctor of the dangers related to the requested prescription for controlled substances, that ANNA NICOLE SMITH should be hospitalized and on a heart monitor, and recommended that ANNA NICOLE SMITH be admitted to an addiction rehabilitation clinic.

Overt Act 15. On or about 9/15/06, with knowledge of ANNA NICOLE SMITH's addiction, KHRISTINE EROSHEVICH was informed by another doctor of the dangers related to the requested prescription for controlled substances, that ANNA NICOLE SMITH should be hospitalized and on a heart monitor, and recommended ANNA NICOLE SMITH be admitted to an addiction rehabilitation clinic.

Overt Act 16. On 9/22/06, after being warned of the danger of such controlled substances, SANDEEP KAPOOR prescribed controlled substances to Michelle Chase, intended for ANNA NICOLE SMITH.

Overt Act 17. On 9/22/06, with no legitimate medical purpose, SANDEEP KAPOOR prescribed hydromorphone, a controlled substance, to Michelle Chase, intended for ANNA NICOLE SMITH

Overt Act 18. On 9/22/06, after warnings of the danger of such controlled substances, KHRISTINE EROSHEVICH prescribed controlled substances in the names of Howard Stem, Howard K. Steam and Wesley Irwin intended for ANNA NICOLE SMITH.

Overt Act 19. On 9/22/06, KHRISTINE EROSHEVICH prescribed controlled substances to Howard Stem, Howard K. Steam and Wesley Irwin, each of whom were not patients.

Overt Act 20. On 9/22/06, KHRISTINE EROSHEVICH prescribed controlled substances to Howard Stem, Howard K. Steam and Wesley Irwin, for no legitimate medical purpose.

Overt Act 21. On 9/22/06, with no legitimate medical purpose, KHRISTINE EROSHEVICH prescribed clonazepam, a controlled substance, and carisoprodol to Wesley Irwin, intended for ANNA NICOLE SMITH.

Overt Act 22. On 9/22/06, with no legitimate medical purpose, KHRISTINE EROSHEVICH prescribed chloral hydrate and clonazepam, controlled substances, and carisoprodol to Howard K. Steam, intended for ANNA NICOLE SMITH.

Overt Act 23. On 9/22/06, win no medical purpose, KHRISTINE EROSHEVICH prescribed chloral hydrate, a controlled substance, to Howard Stern, intended for ANNA NICOLE SMITH.

Overt Act 24. On 9/22/06, KHRISTINE EROSHEVICH prescribed two (2) prescriptions of chloral hydrate, two (2) prescriptions of clonazepam, and two (2) prescriptions of carisoprodol in the names Howard Stern, Howard K. Steam and Wesley Irwin, none of whom were patients of KHRISTINE EROSHEVICH.

Overt Act 25. From 9/11/06 to 9/22/06, HOWARD K. STERN directed KHRISTINE

EROSHEVICH to bring excessive quantities of controlled substances to the Bahamas for ANNA NICOLE SMITH.

Overt Act 26. From 9/11/06 to 9/22/06, HOWARD K. STERN dispensed excessive quantities of controlled substances to ANNA NICOLE SMITH.

Overt Act 27. From 9/11/06 to 9/22/06, KHRISTINE EROSHEVICH prescribed excessive quantities of controlled substances to ANNA NICOLE SMITH.

Overt Act 28. From 9/11/06 to 9/22/06, HOWARD K. STERN acted with knowledge that ANNA NICOLE SMITH was an addict.

Overt Act 29. From 9/11/06 to 9/22/06, SANDEEP KAPOOR acted with knowledge that ANNA NICOLE SMITH was an addict.

Overt Act 30. From 9/11/06 to 9/22/06, KHRISTINE EROSHEVICH acted with knowledge that ANNA NICOLE SMITH was an addict.

Overt Act 31. On 10/17/06, KHRISTINE EROSHEVICH prescribed controlled substances to Charlene Underwood, not a patient, intended for ANNA NICOLE SMITH, using Wesley Irwin's date of birth from a pharmacy in Orange County, California.

Overt Act 32. On 10/17/06, KHRISTINE EROSHEVICH paid cash for and picked up the controlled substances for Charlene Underwood, not a patient, intended for ANNA NICOLE SMITH, from a pharmacy in Orange County, California.

Overt Act 33. On 11/24/06, KHRISTINE EROSHEVICH prescribed controlled substances to Charlene Underwood, not a patient, intended for ANNA NICOLE SMITH, using Wesley Irwin's date of birth from a pharmacy in Orange County, California.

Overt Act 34. On 11/24/06, KHRISTINE EROSHEVICH paid cash for and picked up the controlled substances for Charlene Underwood, not a patient, intended for ANNA NICOLE SMITH, from a pharmacy in Orange County, California.

Overt Act 35 On 12/4/06, KHRISTINE EROSHEVICH prescribed controlled substances to Howard K. Steam, who was not a patient, which were intended for ANNA NICOLE SMITH.

Overt Act 36. On 1/2/07, KHRISTINE EROSHEVICH prescribed controlled substances to Howard K. Stem, who was not a patient of KHRISTINE EROSHEVICH, which were intended for ANNA NICOLE SMITH.

Overt Act 37. On 1/3/07, KHRISTINE EROSHEVICH picked up the controlled substances prescribed to Howard K. Steam, who was not a patient of KHRISTINE EROSHEVICH, which were intended for ANNA NICOLE SMITH.

Overt Act 38. On 1/5/07, KHRISTINE EROSHEVICH prescribed controlled substances to Howard K. Stearn and Ben Stern, who were not patients of KHRISTINE EROSHEVICH, which were intended for ANNA NICOLE SMITH.

Overt Act 39. On 1/5/07, KHRISTINE EROSHEVICH picked up the controlled substances prescribed to Howard K. Stearn and Ben Stern, who were not patients of KHRISTINE EROSHEVICH, which were all intended for ANNA NICOLE SMITH.

Overt Act 40. On 1/5/07, KHRISTINE EROSHEVICH picked up the controlled substances for Howard K. Stearn and Ben Stern, all intended for ANNA NICOLE SMITH.

Overt Act 41. On 1/5/07, KHRISTINE EROSHEVICH shipped the controlled substances via Federal Express overnight to Maurice Brighthaupt in Florida and intended for ANNA NICOLE SMITH.

Overt Act 42. On 1/26/07, KHRISTINE EROSHEVICH prescribed controlled substances to Howard K. Stearn, who was not a patient of KHRISTINE EROSHEVICH, which were intended for ANNA NICOLE SMITH.

Overt Act 43. Between 9/11/06 and 1/26/07, KHRISTINE EROSHEVICH gave placebos to ANNA NICOLE SMITH.

Overt Act 44 Between 9/11/06 and 1/26/07, KHRISTINE EROSHEVICH prescribed excessive amounts of controlled substances to ANNA NICOLE SMITH.

Overt Act 45 Between 9/11/06 and 1/26/07, HOWARD K. STERN administered excessive amounts of controlled substances to ANNA NICOLE SMITH.

OVERT ACTS AS TO COUNT 2

Overt Act 1. Between 6/9/04 and 6/29/04, SANDEEP KAPOOR prescribed hydromorphone, a controlled substance, on three different occasions to ANNA NICOLE SMITH.

Overt Act 2. On 6/29/04, SANDEEP KAPOOR and HOWARD K. STERN discussed the dispensing of medication for ANNA NICOLE SMITH.

Overt Act 3. On 12/7/04, SANDEEP KAPOOR and HOWARD K. STERN discussed referring ANNA NICOLE SMITH to an addiction specialist and weaning ANNA NICOLE SMITH "off the Dilaudid".

Overt Act 4. Between July 2005 and May of 2006, SANDEEP KAPOOR prescribed excessive amounts of sleep aids and benzodiazepines to ANNA NICOLE SMITH.

Overt Act 5. Between 6/09/04 and 9/10/06, SANDEEP KAPOOR prescribed excessive amounts of opiates to ANNA NICOLE SMITH.

Overt Act 6. Between 6/09/04 and 9/10/06, HOWARD K. STERN dispensed excessive amounts of controlled substances to ANNA NICOLE SMITH.

Overt Act 7. Between February 2005 and July 2006, HOWARD K. STERN paid for and picked up prescriptions in the name Michelle Chase, intended for ANNA NICOLE SMITH, from a pharmacy in Los Angeles County, California.

Overt Act 8. On 2/9/06, SANDEEP KAPOOR prescribed alprazolam (Xanax) to ANNA N. SMITH from a pharmacy in Los Angeles County, California.

Overt Act 9. On 2/10/06, SANDEEP KAPOOR prescribed Ambien to HOWARD K. STERN, who was not a patient of SANDEEP KAPOOR, and Ambien and Xanax to ANNA N. SMITH, as well as methadone to Michelle Chase, which were all intended for ANNA NICOLE SMITH, from a pharmacy in Los Angeles County, California.

Overt Act 10. On 2/23/06, SANDEEP KAPOOR prescribed Ambien and Xanax to ANNA N. SMITH from a pharmacy in Los Angeles County, California.

Overt Act 11. On 3/13/06, SANDEEP KAPOOR prescribed Ambien and Xanax to ANNA N. SMITH and Ambien to HOWARD K. STERN, who was not a patient of SANDEEP KAPOOR, which were all intended for ANNA NICOLE SMITH, from a pharmacy in Los Angeles County, California.

Overt Act 12. Between 4/24/06 and 5/2/06, SANDEEP KAPOOR and HOWARD K. STERN saw ANNA NICOLE SMITH, who had been admitted to a hospital in Los Angeles County, California for opiate withdrawal and prenatal care.

Overt Act 13. On 6/7/06, SANDEEP KAPOOR prescribed Ambien, a controlled substance, to HOWARD K. STERN, who was not a patient of SANDEEP KAPOOR, which was intended for ANNA NICOLE SMITH, from a pharmacy in Los Angeles County, California.

Overt Act 14. On 3/13/06 and 6/7/06, HOWARD K STERN paid for the controlled substances prescribed in his name, intended for ANNA NICOLE SMITH, using ANNA NICOLE SMITH's credit cards.

Overt Act 15. Between 4/14/06 and 6/30/06, SANDEEP KAPOOR prescribed methadone, lorazepam, and Xanax in the name Michelle Chase, intended for ANNA NICOLE SMITH, from a pharmacy in Los Angeles County, California.

Overt Act 16. After prescribing methadose to Michelle Chase, which was intended for ANNA NICOLE SMITH on 8/18/06, SANDEEP KAPOOR prescribed methadone to Michelle Chase, intended for ANNA NICOLE SMITH, on 8/25/06, for no legitimate medical purpose, from a pharmacy in Los Angeles County, California.

Overt Act 17. On 8/25/06, HOWARD K. STERN requested that a pharmacy in Los Angeles